tantra
The cult of ecstasy

Kali fighting demons. *Eighteenth century.*

The universities do not teach all things,
so a doctor must seek out old wives,
gypsies, sorcerers, wandering tribes, old
robbers, and such outlaws, and take lessons
from them. A doctor must be a traveller.
Knowledge is experience.' ('Paracelsus')

Ganesaya namah

tantra

The cult of ecstasy

Indra Sinha

hamlyn

For my friend
Marie

Do not weep for me
I am everywhere
I am in the earth
I am in the air
I am in the sea
I am even in the Buddha tree

Gilt Bronze Buddha. *Nepalese, nineteenth century.*

First published in Great Britain in 1993 by Hamlyn, an imprint of
Octopus Publishing Group Limited, 2-4 Heron Quays, London, E14 4JP.

This paperback edition first published 2000.

Distributed in the United States by Sterling Publishing Co., Inc.
387 Park Avenue South, New York, NY 10016-8810

Acknowledgements, text. A comprehensive list of text sources is included with the bibliography on page 146.

Every effort has been made to trace all copyright holders, but in some cases this has proved difficult. Anyone not acknowledged should write to the author care of the publishers so that their details can be included in reprints of the work.

Acknowledgements, illustration. The compilers are grateful to the numerous museums and private collections for their help and assistance. Special thanks are due to The Klinger Collection, Nuremberg (eighteenth-century Dutch and French paintings and twentieth-century Indian portrait); The British Museum (Attic cup); Naturhistorisches Museum, Vienna (Venus of Willendorf); The Victoria and Albert Museum; and most important of all - Lance Dane for his unique collection of Tantric images.

Designed by Grahame Dudley Associates
Typesetting by Inline Graphics
Special photography: Lawrence Bulaitis of Lawrence Photography
Bullfight photograph on page 33 by Cayetano Vega Millán of Córdoba

A catalogue record for the book is available from the British Library.

Produced by Toppan Printing Co Ltd. Printed in China

ISBN 0 600 59998 1

Contents

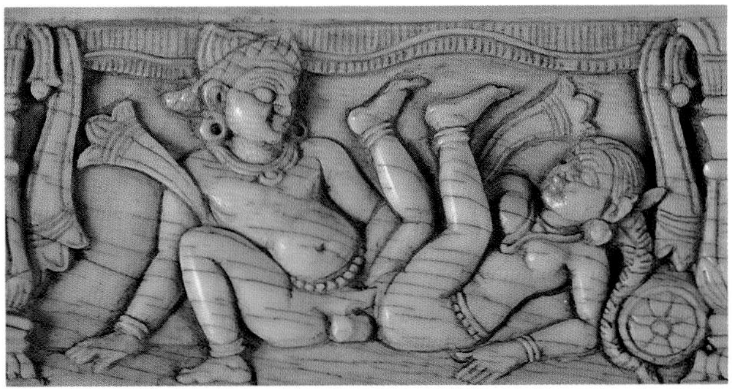

Preface

THE TEMPLE OF KALI

In a Bombay back street, scarcely a hundred yards from the Taj Hotel, is an antique shop above whose doorway is blazoned the legend: 'Live in Oriental Glory of Grandeur'.

Inside, shabby tigers preside glassily over carved rosewood desks and rattan punkahs; bundles of dusty Bhil spears, bound up by some homegoing sahib for a passage to England that never was; beams from old havelis, rescued from being burned as firewood on Gujerat beaches; finials from South Indian temples; dancing bronze Sivas and marble Ganesas; vulgar green chandeliers from Lucknow; a sixteenth-century stone goddess, of hideous mien, still daubed with vermilion; Wedgewood dinner services, brought out from home; canteens of Sheffield silverplate, worn yellow by generations of servants; crystal glasses; heaps of books: gazettes, histories, some fine bindings, monsoon-mildewed or furrowed by the white ant.

In this emporium, at some point during the late fifties, my mother unearthed a fine leather-bound copy of "Hindu Manners, Customs and Ceremonies" by the Abbé Dubois. This was a 1905 edition of the Abbe's 1807 manuscript, with a preface by the great Indologist Max Muller. The frontispiece depicts a European, bearded and turbanned in the eighteenth-century Deccani fashion.

The Abbé, a French missionary and contemporary of Tipu Sultan, worked in India for thirty years following his ordination to the priesthood in 1792. After Tipu's defeat at Seringapatam in 1799, the Abbé was invited by Arthur Wellesley, the future Duke of Wellington, to visit Tipu's capital and re-convert the Christian community there which had, in the words of the Abbé's biographer, been 'forcibly perverted to Mahomedanism by Tippu Sultan'. This sort of fighting talk does not wholly reflect the attitudes of the Abbé himself, who found a certain sympathy for the Indian peoples among whom he worked, even when he could not share their religious convictions. For the next decade, he travelled across south India, questioning, probing and recording his findings. The first draft of his manuscript, composed in French, was considered by the country's British rulers to be of such unusual value that it was purchased by Lord William Bentinck on behalf of the East India Company in 1807 for the exotic sum of 2,000 'star pagodas', equivalent to about 8,000 rupees in the currency of the time.

Like previous European travellers, the Abbe was fascinated and shocked by the explicitness of some forms of Hindu worship, by the erotic carvings that climbed the stone temples and by the connection between temples and sacred prostitutes. Indeed, he wrote:

> 'It really seems as if most of the religious and civil institutions of India were only invented for the purpose of awakening and exciting passions towards which they already have such a strong natural tendency. The shameless stories about their deities, the frequent recurrence of special feast days which are celebrated everywhere, the allegorical meaning of so many of their everyday customs and usages, the public and private buildings which are to be met with everywhere bearing on their walls some disgusting obscenity, the many religious services in which the principal part is

played by prostitutes, who often make the temples themselves the scenes of their abominable debauchery; all these things seem to be calculated to excite the lewd imagination of the inhabitants of this tropical country and give them a strong impulse towards libertinism.'

It was not just Indians whose lewd imaginations were ignited by these things. In my copy of the Abbé's book, a previous owner has marked some passages in pencil. It is impossible not to notice that all of these passages allude to sexual customs. On the very third page, for instance, the reader has heavily scored the following comment on a supposed practice of the Nambudiri caste:

'...if a girl who has arrived at an age when the signs of puberty are apparent happens to die before having intercourse with a man, caste custom rigorously demands that the inanimate corpse of the deceased shall be subjected to a monstrous connection. For this purpose the girl's parents are obliged to procure by a present of money some wretched fellow willing to consummate such a disgusting form of marriage'.

Now this claim happens to be utterly untrue. The Nambudiris do nothing of the sort. The facts are that certain religious rites associated with marriage - for instance the fastening around the bride's neck of a small golden ornament called the 'tali' - are performed over the body of the dead woman before her cremation. This token 'marriage' has nothing to do with

In the eighteenth century, it was common for officials of the East India Company to take native mistresses, which makes European attempts to portray Indians as sexually depraved seem rather hypocritical. *Rajasthan, late eighteenth century.*

consummation. The Abbé's 1905 editor knew this, and said so in a detailed footnote. Unfortunately for Nambudiri reputations, earlier editions of the book did not benefit from this correction and the slur, along with many other mistakes, went unchallenged throughout the nineteenth century. (Interestingly, the annotator of my copy marked the original comment but not the footnote, suggesting that, correction or no, the damage was still done.)

With the passing years, Abbé Dubois himself became aware of the inaccuracies in his early work and sought to revise it. In 1815 he presented to the Directors of the East India company a huge palimpsest of notes and cross-references. How necessary these changes were may be gauged from the fact that his 1907 editor says they would have furnished "material for a substantial volume'. But it was too late. The Abbe's first manuscript had already been translated into English and published. The original edition, mistakes and all, was admired by people like Samuel Taylor Coleridge; Mill, the historian of India; and Professor Wilson, the scholar who founded Sanskrit studies at Oxford. For many, the Abbé's was the seminal work on Hindu life. It helped fix the notion that Hindus were indolent and depraved. This was no coincidence, as Dubois makes quite clear in his preface to the work:

> 'There is one motive which above all others has influenced my determination. It struck me that a faithful picture of the wickedness and incongruities of polytheism and idolatry would by its very ugliness help greatly to set off the beauties and perfections of Christianity.'

The importance of the Abbé's work for our present purpose is that it contains what is probably the first detailed account of Tantric 'sakti' worship - the orgiastic ritual that was to become known as the 'cakrapuja'. This description was passed down from writer to writer throughout the nineteenth century and continues to colour our perceptions of Tantrism to this day. Here is what Dubois wrote:

> 'Among the abominable rites practised in India is one which is only too well known; it is called sakti-puja; sakti meaning strength or power. Sometimes it is the wife of Siva to whom this sacrifice is offered; sometimes they pretend that it is in honour of some invisible power. The ceremony takes place at night with more or less secrecy. The least disgusting of these orgies are those where they confine themselves to eating and drinking everything that the custom of the country forbids, and where men and women, huddled together in indiscriminate confusion, openly and shamelessly violate the commonest laws of decency and modesty.
>
> 'People of all castes, from the Brahmin to the Pariah, are invited to attend. When the company are assembled, all kinds of meat, including beef are placed before the idol of Vishnu. Ample provision is also made of arrack, toddy and opium, and any other intoxicating drug they can lay their hands on. The whole is then offered to Vishnu. Afterwards, the pujari, or sacrificer, who is generally a Brahmin, first of all tastes the various kinds of meats and liquors himself then gives the others permission to devour the rest. Men and women thereupon begin to eat greedily, the same piece of meat passing from mouth to mouth, each person taking a bite, until it is finished. Then they start afresh on another joint, which they gnaw in the same manner, tearing the meat out of each other's mouths. When all the meat has been consumed, intoxicating liquors are passed round, every one drinking without repugnance from the same cup. Opium and other drugs disappear in a similar fashion. They persuade themselves that under these circumstances they do not contract impurity by eating and drinking in so revolting a manner. When they are all completely intoxicated, men and women no longer keep apart, but pass the rest of the night together, giving themselves up without

restraint to the grossest immorality without any risk of disagreeable consequences. A husband who sees his wife in another man's arms cannot recall her, nor has he the right to complain; for at those times every woman becomes common property... Under certain circumstances, the principal objects which form the sacrifice to sakti are a large vessel full of native rum and a full- grown girl. The latter, stark naked, remains standing in a most indecent attitude. The goddess Sakti is evoked, and is supposed to respond to the invitation to come and take up her abode in the vessel full of rum and also in the girl's body. A sacrifice of flowers, incense, sandalwood, coloured rice and a lighted lamp is then offered to these two objects... This done, Brahmins, Sudras, Pariahs, both men and women, intoxicate themselves with the rum which was offered to sakti, all drinking from the same cup in turn. To exchange pieces of the food that they are in the act of eating and to put into one's own mouth what has just been taken from another's, are under these conditions regarded as acts of virtue by the fanatics. As usual, the meeting winds up with the most revolting orgy.'

It remains one of the most complete descriptions of a cakrapuja ever written. Dubois manages to convey the impression ('It has come to my knowledge that certain Brahmins were in the habit of meeting...') that his account is based on information given to him by someone with first hand evidence, yet, as we shall see, there is reason to doubt this.

At about the time of Waterloo, the Reverend William Ward, a man described by his own biographer as 'not endowed with genius', sat down with a brahmin scholar to dissect a tantric text, much in the way that Captain Richard Burton would sit with four pandits, seven decades later, to decode the Kama Sutra. Ward was clearly unprepared for what he learned, for his text (rendered more exotic by his uncouth method of transliterating Sanskrit vowel sounds) throbs with outrage:

"Many of the Tŭntrŭs...contain directions respecting a most extraordinary and shocking mode of worship, which is understood in a concealed manner among the Hindus by the name of Chŭkrŭ (Cakra). These Shastrŭs direct, that the person who wishes to perform this ceremony must first, in the night, choose a woman as the object of worship. If the person be a dukshinacharee, he must take his own wife; and if a vamacharee, the daughter of a dancer, a kupalee, a washerwoman, a barber, a chandalu, or of a prostitute; and place her on a seat or mat; and then bring broiled fish, flesh, fried peas, rice, spirituous liquors, sweetmeats, flowers and other offerings, which as well as the female must be purified by the repeating of incantations. To this succeeds the worship of the guardian deity; and after this, that of the female, who sits naked * * * * '

At this point the thunderstruck Mr Ward seeks refuge in asterisks, continuing, when he has regained his composure:

'Here things too abominable to enter the ears of man, and impossible to be revealed to a Christian public, are contained in the direction of the Shastrŭ. The learned bramhum who opened to me these abominations made several efforts - paused and - and then paused again - before he could mention the shocking indecencies presented by his own shastrŭs.'

Clearly the brahmin was either brave enough - in the face of this censorious sahib - or well-paid enough, to carry on, for Ward was able to embelish his account with the following details:

'...She (the woman) partakes of the offerings, even of the spirituous liquors; and of the flesh though it should be that of the cow... the spirituous liquors must be drank by measure; and the company while eating must put food into each other's mouths. The priest then - in the presence of all - behaves towards this female in a manner which decency forbids to be mentioned; after which the persons present repeat many times the name of some god, performing actions unutterably abominable and here, this most diabolical business closes.'

One cannot help wondering whether the 'shastrŭ' here referred to was none other than the Abbé Dubois's recently translated and published work. The material, even down to the sentence structure, is strikingly similar. But Ward gives his sources. He says that he consulted the Yoni-tantra, the Nila-tantra and the Rudrayamala. If this is true, it raises the interesting corollary: if these were Ward's sources, were they also Dubois's?

The Yoni-tantra certainly provided Ward with the list of women from whom the Tantric worshipper should choose his partner. The text forbids sexual union with one's mother (matryoni) but recommends one's sister or daughter. This tantra is also unique in going into vast detail about yoni-worship. It divides the vulva into ten parts, each of which is dedicated to a particular aspect of the great Mother Goddess.

The Nila-tantra also offers plenty of scope for outrage. Among the acts it recommends are the worship of virgins, aged from one to sixteen years; meditation on a corpse, preferably that of an unborn baby, or a boy of five, or an untouchable (candala); and human sacrifice. The Rudrayamala acted as a treasury for many other Tantras. It contributed some verses to the Yoni-tantra, as noted by another Abbé Dubois fan, Oxford's Professor Wilson.

On the face of it, these Tantras contain teachings that are immoral and repulsive. Whether they were meant to be taken literally is another question. At the centre of all the Tantras is a five-fold sacrament of meat, wine, fish, grain and sexual intercourse. What both

This painting reflects the rumours that abounded about Tantric sexual practices, since a sadhu, or holy man, is shown to be involved in the debauchery. On the other hand, all these acts can be found on the walls of Khajuraho temples (see page 77). Did the painter intend to condemn sexual licence, or to suggest that animal sexuality is to be transcended? *Early nineteenth century.*

Dubois and Ward have described is the ceremonial partaking of these sacraments. The men and women in the circle are in a state of hysterical exhileration, called by the texts 'praudhanta-ullasa', in which all actions are holy. There is some evidence to suggest that the descriptions of this state in the Tantric texts are purely metaphorical. The vast majority of Tantrics were, and are, thoroughly respectable people who would not dream of using sex, alcohol or other intoxicants in their worship. On the other hand, there is no doubt that a few Tantric groups did follow the texts to the letter. What is really difficult to realise is that Tantric sex, even when literally performed, is itself a metaphor for a deeper mystery. Dubois and Ward described the outward form of the rituals, but missed their hidden purpose and meaning. It is easy, and puerile, for writers to condemn what they do not understand, but the real challenge is to illuminate the subject from within, neither condoning nor, condemning.

Dubois and Ward were by no means the first Europeans to make the discovery that in India the mysteries of sex and religion were linked. They must both have been familiar with 'Robertson's India', published in 1791, in which William Robertson, without any first hand knowledge of the country, had condemned the worship of certain 'licentious' Hindu deities:

> 'Their altars were always bathed in blood, the most coftly victims were offered, whole hecatombs were flaughtered, even human facrifices were not unknown,and were held to be the moft powerful expiations. In order to gain the good-will of the deities... recourfe was had to inftitutions of a very different kind, to fplendid ceremonies, gay feftivals, heightened by all the pleafures of poetry, mufic and dancing, but often terminating in fcenes of indulgence too indecent to be defcribed.'

So long as the writer was a mere visitor, the accounts remained travellers' tales, weird and fantastic. But with colonial rule came the opportunity to make conversions and the reports, though still content to record rather than to investigate, began to acquire a moral tone. But if missionaries like Dubois and Ward had religious motives for wanting to denigrate Hindu religion, there were soon political reasons too. The problem of 'thuggee', or religious murder, focussed attention in the early nineteenth-century on some other less than savoury aspects of the Siva-Kali cult. Ward, in particular, documents ritual murders which are clearly linked to tantric practice:

> 'About seven years ago, at the village of Serampore, near Kutwa, before the temple of the goddess Tara, a human body was found without a head; and in the inside of the temple different offerings, as ornaments, food, flowers, spirituous liquors, &c. All who saw it knew that a human victim had been slaughtered in the night; and search was made after the murderers, but in vain'.

Tara, Durga, Siddheswari and Kali, to whom the human sacrifices were offered, were all goddesses worshipped with Tantric rites.

Tantrism acquired a new, political dimension as British fears about civil unrest and mutiny were excited and deliberately linked to the supposed degeneracy of the natives. In early 1857, of the many portents which might have warned the British of the terror to come, none was more bizarre than the phenomenon of the night- runners: watchmen who passed through the land by night, from village to village, town to town, cantonment to cantonment, carrying, of all things, chapattis - round cakes of unleavened bread - accompanied by the message "sab lal ho jayega", "all will become red". It was whispered that the chapattis had originated from a great temple of Siva away in east Bengal. To this day, nobody knows what their significance really was. Possibly, as John Masters conjectured in his 'Night-Runners of

Bengal', they were a code giving a date for the people to rise up and slaughter the Europeans. But all sorts of other strange meanings have been ascribed to them.

> 'The round, flat, unleavened cake represented the female principle. Lotus and chuppaty - lingam-yoni, penis-cunnus - emblems of regeneration.'

So we are told by Allen Edwardes, in his 'The Jewel in the Lotus'. This book, which purports to be a study of eastern sexual mores, is a remarkably silly work. The best thing about it is its bibliography, and it would not be worth mentioning here were it not such a perfect illustration of the process that the Abbé Dubois had begun. On the subject of the cakrapuja, Edwardes develops a bizarre fantasy, far too long and obscene to be quoted here, in which we find certain details oddly familiar:

Nepalese bronze of the god Siva.

> 'The Chosen One is a temple priestess (pudminee, lotus-woman) a wife of Lord Shiva, slave girl to the Abode of Mahadeva with the phallic emblem tattooed on her breasts and groin.' (Edwardes)

> 'The priestesses of Siva are called linga-basavis or women of the lingam, and bear this sign tattooed on their thighs.' (Abbé Dubois)

The approach to the underground cave in which the cakrapuja is to take place is carefully described by Edwardes, but in terms first used by the Abbé Dubois 150 years earlier to describe the vestibule of a typical Hindu temple.

> 'Descending more deeply into the earth, the terrible darkness becomes impregnated with dim eerie light. The air is stifling, sickeningly pungent. Persian camphor, rotting flowers. Cockroaches, bat excrement, lamp oil. Rancid ghee and human perspiration.' (Edwardes)

> 'The low elevation; the difficulty with which the air finds a way through a single narrow and habitually closed passage; the unhealthy odours rising from the mass of fresh and decaying flowers; the burning lamps; the oil and butter spilt in libations; the excrements of the bats that take up their abode in these dark places; finally and above all the fetid perspiration of a multitude of unclean and malodorous people - all contribute to render these shrines excessively unhealthy'. (Abbé Dubois)

It is interesting to notice how the dark entrance passage into a stone temple has turned into an underground cave. Inside this cave lurks, of course, the fearsome 'Kalee', garlanded with freshly severed human heads, each of her many arms bearing a keen edged weapon smoking with the blood of innocents. Anyone who has seen 'Indiana Jones and the Temple of Doom' will recognise the scene at once, the underground cavern, complete with sinister Hindoo priest, the many-armed-to-the-teeth goddess and semi-clad victim.

By the middle of the nineteenth-century, Tantra had achieved the allure that it retains to this day: dark and terrible, shot through with flashes of power and mystery. For Victorians, as for modern readers, it was irresistible. Tantra had something for everyone: exotic sexual rites, forbidden liaisons, intoxication whether by drug, wine or beauty, a profound mystery, silence and dark terror.

PART I

The Evolution of the Sacraments

Twelfth-century sandstone stele of a god.

Chapter 1

The Five-Fold Sacrament

meghāngīṁ sāśiśékharam triṇayāṁ raktāmbarāṁ bibhratīṁ pāṇibhyāmbhayaṁ varaṇca vilasadraktāravindasthitām I nrtyantaṁ puratō nipīya madhuraṁ mādhvīkamadyaṁ mahā- kālaṁ vīkśya vikāsitānanavarāmādyāṁ bhajé kālikām II
(Mahanirvana-tantra V.141)

I adore primaeval Kali; her limbs like dark rain clouds, moon-crowned, three-eyed, clothed in crimson. Her two hands uplifted bless me and free me from fear. Seated on a red lotus, She turns her laughing face to Mahakala who, drunk on madhvika wine, is dancing before her.

There is one Mother, creator of all things. From her everything that exists was born, to her all things will return. Galaxies, stars, mountains, seas, plants, animals, humans, gods: all are her creations. Every leaf, each living cell, every pulse of the blood, every molecular love affair, each fizzing electron, is sustained by her. She gives life and takes it. With a myriad forms, loving and terrible, she is known by untold numbers of names and honoured in countless shrines. She is the primordial ground of being from which everything and even nothing springs. Hers is the primaeval energy of the universe that drives all divine and cosmic evolution. Supreme Being, single source and controller of all the forces and potentialities of nature: She is Sakti, the great goddess of the Tantrics. She is Parvati, lovely beyond imagination, who, because her limbs were dark, was given the pet name of Kali, the dark one. She is the One with whom all creation begins.

sadāśivaṁ sadānandaṁ karuṇāmrtasāgaram I karpūrakundadhavalaṁ śuddhasatvamayaṁ vibhum II digambaraṁ dīnanāthaṁ yōgīndraṁ yōgivallabham I gangāśīkarasaṁsiktajaṭāmaṇdalamaṇditam II vibhūtibhūśitaṁ śāntaṁ vyālamālaṁ kapālinam I trilōchanaṁ trilōkeśaṁ triśūlavaradhāriṇam II āśutōśaṁ jnānamayaṁ kaivalyaphaladāyakam I nirvikalpaṁ nirātankaṁ nirvisésaṁ niraṇjanaṁ II sarvveśāṁ hitakartāraṁ dévadévaṁ nirāmayam I
(Mahanirvana-tantra I. 6-10)

Ever gracious, ever blissful Lord whose compassion is like an ocean of nectar; whose body shines white as camphor and the jasmine flower; purest truth, robed in space, omnipresent; loving and beloved Lord of yogis, whose coiled and matted hair is drenched by spray from the torrents of Ganga; adorned with ashes, garlanded with snakes and human skulls; three-Eyed Lord of the triple-world: trident in one hand, in the other, blessing; embodiment of Gnosis, giver of Nirvana; everlasting; pure; flawless; amiable; benefactor to all that lives, God of Gods.

So the poet describes Siva, consort of the goddess. As Mahakala, he dances for her pleasure, he is also her Lord. He is her strength as she is his. Siva and Sakti cannot be separated, they are eternally One. Each is the Other. When Siva dances, it is Kali who moves within his limbs. When Kali dances, it is Siva who dances within her body. Siva, indeed, is Lord of the Dance, of music and drama, of austerity and yoga. He is the master ascetic, untroubled by desire, yet he is also teacher of the arts of love. If Sakti is all and everything, Siva is the annihilation of opposites. He is simultaneously holy yet outcaste; god yet beggar; sober yet intoxicated; lord of the ever-erect phallus yet supremely detached yogi.

The basis of all Tantrism is the worship of Sakti and Siva, the female and the male principles. This worship can take the simple form of ceremonies to the village Mothers, goddesses of such great antiquity that their origins are forgotten. Their shrines may be no more than rough stones standing as they have for centuries, or perhaps millenia, in the corners of fields, by old trackways, or on hilltops. Or the ceremonies can be lavish and elaborate, taking place in thousand year old temples, with incense and bells and mountains of flowers. The universal outward symbol of this Sakti-Siva worship is the holy 'lingam' standing in the sacred 'yoni'. There can hardly be anyone reading this who is not acquainted with Burton's translation of the Kama Sutra, but in case there is, the words 'lingam' and 'yoni' signify the penis and the vulva, the conjoined creative powers of the goddess and god. Without Sakti there is no Siva, and no Siva without Sakti. Siva is the creative principle, the

The sacred lingam, or phallus, of Siva is surrounded by yoni-symbols and other emblems of the Tantric cult. Part of the remarkable 'ritual' series of eighteenth-century Tantric paintings published in this book for the first time, they were used for meditation and in rituals.

spark, that arises out of the all-nothingness of the primordial Mother. The lingam and the yoni, joined in perfect balance, symbolise the harmony of the cosmos. These linga-yoni images can be unhewn stones dating back to the neolithic, or highly stylised and elaborately carved pillars of great size in temple sanctuaries.

If the missionaries considered the linga-yonis to be disgusting obscenities, they were more disturbed by whispered stories of secret sexual rituals. Most of what they knew about these rites was gleaned from the Tantra texts, often by reading between the lines, for the texts are ambiguous, sometimes purposely obscure, and often speak in metaphor. Nonetheless, there was a secret Tantric tradition, which did include ritual sex, mostly with one's own spouse, sometimes with other people's, often involving prostitutes and people of the lowest caste. Followers of this secret tradition broke caste taboos not only by associating with outcastes, but in accepting a sacred five-fold sacrament of meat, wine, fish, bread and sexual intercourse. This inner tradition was and is a gnostic one, in that it teaches a secret knowledge which leads to a direct experience of God. But unlike the gnostic sects of Rome and Alexandria, the purpose of Tantra is not so much illumination as release: moksa, freedom from the cycle of endless birth, death and rebirth. In this it is uniquely Indian.

Some Tantric schools, the so-called daksinachari, or 'followers of the right-hand path', do not accept the five sacraments in their literal forms. Instead, madya, wine, is seen as symbolic of the knowledge that intoxicates; mamsa, meat, is taken to signify the mastery of speech; matsya, fish, stands for the currents of energy that flow through the body; mudra, parched grain, symbolises the intense concentration of yogic meditation; while maithuna, the sexual act, is transformed into a meditation on the primal act of creation.

In other circles, the meat, wine, fish and ritual sex were replaced, not with intellectual concepts, but by simple substitutes which were considered harmless from the karmic point of view. Thus wine was often replaced by honey, cow's milk or coconut water; meat by garlic or ginger; fish by buffalo's or sheep's milk; and the sexual act by roasted fruits and shoots.

There can be no doubt, however, that in many circles, the real forms of the sacraments were enjoyed. Well respected Tantras like the Kularnava-tantra emphasise that those who take part in the panchamakara ritual mainly for sexual pleasure or out of mere hedonism only defeat themselves. The senses are to be conquered by leaving nothing unexperienced. Classical yoga seeks to overcome the distractions of the senses by ignoring them. Tantra, conversely, not only accepts the senses, but assigns them a central role in the quest for gnosis. Even forbidden acts could be enjoyed by the worshipper, secure in the knowledge that if performed with a pure heart, they incurred no karmic taxes.

Human nature being what it is, any examination of Tantra always dwells on the sexual aspect. But most Tantrics - and there are many different groups who class themselves as practitioners of Tantra - would not regard sex as the most important ingredient in Tantric worship. Just as important is the kundalini yoga, which seeks through posture, breathing and meditation, to raise the body-energy called kundalini through the psychic centres of the spinal column into the brain, where gnosis and liberation are experienced, an achievement which may take a lifetime of practice.

A different kind of yoga, which also involves posture, breathing and meditation, is practised with ritual diagrams, or yantras, which contain within their lines, angles and dots, the knowledge of a particular deity. The most important of these is the Sri Yantra, which is sacred to Adi Sakti herself and which represents the whole universe and demonstrates its mode of manifestation.

These two types of yoga, although essentially Tantric, are not the preserve of any one class or caste in Hinduism, or even of Hinduism itself. The Mahayana Buddhism of H.H. the Dalai Lama, is Tantrism of the most sophisticated kind. This may seem hard to reconcile with cutting chickens' throats over old, weathered goddess stones, or sacrificing a

A carving of the sexual technique 'aurparistaka' or 'sucking a mango'.

A temple hardwood carving.
Eighteenth century.

goat to Kali, yet it is all Tantra. The more closely we examine Tantrism and those who practise it, the more confusing the picture becomes. Tantra, like Hinduism, is not a clearly defined system of belief and practice, but a melange of worship, ritual, meditation, superstition, magic, sexual ritual and the highest forms of spiritual yoga. There are even Vaisnava Tantras, known as samhita. So intimately interwoven is Tantra in the everyday worship of India that even in temples that do not consider themselves Tantric, the content of the rituals is purely brahmanical, but their form and structure is Tantric.

Who practises Tantra? In one sense, the not-very-useful answer is: 'everyone'. But if we confine ourselves to those who speak of themselves as Tantrics, we encounter time and time again the name of the 'Kaula' sect. There are many other schools and sects of Tantrism, including as we have observed, worshippers of Visnu. However, it the Kaulas with whom Tantrism in the form in which it is most widely known, is inextricably associated. The name comes from 'kul', 'family', according to some because the Kaulas honoured Siva-Sakti as a 'family' of deities, or emanations of the Supreme Being. The Kaulas were strongly represented in Assam, Bengal and Kashmir and many of the Tantric texts are specifically addressed to them.

The texts from which the various Tantric sects drew their ritual and moral instruction were written, mainly in Bengal, Orissa, Assam, Kashmir and Tibet, over a period ranging roughly from the fourth century AD to the present. Said to have been expounded by Siva and the great Mother as fit teachings for the fourth and final Hindu age - the Kali Yuga, era of degeneracy and destruction - the texts contain advice to the sadhaka, or Tantric worshipper, on every conceivable subject: cosmology; astrology; different types of men and women; the significance of the 'cakras' or psychic centres in the body; the nerves and channels through which the prana or vital life energy flows; methods of raising kundalini energy through the cakras; various types and forms of worship, including mantras (charms to be muttered) and yantras (abstract meditational designs); rituals involving the worship of the goddess in the form of virgin girls; of the yoni-puja or womb-worship; the rites of purification to be carried out before sexual worship; positions for meditation and sexual practice; prayers and poems to the goddess and her consort; basic health care and how to bring up children. Their magic spells sometimes had unexpected uses, as we read in the Brhad-vimansastra, a hitherto untranslated text on flying machines which is said to date from the medieval period:

> māntrikas tāntrikast dvatkṛtak aścāntarālakaḥ...&c
> (Brhad-vimansastra, I.ii.8)
>
> Only those who have had the knowledge of Mantra, Tantra (and twenty other skills here omitted for brevity) taught to them personally by a guru are fit and proper persons to pilot a flying machine.'

The author quotes the Mahamaya-tantra and other Tantric texts as sources from which the secret doctrines may be learned. The Mahamaya-tantra does indeed contain spells for flying, taking a bird's shape and travelling to any place on earth. It also promises the ability to espy holes in the ground, perhaps marking spots where other, less talented sky-striders came to grief.

What all Tantras have in common is that they are scriptures for the common folk, unanimous in rejecting the elitism of caste Hinduism. This is in part a reflection of the fact that the great Mother Goddess and her consort Siva have dark aboriginal origins, and were for a long time not admitted to the Vedic religion. It is not difficult to see how the subtle philosophising of the ascetic Upanisadic tradition was lost on the uneducated Indian masses.

This charming miniature, part of a set recording Tantric yoga postures, shows adepts maintaining a difficult pose. The spirituality of their lovemaking is contrasted by the animal sexuality of the creatures around the border. A stag chases a doe, two bears meet and ever fecund rabbits eye each other hopefully. *Orissa, eighteenth or nineteenth century.*

Tantra offered them a sort of tabloid religion, full of fun, enjoyment, magic and properly awe-inspiring ceremonial. One modern devotee of the great goddess, quoted by Thomas Coburn in his work on the 'Devi-Mahatmaya', explains why he refuses to permit brahmanical commentators to come between him and the fifteen-hundred-year-old proto-Tantric text.

> 'The commentators claim to worship the Goddess, saying to her "Hello, Mother" and praising her beauty, but then proceeding to reduce her to mere thought (cit) and sound (sabda). In doing this they destroy her beauty...A genuine devotee would never write a commentary. If he or she had to write something, it would be less dessicated and analytical, more an ebullient expression of love.'

This is a message that will strike a sympathetic chord with every Hindu villager in India. After all, the Mother has been worshipped in their homes and fields for thousands of years. The Upanisadic influence lies lightly on the countryside. The Tantras, powerful in their devotion to the goddess, with their promises of liberation from the torment of endless rebirth, of occult powers to be won, and in their frank enjoyment of worldly pleasures, exercised a strong appeal for the masses excluded by birth and caste from the higher levels of

The blue goddess, part of an outstanding set of Tantric 'ritual' paintings. The black cobras of kundalini energy writhe around her body, which is covered in yoni symbols and marked with yantras or sacred diagrams. She is surrounded by erect lingams, the symbols of her consort Siva. Her hands hold severed heads, themselves symbolic of moksa, or release from the world of ideation, and the god Brahma dwells in her heart. This painting is unique in its depiction of centaurs, better known from Greek than Indo-Aryan mythology, where they become 'gandharvas'. *Eighteenth century.*

Vedic worship. As a result, they were often strongly condemned by the brahmanical heirarchy.

> "If at any time in the history of India the mind of the nation as a whole has been diseased, it was in the Tantric age." (B. Bhattacharyya, 'Buddhist Esotericism')

Nonetheless Tantrics can cite ancient authority, in the shape of Kallukabhatta's commentary on Manu, to the effect that at least some Tantras have scriptural status:

> srutiśca dvividhā prōktā vaidikī tāntrikī tathā I

> Two sorts of holy writ: the Vedic and the Tantric.

Which Tantras should be accorded such status? Clearly many of them are little more than third-rate grimoires. It is not an easy question, not least because no-one has ever been able to agree even about how many Tantras there are. According to the 'Nityasodasikarnava' (I, xxii) the number runs into millions. Some scholars gravely quote a figure of one lakh, or 100,000. Others say 64. The number of Tantric texts in Sanskrit, Bengali, Kashmiri and other vernaculars certainly runs into hundreds, the problem being exacerbated by the fact that many quite different works share the same name. For example, there is more than one Kali-tantra.

Furthermore, the texts frequently contradict one another, for Tantrism was by no means a fixed system of belief or practice. There were hundreds of variations. In some cases the worship is so well defined that it deserves to be classified as a religion in its own right. In others, Tantric elements mingled with traditional Hinduism and Buddhism to produce exotic sub-cults. Some Tantras were even agnostic.

The Tantric texts vary greatly not only in subject matter, but in style and literary merit. Some texts were crudely written. The 'Guhyasamaja-tantra', a well-known Buddhist Tantra, is surprisingly coarse. Other Tantric texts contain some of the loveliest Sanskrit poetry:

> dhunōtu dhvāntaṁ nastulitadaliténdīvaravanaṁ ghanasnigdaślakśṇaṁ cikuranikurumbaṁ tava śivé I yadīyaṁ saurabhyaṁ sahajamupalabdhuṁ sumanasō vasantyasmin manyé balamathana-vāṭī-viṭapinām II (Saundaryalahari, 43)

> 'O consort of Shiva, may the mass of your hair, thick, shining and soft as crushed blue lotuses, dispel our dark ignorance; your hair in which the blooms from Indra's garden nestle: from where else should they draw their fragrance?'

> tanōtu kśémaṁ nastava vadana-saundarya-laharī parivāha srotaḥ saraṇiriva sīmantasaraṇiḥ I vahantī sindūraṁ prabala kabarībhāra timira dviśāṁ vrndairvandīkṛtamiva navīnārka kiraṇam II (ibid, 44)

> 'May your parting, thick with vermilion, bright as the ray of the rising sun, caught and framed by your dark, lustrous hair, the falling wave of your loveliness, shine for our well being.'

> Kalankaḥ kastūrī rajanikara bimbaṁ jalamayaṁ kalābhiḥ karpūrair marakata karaṇḍaṁ nibiḍitam I atastvad bhōgéna pratidinam idaṁ riktakuhuraṁ vidhirbhūyō bhūyō nibiḍayati nūnaṁ tava kṛté II (ibid, 94)

A Nepalese Tantric couple in simple standing posture. Nepal was an important centre of Tantrism and many of the old wooden temples in and around Kathmandu are adorned with brightly painted erotic carvings. *About 1700 AD.*

'The moon is a flask of emerald stained with musk, filled with water and camphory light, which you, for your pleasure, empty daily and the creator fills for you again and again.'

These verses from Saundaryalahari, or 'Wave of Beauty' a long and passionate hymn to the great Mother, are said to have been composed in the eighth century by the great Tantric saint Sankaracarya, a Nambudiri brahmin of the caste slandered by our old friend Abbé Dubois (see Preface). It is interesting to compare Sankaracarya's blissful imagery with the Sufism of the Baghdadi poet Abdullah ibn al-Mu'tazz, writing a century later: Quick! Lash out the wine! The moon's a silver dhow, laden with chunks of amber'. India's first Nobel laureate, Rabindranath Tagore loved Saundaryalahari, which he was fond of comparing with Shelley's Intellectual Beauty. Saundaryalahari inspired Tagore's own Gitanjali, the poem which won him the Nobel Prize for Literature and which is itself essentially Tantric in conception.

As a contrast to the elevated mood of Saundaryalahari, we may take the Guhyasamaja-tantra, which declares in robust language:

> mātṛbhāginiputrims ca kāmayéd yas tu sādhakaḥ | sā siddhuṁ, vipuṭaṁ gacchét mahayāṇagradharmatam ||
>
> "Who sexually desires his mother, sister and daughter attains occult powers and successfully reaches the peak of Mahayana dharma."

Greystone stele of Siva and Parvati. *Fourteenth century.*

This couplet is one of those inevitably quoted against Tantrism by its enemies. Its message is flatly contradicted, however, by the influential Mahanirvana-tantra, the 'Tantra of the great liberation':

> Siva! the punishment of those who go with their mother, sister and daughter is death, and if the latter are willing participants the same punishment should be inflicted upon them.'
> (translator: Arthur Avalon)

The Mahanirvana-tantra specifically prohibits sexual activity except between the worshipper and his or her spouse. The text is emphatic on this point. A man who goes with lustful ideas to the bed of his mother's or father's sister, or his daughter-in-law, or mother-in-law, or the wife of his guru, or either of his grandmothers, or of his brother's wife, sister's daughter, or of any unmarried girl, is to be castrated.

> A man who looks with lust at another's wife should fast for a day to purify himself. He who has converse with her in a secret place should fast for four days; and he who embraces her should fast for eight days to purify himself.'

These rules apply equally to women. Furthermore:

> The man who uses offensive language towards a woman,who sees the private parts of a woman who is not his wife and laughs mockingly at her, should fast for two days to purify himself.'

So much for promiscuity. But the Mahanirvana-tantra does encourage the sexual rite between man and wife and gives specific instructions about how it should be performed.

If the conflicting messages of the Guhyasamaja and Mahanirvana Tantras are confusing, a further complication can be introduced by pointing to the statement in the ascetic Jnanasamkalini-tantra, that 'brahmacarya', or perfect celibacy, is the ideal state, being the root of all penance, kindness and virtue. Which is it to be? Incest? Monogamy? Or celibacy? To the Tantric adept, this is a meaningless question. There were even those who saw no intrinsic contradiction between these three positions.

It was the Kaulas, par excellence, who practised sexual rituals, including the rite of 'cakrapuja' in which many couples took part under the guidance of a guru. Experts in sexual yoga, breath control and meditation, they broke taboos and defied prejudices with an astonishing single-mindedness, admitting outcastes and prostitutes to their rites and flouting

Hindu caste law by accepting as their most sacred sacrament the panchamakara, or five-fold communion, of meat, fish, grain, liquor and sexual intercourse.

The deliberate breaking of taboos in esoteric religion very seldom has anything to with immorality. Its purpose is three-fold: first to initiate the worshipper into the circle and to create a bond of shared experience which is, literally, unspeakable to outsiders; second, to defeat beliefs and patterns of habitual thinking which distract the devotee; third, to begin the process of breaking down and dissolving the emotional and psychological blocks to gnosis. But the five-fold sacrament of meat, wine, bread, fish and sexual union cannot simply be seen as psychic deliquency: these sacraments had evolved over many thousands of years and each one is the centre of a mystery of transformation. The search for their origins reveals how such an extraordinary melange of beliefs and customs came into being and why many, including the great Tantra scholar Sir John Woodroffe (Arthur Avalon) believed that Tantra originated outside India, in Scythia or Sakadvipa.

Tantra is like a broad river, into which many different streams have flowed. If we taste carefully, we may detect the muddy waters that swamped the ancient cities of the Indus valley; and the waters from the rivers of the Punjab, poured out in Vedic sacrifice; we may identify the icy snow-melt of the Himalayas, tasting of asceticism and Upanisads; water from the marshes of the high Tibetan plateau and from the swamps of the Bengal Sunderbans; we shall find Ganges water that has sluiced through the paved mains of Gupta cities; and we should definitely find water from hundreds of small village ponds and wells all over India. Some of this water - to strain the poor metaphor beyond redemption - has fallen from rain-clouds that have been blown eastward from distant countries.

Closer examination of Tantric ideas and rituals suggests that we must explore their relationships with:

1. Palaeolithic worship of fertility deities
2. Bronze age mystery cults
3. The culture of the Indus valley
4. The Vedas, the Soma sacrifice
5. Atharva Veda, Vamadeva, magical traditions
6. The India of the 'Mahabharata'
7. Mystery cults of the classical period
8. Indigenous tribal cults of India: Kalika, Yellama
9. Sacred prostitution
10. The Upanisads
11. Early Buddhism
12. Tibetan shamanism and bon beliefs
13. Yoga sutras
14. Mystery cults of the Roman empire
15. The secular tradition of the Kama-shastras
16. Gnosticism in Egypt, Rome and Asia Minor
17. Tibetan and Mahayana Buddhism
18. Kashmir Saivism
19. Tantra texts in Bengal and Orissa

Gilt bronze figure of a deity. *Nepal.*

In searching for the meaning of the meat, the fish, the wine, the bread and the rite of sexual union, we find that Tantra cannot contemptously be dismissed as a 'licentious' Indian cult. It is the Indian manifestation of a universal quest for gnosis that is as old as humanity itself.

Chapter 2

The Death of Pentheus

Tantrism, often accused of 'licentiousness', has its roots in the most ancient of all human lusts, the lust for survival. In cultures from the palaeolithic onwards, we encounter figurines carved in stone and bone, of a fecund Mother Goddess, one whose womb is full and whose breasts are heavy and full of nourishment. The best known of these statues is the Venus of Willendorf, but the figurines have been found from Siberia to the Pyrenees. Many have prominent sexual organs, wide opened vulvas, clearly intended to invoke the blessings of fertility. For early humans, ignorant of the mechanisms of sex, the vulva must have been the most miraculous thing in the universe. In India to this day the 'yoni' of the great Mother Goddess remains the most revered of all sacred icons. From this cavern of flesh, analogous to the narrow limestone passages and caves in which the clan lived, came new life. Woman was magician, creator. All female things brought forth young. The wild animals on which the hunters preyed had their own magical wombs. Out of this mystery came the concept of a universal Mother: Mother of all life. It is a beautiful idea, which deserves to be honoured.

The famous 'Venus of Willendorf', carved some thirty thousand years ago and exhibiting the characteristics common to Mother Goddess figurines right down to historical times. What looks like a woollen hat is probably a head of peppercorn curls.

We can distinguish three stages in the worship of the great goddess of fertility, a cult so widespread that it is probably the only religion the world has ever known which can truly be called universal. The first and oldest phase was the worship of the Great Mother as the mother of animals: the symbol and source of that fertility which led prey animals to multiply and be plentiful.

> 'After her came grey wolves, fawning upon her, and grim-eyed lions, and bears, and fleet leopards, ravenous for deer; and she was glad in heart to see them, and put desire in their breasts, so that they all mated, two together, about the shadowy vales.'
> (Homer, 'Hymn to Aphrodite', translator: Eveyln White)

At first She was alone. There was no other deity. She alone brought forth the herds and the carnivores. If there were other spirits in the world, they were not of human shape, as She was. They would have been the Mothers of the clans of animals, the animal-wombs - an idea preserved to this day in the rituals of Tibetan Tantrism, which is heavily influenced by the old Bon shamanism - totems of elk, mammoth, bison and cave-bear. At some distant point in history, it would have dawned on the scattered human clans that there was a connection between the birth of children and the act of copulation, which they felt so strangely urged to perform and which, when they did, they found so pleasurable. In the modern witch-cult the goddess says: 'All acts of love and pleasure are my rituals'.

From a very early date, the Mother Goddess must have had a male consort. We can tell this very simply, by the fact that these old palaeolithic statuettes demonstrate extreme steatopygia or prominence of the buttocks. The buttocks were, like the vulva, symbols of fertility when ritual copulation began to be practised as a magical fertility rite. Mating, obviously, took place from behind, mimicking the behaviour of prey animals. The goddess's consort makes one of his earliest appearances in a palaeolithic rock drawing from Algeria. An ample Mother Goddess stands with arms raised in benediction over a hunter who points his sharp arrow at a variety of game, including an antelope, a leopard and an ostrich. The goddess and the hunter are united, genital to genital, by his penis, which is of exagerrated length. Here is a crucial connection: the male hunter draws his strength from the goddess. It is she who stands with arms upraised in blessing. This is a motif found virtually everywhere that the archetypal female figure appears, even in early stone age daubings. He is the active principle, purusa, she is his sakti, his foundation and strength: as an expression of the Sakti-Siva equation, it is entirely accurate.

The great Mother's consort wore horns. Gradually he assumed the role of Lord of Beasts, specifically of those prey animals on which his clan depended for meat and hides; and bones for needles and combs and ornaments. San, or 'bushman' paintings from Tassili in the Sahara and elsewhere depict horned gods of the hunt. From Celtic prehistory comes the horned Cernunnos, known to certain sections of the contemporary witch cult as Karnayna, although they probably cannot say why. In fact the word, Maghribi for 'horned', was a north-African epithet of Alexander the Great, whom the Arabs knew as 'dhu al'Karnayna', the 'two-horned one'. The earliest paintings of the horned god are the magical horned dancers of palaeolithic cave frescoes. The images of these horned deities, men-made-divine-by-dance, would have bounded and leapt in the flickering firelight of the caves, guaranteeing the fertility of the wild herds upon which the clans fed, and the carnivores they killed for their fur and claws. The horns they wear are typically those of deer, elk, or bison: they would have worn the skins of elks, deer, bears, lions and tigers. A specially gifted dancer, the strongest male perhaps, would have danced around the fire in hide and horns, working himself up to an ecstasy, calling on the herds to be fertile and multiply. His shadow would have leapt around the walls of the cave on which the horned deities and the Mother themselves danced. At what point in history did people discover that throwing onto the fire stems and leaves and seeds of certain plants induced euphoria and visions? Cannabis sativa was certainly used this way by the Scythians thousands of years before Christ. The seers of the Vedas were inspired to their flights of poetry by the narcotic drink 'soma', whose active ingredient has never been identified. Tantric rituals made liberal use of 'bhang', a drink made from cannabis resin or oil stirred into milk or alcohol. In their state of exalted intoxication some Tantric sects practised orgiastic sex. These rites are the descendants of the stone age cave dances, which would have ended with ritual copulation between the chief horned dancer and the representative of the Mother, and sometimes between all the stag-dancers and hind-dancers: sacred orgies, acts of sympathetic magic to ensure the fertility of the prey.

When the dancers were successful, children would be born and the clans would notice something interesting: that the female's monthly flow of blood suddenly ceased. Blood was clearly the price of conception. A woman had to bleed to conceive. In fact, the most critical moments of her life - menstruation, deflowering and childbirth - were all attended by a significant loss of blood. Blood is the sacred life force - not for nothing are burial goods and holy figurines from the stone age onwards coloured with red pigments. The loss of blood is an offering by the female of her vital life force. The cave clans saw that before a woman can conceive, she must first bleed. It must have seemed to them that she shed her blood in order to bear a child: that the monthly moonblood was the price of children, fertility and life, and was therefore sacred and deserving of reverence. The same idea is found to this day in Tantric sects, where a woman in her menses is seen, not as unclean, but holy. The Tantric name for menstrual blood, 'kundapuspa', means 'flower-of-the-holy-well'. Sanskrit 'kund' or 'kunt' meaning a spring, well, fount or basin of water consecrated to some holy purpose or person, and carrying also the meanings of pitcher, or pot, is essentially the same word as Old English 'kunte', better known to us as the 'C-word' of which the dramatist Fletcher wrote: 'They write sunt with a C, which is abominable'. So terrifying is this word, so powerful its

Greystone stele of Siva and Parvati. *Fourteenth century.*

Invading warriors dressed in Scythian style desecrate the holiest symbol of the culture they are overthrowing, the female organ on which the taboo is so strong that to this day we dare not pronounce its oldest and most sacred name.

taboo, that it is not given even in the great Oxford Dictionary. The Penguin Dictionary of Modern Slang finds its etymology mysterious: 'The -nt, which is difficult to explain, was already present in Old Engish kunte'. The link to Sanskrit explains the '-nt', and not only demonstrates the antiquity of the word - it has existed in the Indo-European vocabulary since prehistoric times - but also shows beyond doubt that it was a sacred concept, as the survival of the root in the word 'kundalini' also confirms. No wonder we feel such deep, atavistic revulsion when we hear this word used as an obscenity: it is a desecration of something holy.

Since all females, human and animal, represent the Mother, it is the Mother herself who bleeds, her life flowing away out into the world to create new generations of humans and animals. If her strength and energies are not replaced, the Mother may grow weak and die. Sacrifice begins here.

A life taken must be paid for. To the human aboriginal, all lives are sacred. All are part of Her life. He recognises that his own life is made up of millions of tiny lives flowing into his body, meals made of grubs and insects, of plants and birds, of small animals and large. Life flowed into him from animals who gave their hides and fur, tusks and teeth, that he could survive. He needed to honour those lives and repay the debt.

> 'Every part of the earth is sacred to my people. Every shining pine needle, every sandy shore, every mist in the dark woods, every clearing and humming insect is holy in the memory and experience of my people.' (Chief Seattle of the Duwamish tribe)

'When Indians referred to animals as "people" - just a different sort of person from Man - they were not being quaint. Nature to them was a community of such "people" for whom they had a great deal of genuine regard and with whom they had a contractual relationship to protect one another's interests and to fulfill their mutual needs. Man and Nature, in short, were jointed by compact - not ethical ties - a compact predicated on mutual esteem. This was the essence of the traditional land relationship.'
(Ojibway Indian, quoted in 'The Gaia Atlas of First Peoples')

Just as in thermodynamics the total energy of a system is always conserved, so in psychodynamics there is conservation of psychic energy. Life taken must be paid for. The debt of blood must be repaid. Sacrifice exists in order to complete the mutual exchange of life force, between humans and other species and also between humans and deities - to seal a psychic bargain. If the bargain was not kept, the animals would die, the Mother herself

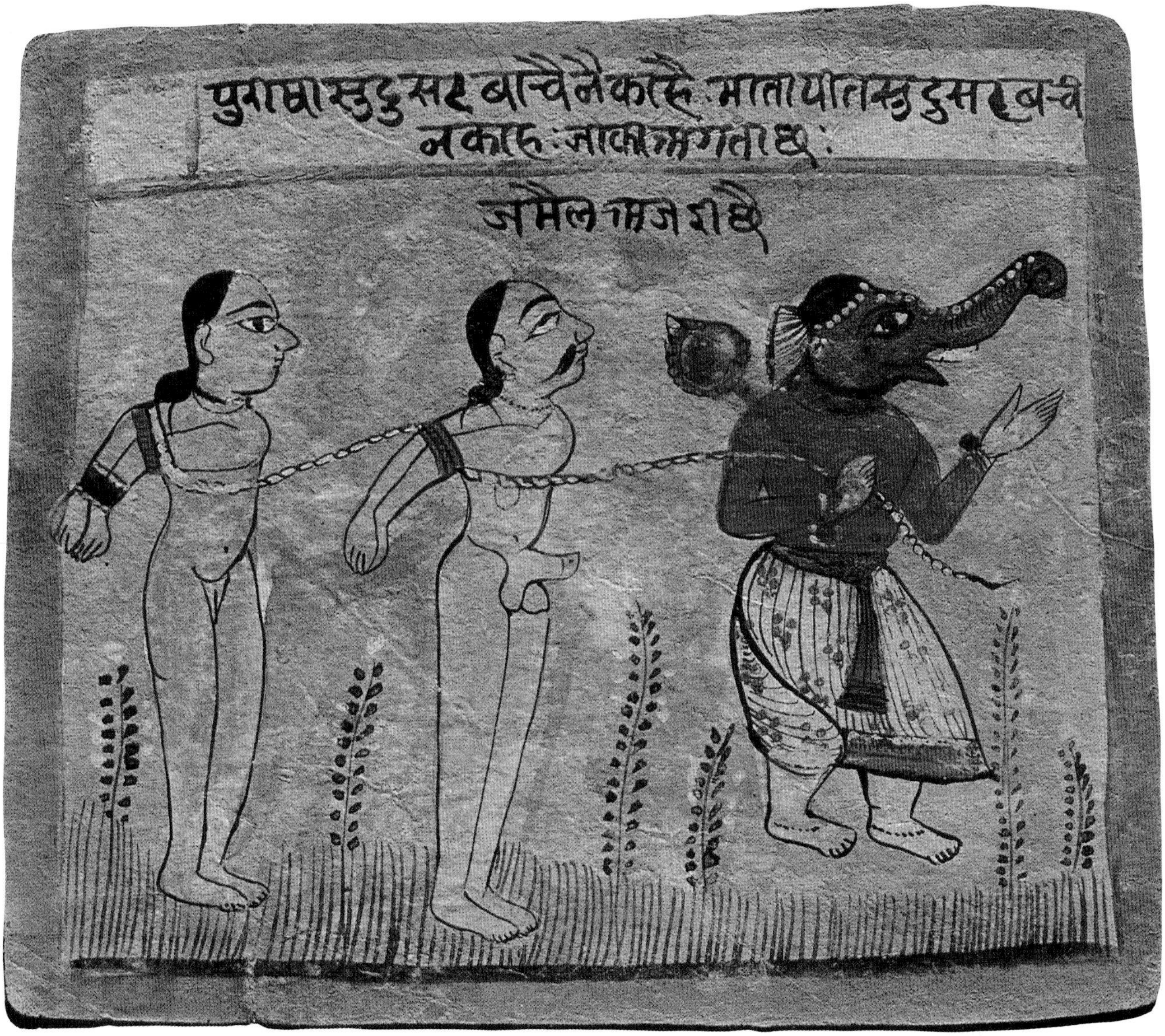

Slaves to passion: in this painting, part of a set designed as dire warnings against the deadly sins of the senses, a man and woman are led away by an animal-headed demon to meet their fate. *Eighteenth century.*

might die. We encounter the same idea in the crude Tantric blood sacrifices still widely practised in India, especially in the villages. If the goddess is not propitiated; if nature is plundered and nothing returned, then calamity follows. The multinational corporations, governments and banks who are raping the rainforests need to learn this lesson.

This page and opposite: Eighteenth-century carvings in hardwood which take woman as their subject. Details of Indian village life, from the ubiquitious pet parrot to the worship of Mother Goddesses, have changed little in over six thousand years.

> Now the Mama grows sad,
> He feels weak.
> He says that the Earth is decaying.
> The Earth is losing its strength
> because the Younger Brothers have taken away much petrol.
> coal, many minerals...
> We tell you,
> we the people of this place,
> Kogi, Asario, Arhuaco:
> that is a violation...
> The Earth feels.
> They take out petrol,
> it feels pain there.
> So the Earth sends out sickness.
> There will be many medicines,
> drugs,
> but in the end the drugs will not be of any use.
> (Divination by a Mama, a holy man, of the Kogi tribe, Colombia. Collected by Alan Ereira 'The Elder Brother')

The Mother's life force flowed visibly as blood. The females of the clan gave their blood ceaselessly before they could conceive. The animals surrendered their meat, hides and horns in pools of blood. It was blood which must be returned to animals and to the Mother. Blood-ritual grew out of the mimic-dances. At a moment in psychic history, the dancers stopped pretending to be hunters and hunted. The hunt became real and a victim died. The victim was a healthy male, dressed in horns and animal skins to play the part of the prey animal. At first he was simply chased. Later, he was chased and then killed. It might have happened by accident, the first time, or the first thousand times, and the accident had to be explained. It would be seen that such a victim was sacred, holy, the representative of those who killed, of the horned god himself, who was sent back to the animals to replenish their energies. So also, the victim would have been offered to the Mother, to compensate her for her constant and selfless sacrifice of blood. To play his role, the victim would need to be intoxicated with drink, or drugged with hashish or mushrooms, or by drumming and dancing, into a state of ecstasy. The hunters too, would need to be lifted out of their everyday consciousness and possessed by a holy madness. From beginnings such as these, we may conjecture, arose the Bacchic chase: the frenzy which overwhelmed worshippers who, in the grip of its madness, chased animals and humans across wild mountainsides and tore them to pieces, even eating fragments of the bloody corpse, in a violent but holy sacrament.

> 'To the earth Pentheus fell, with one incessant scream
> As he understood what end was near.
> His Mother first,
> As priestess, led the rite of death, and fell upon him.
> He tore the headband from his hair, that his wretched
> Mother

Might recognise him and not kill him. 'Mother', he
cried,
Touching her cheek, 'It is I, your own son Pentheus,
whom
You bore to Echion. Mother, have mercy; I have sinned,
But I am still your own son. Do not take my life!'
Agave was foaming at the mouth; her rolling eyes
Were wild; she was not in her right mind, but possessed
By Bacchus, and she paid no heed to him. She grasped
His left arm between wrist and elbow, set her foot
Against his ribs, and tore his arm off by the shoulder.
It was no strength of hers that did it, but the god
Filled her, and made it easy. On the other side
Ino was at him, tearing at his flesh; and now
Autonoe joined them, and the whole maniacal horde.
A single and continuous yell arose — Pentheus
Shrieking as long as life was left in him, the women
Howling in triumph. One of them carried off an arm,
Another a foot, the boot still laced on it. The ribs
were stripped, clawed clean; and women's hands, thicl
red with blood,
Were tossing, catching, like a plaything, Pentheus's
flesh.'
(Euripides, 'The Bacchae', trans Phillip Vellacott)

Euripides does not say so but, in the earliest sacred hunts, the most prized of all the fragments of the body would have been the generative organ. The object of all the killing was, after all, to ensure fertility. Not just the life force but the potency of the victim must be given back to the Mother and to the world. The tearing to pieces of the sacred victim survives in symbolic form to this day in the Chöd ritual of Tibetan Tantrism.

As the domestication of cattle and the cultivation of crops began to replace the old hunter gatherer culture, the nature of fertility, and therefore the role of the goddess, changed. She acquired new children: in addition to being Mother of the wild beasts, she became supreme progenitor of cattle, sheep, goats and other domesticated animals.

'Her names are innumerable - Britomartis and Dictynna, Cybele and Ma, Dindymene and Hecate, Pheraia and Artemis, Baubo and Aphaia, Orthia and Nemesis, Demeter, Persephone, and Selene, Medusa and Eleuthera, Tacit and Leto, Aphrodite and Bendis. And Hathor and Isis, and all other Great Goddesses who appear in animal form, are in reality the Lady of the Beasts. All beasts are their subjects: the serpent and scorpion, the fishes of river and sea, the womblike bi-valves and the ill-omened kraken, the wild beasts of wood and mountain, hunting and hunted, peaceful and voracious, the swamp-birds - goose, duck, and heron -the nocturnal owl and the dove, the domesticated beasts - cow and bull, goat, pig, and sheep - the bee, and even such phantasms as griffin and sphinx.' (Erich Neumann, 'The Great Mother')

With the beginnings of agriculture, the Great Mother became the fruitful womb which gave birth not just to humans and animals, but to wheat, vines and cotton and all harvests. The fertility expressed by the divine lovers was now that of the soil, the fields and the land itself.

An exquisite smooth-limbed bronze statue of the goddess Parvati in her aspect as Uma. It was made in Thanjavur (Tanjore) by the lost-wax process. *Seventeenth century.*

There is a long gap between the stone age and the first historical cultures of the Near East. But the figures found at Tell Halaf, clay goddesses fashioned some time before the fourth millenium BC, demonstrate no significant differences. The voluptuous curves and bulging sexual organs are as emphatic as ever they had been twenty centuries earlier. Indeed, as one eminent Jungian psychologist has pointed out, the archetype is alive and well, as may be seen from a cursory examination of the works of Henry Moore. In some places the animal horns of the old deities survive as relics of the hunter culture. In others the horns turn into wreaths of leaves that sprout from the head, nose and mouth and other parts of the body.

From Harappa, a city-state in the Indus valley that was already thriving in the third millenium BC, comes a seal showing the goddess with the green shoots of new plant growth issuing from her womb. The nude female figure, on the obverse of the seal, is head down with legs stretched outward and upward. Some Indian scholars regard her as the prototype of the earth Mother Sakambhari of the Purana texts, out of whose body grow the food plants that sustain human life. The reverse of this seal carries darker imagery. A female figure with disordered hair and raised arms confronts a threatening male figure carrying a shield and a sickle-shaped knife. This may simply refer to some incident now forgotten in the history of the city, but some have seen in it the portrayal of a human sacrifice connected with the earth goddess depicted on the obverse. If they are right, then the ritual killings in the names of Kali, Durga and the Taras may well have been foreshadowed in Harappa.

We do not know what the goddess was called in the cities of the Indus, but there is no doubt that she was there. Hundreds of steatite amulets and seals bear her image. Typically,

Strange, grim warriors with drawn scimitars threaten a woman who is trapped, head down, between two palm trees. Whilst this may depict the overthrow of one religious orthodoxy by another (see also the painting on page 26), the woman here may be the victim of a human sacrifice.

she is nude, save for a very short skirt secured about the waist by a girdle. Usually, she is weighed down with jewellery: elaborate neck collars, chains, bangles, armlets, anklets and earrings. She has a distinctive head-dress, which rises from behind the head, or perhaps out of her hair. In addition to these goddess figurines, a god generally taken to be an early form of Siva seated in meditation, surrounded by beasts, is well known from Indus valley seals. Some scenes on seals, and ritual objects like large stone lingams and round pierced stones which might have been yonis, suggest that religio-magical fertility rites were well established in a pattern we can recognise from later Tantric worship. In fact there is every reason, as we shall see, to suppose that the Indus civilisation was a major centre in India of the worship that would evolve into Tantrism.

From a tomb near Lauriya in the far north-west comes a small gold tablet upon which is represented a naked woman with voluptuous hips and swollen sexual organs. The figure dates from the seventh or eighth century BC, by which time the Harappan cities had been in ruins for half a millenium. The goddess of the tablet may have been the Mother Goddess, Umadevi, who was worshipped by the Maurya kings, particularly the Emperor Asoka, before his conversion to Buddhism. We learn from Asoka's biographer, the Buddhist Lama Taranatha, that the king used actively to encourage the orgiastic sexual rites which were a part of the cult of the Mother Goddess.

In its present form, Tantrism is essentially a medieval religion, but it is a direct descendant of the old Mother Goddess worship. which was the religion of the agricultural peoples whose social sytems were based on the principle of Mother-right, as those of the Indus Valley peoples were.

Baron Omar Rolf Ehrenfels observes that Mother-right elements in India are stronger, both in extent and in degree, than in any other part of the world and that, in spite of the ruthless efforts to establish male supremacy through hypergamy, child-marriage and sati (widow-burning), it has proved impossible to stamp out Mother-rights from the life of the Indian masses. The violence of these methods used against the feminine principle in India has no parallel anywhere else in human history.

Something of the nature of the Indus goddess may be deduced by comparisons with goddesses of western Asia and the Mediterranean. There are haunting similarities between the Harappan goddess seals and those of ancient Crete. The Sumerian Mother Goddess, who later became Nana of Uruk, Nina of Nineveh, Inanna of Erech, Bau of Lagash, Ninlil of Nippur, Annuit of Akkad, Zarpaint of Babylon and Anatita of Persia; who was also supposed to be the Mother of Attis and who was identified with Ishtar, Astarte, Anaitis and Aphrodite; was also worshipped in India. Her name is found on coins of the Kushana period and she survives to this day as Bibi Nani of Baluchistan, Naina Devi of the Kulu Valley, Sirmur and Bilaspur, and Naini Devi of Nainital. According to one scholar the goddess name 'Nana' can be identified on some Indus valley seals, but we must take this 'cum grano salis'. The Indus valley script remains enigmatic and continues to foment academic feuds.

Some scholars have been struck by the similarity of the word 'Tara', a name shared by an important group of Tantric goddesses, with the names of Astarte, Ishtar, Atargatis and Ashtaroth, the renowned Mother Goddess of Canaan. It is not just the goddess names which resemble one another, but the manner of their worship. It is clear that, from the very earliest times, sacred sexuality has played a part in the worship of the great Mother. An ice-age rock painting from Cogul, in Spain shows a group of women dancing round a phallic male figure. Robert Graves, in his 'White Goddess', mythopoeically identifies this figure as a dancing Dionysus.

In the context of Dionysian worship, castration, one of the oldest rituals of the Mother Goddess in western Asia, acquires a new significance. It was particularly associated with the cult of Cybele, the Mother Goddess of Phrygia, who was connected with Dionysian worship.

Was castration a development from the older and more primitive Bacchic chase? Was the sacred victim spared, if he would voluntarily give up the vital part of his body, his generative organs? We shall return to this theme in considering the evolution of the sacrament of Tantric maithuna, or ritual sex.

The sacrifice of a bull is often encountered in cults which practised castration. It may have been that sparing the life of the human victim made it necessary to kill a substitute of suitable power and magnificence. The White Yajur-veda describes a crop-fertility ritual in which the country's queen has sexual intercourse with a high priest in front of a congregation. In each verse, an aspect of the sexual union is linked to a specific agricultural operation. The ritual was originally a 'naramedha', or human sacrifice, in which the priest was slaughtered after his copulation with the queen. In later ages, the priest's life was spared and a horse was offered instead. This is the origin of the famous 'asvamedha', or horse sacrifice. The ritual copulation was now mimed, with the queen lying down in the field beside the dead horse. In the same way, Himalayan Tantric sects which once practised human sacrifice still slaughter buffaloes in honour of the great Mother Kali. Bull-fighting and other dangerous games with bulls, like the bull-leaping practised in Crete, were among the great rituals of the Mother Goddess. In Crete the goddess demonstrated her control over the wild forces symbolised by the bull, by toying with him and thus taming him. In her form as the great goddess Tauropolos, she is the Lady of the Bull; as Pheraia or Europa, riding on a bull, she tames the masculine and bestial. The earliest consort of the great Mother Goddess is, indeed, a blend of beast and man. Siva and Dionysus, both central to our understanding of the worship that became Tantra, were both consorts of the great Mother who began as horned gods of the hunt. Both, in later incarnations, became bull gods. Dionysus was 'taurokeros' (bull-horned), and 'tauroprosopos' (bull-faced) and was the

A matador in Andalusia makes a pass with the muleta, or killing cape. The bullfight is the last surviving vestige of the religious rituals that surrounded the ancient and widespread bull cult. The bull was associated with both Dionysus and Siva and was the holy animal of the mysterious Indus valley culture. It remains sacred in India to this day.

Nandi, doorkeeper to Siva and Parvati and first source of the love-teachings that eventually became codified as the Kama Sutra. *Black granite, twelfth or thirteenth century.*

spirit of the sacrificial bull. Siva, whose earliest forms are all horned, but whose horns became coils of matted hair and twining snakes, to this day retains the services of the excellent Nandi, the white bull who is his mount and doorkeeper. Nandi it was who stood watch outside the divine bedchamber where Siva and his consort the goddess Parvati, 'daughter of the mountain', one of the names of the Great Mother, were making love - a lovemaking which, according to legend, lasted for a thousand divine years and whose passion literally shook the world. From Nandi's lips came the description of this lovemaking, secrets which became codified in the Indian kama-shastra tradition. Throughout the ancient world, the bull was both sacrificial victim and symbol of potency, uniting in his body and blood the themes of death and sexuality. The bull was the single most important animal in the Indus valley cities, appearing on more seals than any other beast and remains sacred and protected animal in India.

It is a long road from where Pentheus' body lies, in fragments on the mountainside, and the cakrapujas of the Tantrics. But all later rites and rituals are an evolution of the Mother worship of the first humans, and even the sacraments of later times, whether of meat, burnt offerings, bread, wine or ritual sex - all the Tantric sacraments - are in essence a re-enactment of the primal sacrifice: the bloody body of Pentheus. Secret forms of worship, resembling Tantric rites, were used in Phrygia, Syria, Lydia, Cappadocia, Pontus and Galatia, all places where the cult of the Mother Goddess was popular. There were 'Tantric' elements in the

Zeus, chieftain of the Greek gods, assumes human form to enjoy one of his many mortal conquests. The cult of Zeus and Demeter was associated with sacred orgies. In this oil painting, the unknown artist has carefully included an interesting antelope-legged table and Zeus's eagle with its talons full of thunderbolts – now part of the official regalia of the USA. *French, school of David, eighteenth century.*

orgiastic worship of the Phoenician Mother Goddess Astarte of Hierapolis, the Eleusinian, Phrygian, Dionysian rites, the rituals of Isis and the Marian mysteries.

The rituals connected with the union of Cybele and Attis, Aphrodite and Adonis, Ishtar and Tammuz, Demeter and Zeus, were markedly sexual in nature and are mirrored in the orgiastic 'cakras', circles, of Tantrics of the left-hand path. Promiscuous sexual intercourse was a feature of the Greek festival of Demeter and Persephone. On the headdress of the Cyprian goddess, adorned with Hathor-horns and floral rosettes, fauns and women danced in orgiastic abandon. On the Greek island of Delos, huge erect marble phalluses, each several feet high, crouch on pedestals like a row of lions, guarding a ceremonial highway.

The Isis mysteries are supposed to have been entirely without sexual content and, on the surface, presented an ascetic picture strangely reminiscient of Brahmanical Hinduism: shaven-headed, white robed priests offering prayers, incense and water from the sacred river - in this case, of course, the Nile. Yet the cult had as its most secret mystery a rite performed in a sacred marriage bed. Isis-worship had a particular fascination for the hetairai, or courtesans, of the classical world. It was to the temple of Isis that the Roman noblewoman,

'Offering to Priapus': A young woman helps her friend mount the phallic statue of the Roman god Priapus in order to gain the blessings of fertility. *Oil painting by an unknown French artist, eighteenth century.*

Paulina, went to spend the night with the god Anubis, who had summoned her there. But this was no divinity, of course. Beneath the jackal's mask was the grinning face of the eques Decius Mundus. In the ensuing scandal the emperor Tiberius banned the priests of Isis from Rome.

The early travellers to India were invariably shocked by the widespread Tantric worship of 'Siva-lingas', or representations of the erect phallus of the god. Very few of them remembered that the streets of Rome and Pompeii were dotted with erect phalluses carved on stone plaques with inscriptions like 'HIC HABITAT FELICITAS': 'here dwells happiness'. It was at one time thought that these were signs or advertisements for brothels - Pompeiian and Roman equivalents of the English pub sign - but as scholarship has emerged from the self-imposed censorship of the eighteenth and nineteenth centuries, it has been possible to accept that these phallic representations were much more than evidence of immorality.

Also in use throughout the classical world were herms, or boundary markers, phallic stone pillars sometimes topped with carved goat horns but always embellished with an erect penis. The Romans used to worship these stone phalluses with offerings of flowers, fruit and libations of honey, milk and wine. Women brought garlands of roses in spring, ears of corn in summer, grain in the autumn and olive branches in winter. This is, of course, reminiscent of the worship of the Siva-linga in India, which is bathed with perfumed water, ghee, honey and sugarcane juice and adorned with flowers, perfumes and ointments.

Criticism of Tantrism has been fierce over the years and apologists for the cult have repeatedly been driven to remind us that Indian Tantric sects were not the first and will not be the last to make use of sexual rituals in worship. They point to the evidence we have just mentioned: of promiscuity in the cult of Phrygian Cybele and ritual sex in the mysteries of Dionysus; of holy whores at the temples of Aphrodite and Astarte. This is all very well, but it misses the point, which is that the Tantric cult is nothing more or less than the same Mother-goddess worship, in a purely Indian manifestation.

If the Indus cities were the first centres of Mother Goddess worship in India, it is worth remembering their geographical location. The Tantric texts of the second millenium AD may have come from Bengal, Orissa and Assam, in the far east of the country, but earlier Tantras come from the mountains of Tibet and Kashmir. Of the Indus cities, Harappa stood within sight of the snow peaks of the Hindu Kush, while Mohenjo-daro was a day's march from the mountains of Baluchistan. There is a verse in the Kubjikamata-tantra, which suggests that Tantrism may have entered India through these mountains, perhaps brought by the Magi priests of the Scythians. Sir John Woodroffe, the pre-eminent scholar of Tantrism, was convinced that Tantrism came to India from Scythia, the Sakadvipa of tradition, which is shown on old maps as lying just across the Hindu Kush in Central Asia. The goddess Nana-Inanna who, as we have seen, is still worshipped in India today, is thought to have entered India with the Scythians in the same way.

Tantra has its deepest roots in the universal prehistoric fertility cult. The magical and psycho-sexual practices of the Tantric sects evolved from the experiences of various cultic and mystery traditions which in turn arose out of the worship of the great Mother and her consort. But these mysteries were not contemporary with one another. Many thousands of years separate the death of the first Pentheus - the primaeval forerunner of Pentheus, King of Thebes - from the desert speculations of the gnostics. Yet both are in the direct line of descent that leads to Tantra. In tracing that line of descent, one is irresistibly drawn, time and again, to the knot of mountains in the northwest of the subcontinent - the icy granite gates through which every ancient invader entered India - the peaks of Afghanistan and the Hindu Kush. It is in this wild landscape of summits that we must look for the mountainside on which Pentheus's body still lies.

Chapter 3

ENCOUNTER ON THE THREE-HORNED MOUNTAIN

> 'Father and son, mother and mother-in-law, father-in-law, maternal uncle, son-in-law, daughter, brother, nephew, and other kindred, friends, guests and others, slave-men and slave-women - all pair, one with the other. With the men the women mingle, known or unknown, just as the longing comes on them.'

This is not yet another nineteenth-century European fulminating against the depravity of Tantric practices. It is a two-thousand year old diatribe by Prince Karna, speaking to us from the pages of the Indian epic 'Mahabharata' (Karna Parva XL). The people he speaks of with such contempt are members of the Madra and Bahika tribes living in the mountainous regions of the far northwest - near the Indus and Jhelum rivers.

> 'How should there be virtue among the befouled Madras, a byword for their unlovely deeds, among these untutored eaters of groats and fish, who drink heady wine in their homes, and with it eat cow's flesh, and then shout and laugh, sing unrhymed rubbish, follow their lusts and chatter such things at one another as they choose? How should the Madra man speak of virtue, the son of women that throw off their clothes, and so dance, clouded by heady drink, that pair without heed of any barrier, and live as their lusts lead them; that make water standing, like the camel and the ass, have lost seemliness and virtue, and in all things are without shame?...If the Madra woman is asked for sour rice gruel, she shakes her buttocks, and utters — she, infatuated with giving — these dreadful words: 'Let none ask me for my beloved sour rice gruel. My son I would give, my husband I would give, but I would not give sour rice gruel.' Pale-faced (gauryas), big shameless are the Madra women, clad in woollen wraps, greedy, and without cleanliness or neatness. Thus do we hear.' (Translator: Johann Jakob Meyer)

Leaving aside the Madra lady's peculiar attachment to her 'sour rice gruel' - for which we may read the sour rice beer still enjoyed in these parts and nowadays known as 'chang', and which the Kularnava-tantra calls 'sauvira' and recommends for use in its rites - we find in this one passage groats, fish, wine, meat, sexual intercourse: all the five sacraments of the Tantric panchamakara ritual. How old is this passage? And what is the significance of the customs it describes?

The written form of Mahabharata is generally held to have evolved during a period between 400 BC and 200 AD. But it draws on a much older oral tradition which recorded real events - a great war between two princely dynasties - thought to have taken place in the bronze age, some time between 1400 and 1000 BC.

The Kama Sutra of Vatsyayana, composed probably in the third- century AD but, like the Mahabharata, heir to a much older tradition, says that the Bahika women hate kissing, but enjoy 'citrarata', that is, making love in elaborate and difficult standing postures (Kamasutram, 5, xxii-xxiii). It adds that the women living around the Indus, Shatadru and

Two charming miniatures of the Orissan 'Tantric yoga' set. (See also page 18.) On the left the expert couple perform a difficult standing 'bandha' or knot. On the right is an equally virtuoso performance of a variation of the posture which Vatsyayana in Kama Sutra calls 'kakila', the Crow. *Orissa, eighteenth or nineteenth century.*

Iravati rivers are exceedingly passionate, and fond of oral sex. The kama-shastra tradition, of which the Kama Sutra was part, dates back at least to the seventh-century BC.

> 'A husband of these foul, evil women of the Bahikas, one that dwelt in Kurujangala, sang with but little rejoicing soul: "She the tall one, the fair (gauri) one, clad in a thin wool wrap, lies, I know, and thinks of me, the Bahika in Kurujangala. When I have crossed the Shatadru and the delightful Iravati and come into my home, then shall I see them, the great-shelled (shell = vulva), splendid women, the outward corners of whose eyes shine with red-lead, the light-skinned women anointed with ointment from the mountain of Trikakud, wrapped in woollen cloaks and skins, screaming, fair to look on".'

Many times during his outburst, Karna refers to the tribespeople as 'mlecchas'. The word 'mleccha' does not help us very much, as it simultaneously means 'unclean', 'outcaste' and 'foreigner' or 'barbarian', in effect anyone who does not speak Sanskrit. In India, foreigners were automatically regarded by upper-caste Hindus as untouchable, an irony which tended to be lost on high-minded missionaries like Abbe Dubois and William Ward. In this, the ancient Indians were very different from their Greek contemporaries, for whom the word 'xenos', or 'stranger' also signified 'guest'.

But the writers of the Mahabharata did not mean that the Madras and Bahikas were literally foreigners. They too were Aryas, but outside the mainstream of brahmanical society. Very likely, they were tribes which had entered the northwestern valleys long after the first waves of Aryas had passed through and established their Vedic sacrifice in the plains of the Ganga-Jamuna doab. Although the Rg Veda, oldest of the four Vedas, and most sacred of Hindu scriptures, recalls a time before the Aryas entered India, its hymns were not actually composed until the first tribes had been settled for some centuries.

Latecomers like the Madras and Bahikas may have been Aryas, but they had not participated in the creation of the Rg Vedic tradition. It is possible that in the wild frontier regions where they settled, they encountered an ancient Mother Goddess religion, which probably predated even the cities of the Indus; that they were seduced away from the worship of their Arya sky-gods, Indra and Varuna; that the term 'mleccha' was applied to them because in the eyes of other Aryas their worship had become impure. It is made clear elsewhere in Karna's attack on the Madras and Bahlikas that his concern was not primarily with sexual matters, but to maintain the purity of the brahmanical sacrifice.

Karna's great contempt for the Madras, it must be said, did not prevent him from accepting their help in battle. His chariot was driven by Salya, king of the Madras. And when he took his place at the front of the army beside the Kuru prince Duryodhana; it was powerful Madra chariot-warriors who protected them. Salya gently admonished Karna, telling him that: 'Everywhere are kings devoted to their respective religions. Everywhere may be found virtuous men. There are men in many countries that surpass the very gods by their behaviour.'

A sandstone temple carving showing a loving couple entwined in a tight embrace, her face raised to his in a 'lifted kiss'. *Twelfth century.*

If the Madras had learned Mother-worship, who taught it to them? Could the origins of the word 'mleccha', lie in the name of the Indus valley civilisation? It is recorded in Sumer and Elam that the name of this old Indian realm was Meluhha. Were the 'mlecchas' originally the 'Meluhhas' - people of the Indus culture? Certainly, these were the first civilised Indians with whom the Aryas came into contact and the same people whose cities they destroyed, as told in the Rg Veda. They were non-Sanskrit speaking and their matrilinear society with its orgiastic goddess worship must have seemed depraved.

> 'When the women have taken heady drink of corn and molasses and taken cows' flesh with garlic - they, who eat cakes, flesh and roasted barley, and know not the ways of goodness, sing and dance, drunk and unclothed, on the earth-walls of the city and of the houses, without wreaths and unanointed, and amidst drunken, lewd songs of various kinds, which sound like the noises of asses and camels. They know no bridle in their pairing, and in all things they follow their lust. They utter fine sayings against one another, they, who hold forth maddened by the drink: "Ho there, ye outcasts! Ho, ye outcasts! Cast off by your husband, cast off by your lord!" Screaming, this refuse of women dance at the festivals, putting no restraint upon themselves.'

Was it the thick mud walls of Mohenjo-daro and Harappa that the poet of the Mahabharata had in mind? Did the women of Meluhha dance in abandon? To which deity were these festivals dedicated? The orgiastic dances and love feasts described in the epic, while on the one hand seeming so close to later Tantric rites, also call to mind descriptions of bacchic frenzy. Siva and the great Mother, in her forms as Kali or Tara, were not Vedic divinities. They were older, indigenous deities. Were these orgiastic dances, described with such abhorrence in the Mahabharata, the earliest recorded rites of Sakti-Siva?

An early form of Siva, it is customary to accept, is found on seals from Mohenjo-daro, his identity proclaimed by his yogic pose, by the animals that surround him in his form as Pasupati, Lord of Beasts, and by his erect phallus. Lingams and what may have been yoni-stones have also been found in great abundance. Furthermore, the word 'mleccha' in Sanskrit can have another meaning. According to Sir Monier Monier-Williams, author of the great Oxford Sanskrit Dictionary, it can signify 'a savage mountaineer'. He gives the example of 'a Sabara'. The Sabaras were an aboriginal hunter tribe, like the Nisadas, who from the beginning of the first millenium BC, were strongly associated with the worship of the god Siva. The Mahabharata records that Siva once took the form of a forest-dwelling Sabara.

The religion of these people was probably closely related to the religion of the Indus valley cities.

At the time of the Arya invasions, if we agree with a date of roughly 1200 BC, the cities on the Indus plain had already been standing for over a thousand years. Given that they were agricultural centres, with outlying towns, villages and tiny hamlets scattered throughout the forested countryside, it is inconceivable that there would not have been the closest contact between the townsfolk and the wild tribes living in the hills and forests as there is today between townspeople and tribes living in the Santal areas of Bengal and Bihar. From the hunters, the Indus people would have learned about the horned Siva and the village Mothers who are still worshipped all over India today, even if the official Harappan religion was influenced by the Mother goddess worship of further west, in Elam and Sumer, Babylon, Tyre and Knossos.

One clue to the nature of the pre-Arya religion and its deities crops up again and again. In the passage, quoted above, Karna sneers at the lovelorn Bahika man who, alone in Kurujangala and missing his Bahika girlfriend, nostalgically recalls:

> "...the light-skinned women anointed with ointment from the mountain of Trikakud."

'Trikakud' means 'three-horned', clearly signifying a triple-peak. In searching for this mountain we encounter one of the wildest denizens of the mythical landscape, the horned god himself.

The connection between Indian Siva and Greek Dionysus, indeed their complete identification, was long ago acknowledged by Greek and Indian alike. Neither the Greeks nor the Indians of the post-Macedonian conquest had the slightest hesitation in identifying Dionysus as Siva. In particular, they pointed to the similarity of the Bacchic processions with drums and cymbals to the dances of the Sydrakoi (Sydrakoi = Oxydrakoi = Kshudrakas:

Demons of the senses, possibly disfigured by smallpox as a punishment, lead an enslaved victim astray. *Eighteenth century.*

a tribe encountered by Alexander, but whose history dates back like those of the Madras and the Bahikas, to the heroic age of the epics).

Dionysus and Herakles, according to a tradition current in India, were the only foreigners before Alexander ever to have conquered India. (In this, of course, they were mistaken, but for our purpose this makes no difference.) Strabo reminds us that, in his younger, wilder days, Dionysus had led his band of marauding maenads across Asia. As a consequence of this, in his later Greek and Roman days, the god was often shown accompanied by a tiger.

The courtiers of the Indian emperor Chandragupta Maurya even provided Megasthenes, the inquisitive Ambassador of Seleuces I, with a list of the 153 kings who had preceded their master on the throne of Pataliputra. The list, which was supposed to go back 6,000 years, began with the name Spatembas, who, Strabo tells us, was the most 'Bacchic' of Dionysus's companions.

Dionysus is the god of the bacchantes. In lost aboriginal times he may have been worshipped in a symbolic hunt in which his followers ritually pursued a man clothed in animal skins and horns and tore him to pieces: the original frenzy of the maenads. He is said to have come from the east. His worship flourished in Asia Minor, particularly in Phrygia, home to the terrifying cult of Cybele, and Lydia of the soft musical airs. Also called Bacchus, (in Rome, Liber, whence 'libertine') for the Greeks and Romans he was a god of fruitfulness, especially associated with wine and ecstasy. Although he came to Greece via Thrace and Phrygia, the strange legends of his birth and death, and his marriage to Ariadne, a Cretan goddess, later mistress of the labyrinth, suggest that his cult may have been a reversion to a pre-Hellenic nature religion that flourished in Minoan Crete and elsewhere.

Legend tells that Dionysus was the son of Zeus and Semele, daughter of Cadmus, King of Thebes. Semele was originally a Phrygian earth goddess. Zeus' wife Hera was jealous of Semele and goaded her into asking Zeus to prove his divinity by appearing to her in his divine form. When Zeus complied, the power of his presence proved too much for Semele, who was destroyed. Zeus saved his son, the baby Dionysus, by sewing him up in his thigh, where he remained until he reached maturity. Dionysus was thus 'twice born'. He was taken by Hermes, the master of magic, to be brought up by the bacchante Maenads of a place called Nysa. This Nysa, which was thought to be somewhere in Asia or Asia Minor, was the site of the god's holy mountain, across whose slopes the horned god roamed with his maenads, as in the well-known verse of Sophocles:

> "Whence I beheld the famous Nysa, ranged in Bacchic frenzy by mortals, which the horned Iacchus roams as his own sweetest nurse, where— what bird exists that singeth not there?"

Where was Nysa? Some had identified it in ancient times with the village of Isa in Boetia on the basis of the line in the Iliad that speaks of 'sacred Isus'. But Apollodorus, in his 'On Ships', put paid to this notion, saying that there was no 'Nisa' to be found in Boetia. There was a Nysa, vastly more promising, in Phrygia, the site of a cavern called the 'Plutonium' (lit 'ploutonion') which was full of poisonous vapours. It was, according to the geographer Strabo, an opening of only moderate size, large enough to admit a man, but reaching a considerable depth. The depths of the cave were filled with a vapour too misty and dense to see through. Strabo then tells of an experiment he performed here:

> 'Now to those who approach the handrail anywhere round the enclosure the air is harmless, since the outside is free from that vapour in calm weather, for the vapour then stays inside the enclosure, but any animal that passes inside meets instant death. At any rate, bulls that are led into it fall and are dragged out dead; and I threw in

Another in the series of 'Deadly Sin' paintings. (See also pages 27 and 41.) Here an elephant-headed demon feeds his victim to a hungry tiger. In a memorable verse from the Kularnava-tantra, old age is said to stalk mankind like a tiger, waiting to pounce. Perhaps the sin being expiated by this victim is that of indolence.

A greystone sculpture of Durga, her hand raised and fingers shaping a mudra of blessing. One foot rests on a donkey; the goddess is receiving the worship of a small animal.

> sparrows and they immediately breathed their last and fell.'
> (Translator: Horace Leonard Jones)

The cavern was sacred to the cult of Cybele, who in her Cretan form of Semele, was mother of the god Dionysus, and we may infer that the bulls led in were sacrificial beasts. But the castrated priests of Cybele, the 'galli', seemed to have an immunity to the vapours.

> 'The galli, who are eunuchs, pass inside with such impunity that they even approach the opening, bend over it, and descend into it to a certain depth, though they hold their breath as much as they can (for I could see in their countenances an indication of a kind of suffocating attack, as it were), — whether this immunity belongs to all who are maimed in this way or only to those round the temple, or whether it is because of divine providence, as would be likely in the case of divine obsessions, or whether it is the result of certain physical powers that are antidotes against the vapour.'

The castrations of the 'galli' were bloody self-sacrifices in which the ecstatic, or crazed, would-be priests, emasculated themselves with sharp sickle-shaped blades and threw their severed genital organs onto the altar of the goddess, in rites which strangely prefigured the

Temple carving in hardwood of a goddess. *Eighteenth century.*

A pale-skinneed goddess: another of the outstanding 'ritual' series of eighteenth-century Tantric paintings. (See pp 15, 19.) Once again the painting is alive with kundalini energy symbolised by the snakes. The goddess is surrounded by severed lingams and served by attendants who appear to be eunuchs. Below is the face of Bhairava, with the yoni.

'sacrifice' still made by many young boys in India today. Cybele was once Semele, of Crete and the bull- labyrinth. Dionysus, a 'bull-faced', 'bull-horned' god, was her son. Did her bull and castration rituals have their origin in the Bacchic chase? In dim prehistorical times, the holy victims, representatives of the horned god, gave their own lives in order that the maenads could tear from them their life-giving organs of procreation: the life force of the god replenishing the life force of the Mother. Had this sacrifice, by the historical period, been transmuted to the twin offerings of a bull, and their own, voluntarily given-up, manhood? Maybe this is the meaning of that ambiguous Harappan seal - the one where the man with a sickle shaped knife stands before the woman with upraised arms and unkempt hair.

But we must return to our search for Dionysus's holy mountain. The Nysa of Phrygia was sacred to the cult of Cybele. But it was not the place where Dionysus grew up and the mountain, Mesogis, on which it stood, was not his sacred mountain. Even in ancient times, nobody was able to pinpoint a satisfactory location for 'famous Nysa'. According to one authority, writing for the Encyclopaedia Brittanica, it was 'a purely imaginary spot'.

Only once in history has a place called Nysa been unequivocally identified as the holy mountain of Dionysus. The geographer Strabo records that when Alexander's Macedonians were threading their way through the Hindu Kush on their march towards the valley of the Indus, they came across a place called Nysa. There, in that wild mountain landscape, they encountered a people who greeted them as long-lost brothers. These people told the startled Greeks that they were the descendents of a western people who had come into those parts in ages past with the god Dionysus.

In the god's legend, the Greeks recalled, Nysa was the name given to the place of his holy hill. The name of this little town in the Hindu Kush, as it was pronounced to Alexander, had a similar ring. The settlement of Nysa, or 'Nisha', stood on the lower slopes of a distinctive triple-peaked mountain. That this was indeed the sacred mountain of Dionysus was confirmed for the Greeks when they were told that a nearby peak was called 'Meru'. Was this not a clear reference to the divine thigh, or 'meros', from which the infant god had sprung?

What escaped Strabo was the significance of 'Meru'. In Sanskrit, the name means 'mountain', but not just any mountain. Meru was a sacred mountain: the mountain of Siva.

Let us describe mount Meru. In its dazzling golden splendour, it surpasses even the sun. Devas and gandharvas (for cognate Greek words read 'gods' and 'centaurs') attend it on all sides. The air on mount Meru is always alive with bird song - 'what bird exists that singeth not there?' Rare medicinal herbs grow on its slopes and sacred snakes guard its approaches. A man burdened with sin cannot approach the holy mountain. Those who do go to great Meru, it is said, never return.

Eight tall mountains surround mount Meru. To the east are the peaks Jara and Devakuta, to the west Pavamana and Pariyatra. To the south rise Kailasa and Karavira. On the northern side, there are two mountains, Makaragiri and Trsrnga.

To identify the mythological Meru is as hopeless a task as finding mythological Nysa, yet many have tried. The Mahabharata describes Mount Meru as being in the far north of the country, at the centre of the world, directly beneath the immovable point of the north star. Scholars have sought Meru without success among the mountains of the Pamirs, the K'un-lun, the Karakorum and the Hindu Kush.

One detail teases, however, in the traditional descriptions of Meru. We are told that to the north of Meru stood the mountain Trsrnga. The name 'Trsrnga' means 'three-horned'. Obviously, it refers to a triple-peak. According to another tradition, one of the subsidiary peaks of Meru is known as 'trikuta', again meaning 'three-peaked'. The great serpent Vasuki once coiled himself around mount Meru, when he uncoiled himself, the triple-peak of 'trikuta' was broken off from Meru. 'Trikuta' is another name for 'trikakud', meaning a 'three-peaked' or 'three-horned' mountain.

There is such a mountain in the Hindu Kush and today it is called Koh-e-Mor. Was this the triple-mountain of Strabo's account, which Alexander's Greeks accepted as Dionysian Nysa and which stood near a peak called Meru? Was it the same triple-peak that the Bahika man called 'trikakud'? Did its unique shape lead to its being called by the names of 'trsrnga' and 'trikuta', which are spurs of Siva's mythological Meru? Was this triple-peak in the mountain country of the Madras once sacred to the horned god of beasts, consort of the great Mother, whose seals we find in nearby Harappa and whose rites were celebrated with wine and meat and fish and cakes and orgies?

The god Siva is attended by Vasuki, king of snakes and by his son, the elephant-headed Ganesa.

If it was, then it confirms the opinion of Megasthenes and his Indian hosts, albeit at a level far more profound than the political ecumenism of ancient empires, that Siva and Dionysus were indeed once the same ancient divinity. The legend of each illumines the other. When Coleridge remarked that: 'The conquest of India by Bacchus might afford some scope for a very brilliant poem of the fancy and the understanding' ('Table Talk', 4 September 1835), he had no idea that the poem had already been written: it is the Siva-samhita. Although Coleridge may not have realised it, he himself, forty years earlier, had begun writing such a poem. It still lay incomplete, interrupted forever by the 'person from Porlock'.

> In Xanadu did Kubla Khan
> A stately pleasure dome decree:
> Where Alph the sacred river, ran
> Through caverns measureless to man
> Down to a sunless sea.
> ('Kubla Khan', 1797)

What is 'Alph' but the holy river Alpheius, which ran through the very caverns sacred to Cybele that we have just visited? As our theme develops, we shall discover the meaning of the 'sunless sea' and of the 'holy dread', 'honey-dew' and 'milk of Paradise'. The poem resounds with the imagery of Siva-Dionysus. As we shall see, Coleridge's description of Kubla Khan's entranced state applies precisely to the intoxicated exaltation of Tantric worshippers.

The very name 'Dionysus' may have an Indian origin. 'Dio-Nysus' means nothing more than 'the God of Nysa'. The Greeks did not know where Nysa could be found, or indeed if it was a real place. Their traditions told them only that it was somewhere out east. What if the old horned god had once been called in Sanskrit 'nisa- deva', 'god of the dark people, the Nisadas'? Or turning it round into Greek: 'dio-nisa'? According to a number of Puranas and also the Mahabharata, the first ancestor of the Nisadas was, like Dionysus, thigh-born. He was a typical wild hunter: 'a man like a charred log with a flat face and extremely short'. The Matsya Purana says that he was also the ancestor of the mlecchas. Wild mountain and forest tribes, fisherfolk - all those who were outside the Arya dharma - these were the children of this dark man. Rudra, the wild god of the hunter tribes, who was grudgingly given a place in the Vedic pantheon, was identified as a form of Siva and in the old texts, was often referred to simply as 'isa-deva', or 'that god', as though they could not bear to name him.

If Dionysus was indeed 'nisa-deva' or god of the dark people, then he was one and the same as this proto-Siva. Follow the histories of the two gods back far enough and they merge in the figure of a shadowy, dark, aboriginal god who was not yet either. Even the Indus valley dwellers, whose seals Pasupati adorns, did not know this original god, who was the god of the before-people, the aboriginals who had inhabited the country for millenia before the forefathers of the Indus Valley people had settled the flood plain of the great river. The

Bacchic mysteries begin here, although they have not yet evolved into the rites of Cybele and the Dionysian frenzies of Thessaly. Nor has the worship of Siva and the Mother yet evolved into Tantra.

That day on the slopes of the three-horned mountain, what happened was this: in the meeting of Alexander's men and the Nysaeans, two strains of the same ancient worship regained contact after long separation. The Nysaeans, to judge by Strabo's description, practised a religion that was intrinsically still that of the old hunter-culture. The Macedonians brought back to India Bacchic mysteries which had long since outgrown the blood ritual and had entered what we may call the 'classical' mystery phase, in which the blood sacrifice is transubstantiated.

The essential point here for the student of Tantra is not the truism that Tantra began with the fertility blessings of conjoined Siva and Sakti. It is that the distant origins in dark, bloody rites, in the incessant struggle to survive, make it possible to examine afresh the 'morality' of Tantra. It is no good simply accepting at face value that for some Hindu sects, sex and liquor and drugs could be sacramental. One may accept this and still find it abhorrent, as the Abbe Dubois and William Ward did. But we should not forget that some Roman commentators found the Christian sacrament revolting and barbaric. Of the five-fold Tantric sacrament, we can now see how three - 'matsya' (meat), 'madya' (wine or any intoxicating substance) and 'maithuna' or ritual sex, might have begun their evolution in magical rites to ensure the survival of the body and the clan. What of the others? What of the loaves and fishes? We cannot answer this without questioning the very nature and meaning of sacramental experience.

Professor E.R. Dodds, writing about Euripides's 'The Bacchae', says:

> 'The moral of 'The Bacchae' is that we ignore at our peril the demand of the human spirit for Dionysiac experience. For those who do not close their minds against it, such experience can be a source of spiritual power and eudamonia. But those who repress the demand in themselves or refuse its satisfaction to others transform it by their act into a power of disintegration and destruction.'

In the primitive worship of the horned god of the hunters, sacrifice is still the sacrifice of living flesh, not yet transubstantiated by mystery. The blessings of the goddess are still those of fertility and plenty, not yet the escape into gnosis. After the Nysa meeting, each strain of Siva-Dionysus worship would continue to evolve separately, the goddess worship into the cult of Siva and Parvati; the Bacchic and related mysteries into early first millenium gnosticism. The two traditions would meet again several hundred years later and merge together in the beginnings of modern Tantra.

Chapter 4

Devagiri: Mountain of the Gods

Ellamma, Kaliyamma, Mariyamma, Mutyalamma, Ponnamma, Ankalamma, Kolumamma, Selliyamma, Pattalamma, Vandi-Kaliyamma, Poleramma, Gangamma, Chaudamma, Durgamma, Nukalamma, Paidamma, Asiramma, Padalamma, Gontyalamma, Paradesamma, Neralamma, Kollapuri-amma, Mallamma, Peddintamma, Somalamma, Talupulamma, Sellandiyamma, Patallamma, Bangaramma, Alagiyanachchiyamma: these are a handful of the local village names by which the Mother goddess is still worshipped in India today.

Some of these names are epithets: 'Bangaramma' = 'the golden Mother'; 'Mutyalamma' = 'pearl Mother'; Alagiyanachchiyamma = 'the beautiful queen mother'. Others are short forms of older names: 'Mariyamma' = 'Mother Marika', who was the goddess of smallpox. 'Kaliamma', of course, is none other than 'Mother Kali', and 'Durgamma' is 'Mother Durga': both names of the great goddess of the Tantras.

These village Mothers have been established since long before the Arya conquest of India. In the 'Harivamsa', a coda to the Mahabharata, Durga is described as the goddess of the Sabaras, Pulindas, Barbaras and other wild tribes, some of whom we have already met. She was fond of wine and flesh. There is essentially no difference between this ancient goddess and today's village Mothers.

The shrines of the village goddesses are often associated with malevolent demons and they demand offerings from their worshippers of chickens, sheep, goats and buffalos. Almost every village in South India, where the old worship was least affected by Vedic and, later, by Islamic ideas, has a shrine sacred to one or other of these Mother goddesses. Often they are situated outside the village, in groves of trees, recalling the original forest home of the great goddess. As in the very earliest days, there may not even be a temple, merely crude structures, within which stands a rough unhewn stone representing the 'amma', or Mother, sacred to that village. Sometimes there is nothing but a spear, typically three-pronged, stuck in the ground. But her oldest symbol is the one that goes right back to the palaeolithic: the yoni. The museum of Alampur, in the southern state of Andhra Pradesh, houses an eleventh-century stone sculpture of the universal mother. The goddess's thighs are widely parted to reveal her yoni, which would have received the touches, flowers and kisses of her worshippers.

The holy places of the great goddess are known as 'yoni-pithas' and are found all over India, often at sites where nature itself seems to have assumed the form of the goddess's sacred symbol. Of these 'yoni-pithas' the most famous is that of Kamakhya, near Gauhati in Assam. Here the goddess is worshipped as Mahamaya in her erotic aspect. The idol within the temple shows a golden skinned woman in the prime of her beauty. Her body radiant with anticipated pleasure, she stands on a red lotus holding a garland of flowers. At her side are her special animals, the bull and the lion.

But the holy place lies not within the temple but inside a cave called Manobhava on the slopes of mount Nila, the 'blue' mountain. Inside the cave is a natural cleft in the rock. Shaped like a huge vulva, at certain times of year this cleft weeps a red and reputedly intoxicating water. According to the Yogini-tantra, the water is considered very holy and is

Adi Kali: part of the fine 'ritual' series of eighteenth-century Tantric paintings. Here the goddess is accepting animal sacrifices. She thirsted for blood; her temple as Kalighat in Calcutta slaughtered hundreds of animals every week. She is attended by men of the four castes. (See also pp 15, 19, 44.)

thought to well up from the underworld. This cave with its mysterious and sacred menstruating yoni, is held by devotees to be the centre of the universe.

The yoni-pithas have been places of pilgrimage since the earliest times. The natural places, caves and clefts, standing stones and mountains, were hers long before the Arya came into India. Their sanctity was never questioned. The great epic Mahabharata mentions two of these sacred yoni-pithas. One is sited in the east, in the 'mountains of sunrise' which have never been conclusively identified.

> 'One should next proceed to the Udyanta mountains, resounding with melodious notes... there, O bull, of the Bharata race, is the famous Yonidwara. Repairing thither, a person becometh exempted from the pain of rebirth.'
> (Mahabharata, Vana Parva, 84, trans. Kisari Mohan Ganguli)

It may have been the shrine also known as Purna-pitha, or the 'yoni-pitha of the east'. But the famous 'Yonidwara', or 'yoni- door' referred to may have been that of Kamakhya, which was seen as a doorway to another world.

In the region called 'Bhima' also there is a sacred yoni-site:

> 'Then, O King, one should go to the excellent region of Bhima. O best of Bharatas, by bathing in the tirtha there, that is called Yoni, a man in his next birth becometh, O king, the son of a goddess, bearing ear-rings decked with pearls, and obtaineth also the merit of the gift of a hundred thousand cattle.'
> (Mahabharata, Vana Parva, 82)

The god Siva rests on the gigantic coils of Vasuki, the king of serpents, and is sheltered by the snake's many hoods. Siva is the arch-ascetic, teacher of the science of yoga: this difficult pose demonstrates his mastery. *Eighteenth-century temple carving.*

At each holy site, the Mother was worshipped in a specific form. At Kamakhya, for example, she was the eponymous erotic aspect of the goddess Mahamaya. Not only her name, but her appearance, proclivities, temper and preferred offerings varied from village to village. It is impossible to keep track of her manifestations: there are eight hundred thousand villages in India. In searching for the distinctive Indian form of the great Mother, we experience something of the confusion felt by Lucius Apuleis in Rome when, wanting to invoke her, he did not know which name to use:

> 'Regina caeli—sive ti Ceres alma frugum parens originalis, quae, repertu laetata filiae, vetustae glandis ferino remoto pabulo, miti commonstrato cibo, nunc Eleusiniam glebam percolis; seu tu caelestis Venus, quae primis rerum exordiis...' &c
> (Apuleis, Metamorphosis, IX, 2)

> 'O queen of heaven — whether you are bountiful Ceres, the primal mother of crops, who in joy at the recovery of your daughter took away from men their primeval animal fodder of acorns and showed them gentler nourishment, and now dwell in the land of Eleusis; or heavenly Venus, who at the first foundation of the universe united the diversity of the sexes by creating Love and propagated the human race through ever-recurring progeny, and are now venerated at the illustrious shrine of Ephesus; or dreaded Prosperpina of the nocturnal howls, who in triple form repress the attacks of ghosts and keep the gates to earth closed fast, roam through widely scattered groves and are propitiated by diverse rites — you who illumine every city with your womanly light nourish the joyous seeds with your moist fires, and dispense beams of fluctuating radiance according to the convolutions of the Sun — by whatever name, with whatever rite, in whatever image, it is meet to invoke you: defend me now...'
> (Translator: J. Arthur Hanson)

The goddess Kalaratri, a form of Durga, the Great Mother Goddess: she rides an ass, holding in her left hand a severed human head. *Thirteenth-century sandstone carving.*

The goddesses of village India are very old. Many of the goddess forms mentioned in the Tantras are very likely nothing more than Aryanised versions of aboriginal deities still worshipped in the south and elsewhere.

Tvarita is a goddess of the 'kiratas' or hunters. She is clothed, like some tribal people even today, in leaves. Her necklace is a string of cannabis seeds. She wears peacock feathers in her hair and eight cobras coil around her brow and shade her with their hoods. She has been identified with the Scythian goddess Tavita, and also with Nagamata, the Mother of snakes.

Kalaratri is identified as one of the nine forms of the goddess Durga. Wearing a single plait of hair and japa-flowers for ear- rings, she has pendulous lips and rides naked on an ass, holding in her left hand a severed human head.

Sitaladevi, also known as Mariyamma, the goddess of smallpox, is another who rides naked on an ass. She carries a winnowing fan on her head and her hands hold a broom and a waterpot.

Srividyadevi has fierce fangs that protrude from her lips. Wearing necklaces fashioned from human bones, she sits on a couch of snakes. Trikantadevi has four faces, each with fangs so frightful that they curl down and outwards piercing her own belly. Her body below the navel is black, red between navel and neck and white above the neck.

Dhumravati, or Dhumra-Kali has a red body and is draped in a red garment. Her ear-rings are of the thickness of an elephants trunk and she too has terrible fangs. Wearing a necklace of human skulls and holding in her hands a naked sword and a skull, she is depicted surrounded by devils.

Many of these goddesses, as their terrifying images suggest, demand fierce sacrifices. Four-armed Tripura-Bhairavi wears a garland of human heads and her breasts are bathed with blood. Vajraprastarini is seated on a lotus, in a bloody boat that floats on an ocean of blood. Her head and limbs are bathed in blood. Jyeshtha is a black goddess with hanging lips, a snub nose and breasts that droop over a huge belly. She revels in blood.

Similar goddesses are found in Tantric buddhism, where their demonic aspects are magnified to the extreme. Horrified Europeans thought - and we cannot contradict them - that their rites were tantamount to devil-worship. The visions suffered by the newly-dead person in the well-known 'Bardo Thodol' or so-called 'Tibetan Book of the Dead', are truly nightmares from hell. The difference is that in India even the simplest people have always recognised that hell is not something outside ourselves. Hell is our own creation in every detail. These dreadful, fear-inspiring forms are nothing more than projections of our own mind, acting out the endless drama of the soul's struggle to escape its own bad karma, the consequences of its actions. Such a struggle will take many many lifetimes - nearly ten million, according to tradition - before through good works, devotion to the gods and enlightenment, we are exempted from the pain of further births.

In brahmanical Hinduism, and in Tantrism, a technology of gnosis has been evolved and developed to allow the worshipper a quicker road to 'moksa' or release. But the village folk of India still practise rites and worship that has remained virtually unchanged for three millenia.

The goddess Kali in her hideous aspect copulates with her consort, the ascetic Siva. Their lovemaking takes place on the body of a corpse which is burning in a funeral pyre. Cemetaries were favourite places for Tantric rites, because it is out of the symbolic death of the body that the spiritual human being arises shining. *Eighteenth century.*

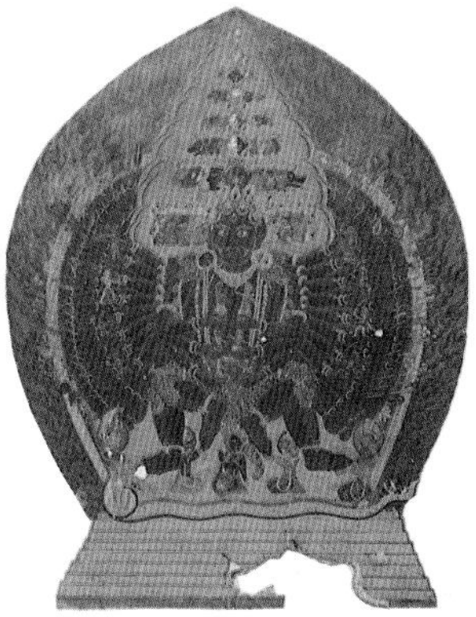

A thousand-armed, many-headed deity, who subsumes within himself the whole of living creation – perhaps an aspect of Rudra, the forerunner of Siva, who was called Pasupati, Lord of Beasts. He has Siva's third eye and a shining snake, symbol of wisdom and enlightenment, crawls at his feet. *Tibet.*

The village Mothers began as hunter-goddesses, and they are still fond of animal sacrifice. The goddess Vattapirai-amman who, like Isis, wears a crescent moon as a forehead ornament, is worshipped at Tiruvottiyur near Madras with buffalo sacrifices on certain days of the year, when a priest of the sudra caste - the lowest of the four castes of Hinduism - replaces the usual brahmin priest. Other atavistic ceremonies peculiar to the worship of the village Mothers are firewalking; running in procession carrying blazing pots of ghee on one's head; falling into an ecstatic state during which one's cheeks, tongue and eyelids may be pierced with metal skewers; piercing one's own abdomen with a metal spear; slashing at one's own breast and forehead until the blood runs; suspending oneself from hooks driven into the breast and shoulders and back; and lashing oneself with a whip. These are traces of the cruel rites once common to the worship of the goddess throughout India and the near-east. The priests of Cybele also scourged themselves, as certain revivalist witch-covens do to this day, albeit with skeins of silk thread. The tradition of self-mutilation also survives in the Shi'a version of Islam. These blood rites are probably relics of the human sacrifices that were common well into the nineteenth century and which are still reputed to occur from time to time.

Reading a book about Tantra from the comfort of our armchairs in our warm, twentieth-century homes, such rituals may seem repulsive and the people who conduct them morally reprehensible. We have to give up such notions. Writing of the goddess Pranasakti who, like some of the deities described above, floats in a 'boat-of-blood', on an ocean of blood and holds among other things a human skull filled with blood, one author disarmingly observes: 'This is as it should be, in the case of a goddess who presides over the centre of physical life'. Pranasakti is, in fact, a goddess of the life energy symbolised by blood and is invoked whenever that energy has to be transfused into a human body. This is the point: until blood-transfusions are available in every tiny hamlet in India, there is need for Pranasakti.

The ritual slaughter of a buffalo may seem obscene, but is it, if the life is taken with reverence and offered with reverence and the meat is a once-in-a-season treat for malnourished villagers? Our western abattoirs do not honour the animals they kill; nor when we buy the flesh do we acknowledge our spiritual debt to the natural world; and the meat is eaten, for the most part, by people who do not need it. And if images of pot-bellied women with pendulous breasts are thought unattractive, we might with humility recall that we are far more likely to meet people (of both sexes) answering to this description in the well-fed West than in the underfed East. Without any insight into how harsh life is for the lower-caste people of India; existing on the edge of starvation, at the mercy of illnesses for which there are still no ready cures, in the grip of a repressive social system: we have no hope of understanding Tantra.

A remarkable piece of field-research carried out within the last ten years by socio-anthropologist Tribhuwan Kapur has vividly documented the survival of the old worship alongside orthodox Hinduism and demonstrates how it continues both to serve and to shape the lives of village people. He shows us why this worship, which we can trace back to the Indus valley cities of the third millenium BC, looks set to continue undiminished and largely unchanged into the third millenium AD.

In the hilly landscape of Kumaon and Garhwal in the Himalayan foothills, the 'Dom' villagers have their own deities and spirits, which are quite separate from those of their higher-caste 'Baman' neighbours. The countryside is magnificent, still thickly forested - the jungles in which the hunter Jim Corbett shot many man-eating tigers and leopards. Here Bageshwari, the 'tiger-goddess', is at home. In one village, Devagiri, 'god's mountain', the Bamans worship the deities of the Hindu pantheon while the Doms pay homage to older, darker entities: Runia, Airi, Chaumu, Bhumiya, Masaan, Khabish, Shaitan, Churail - names that will never be uttered in any Vedic ritual.

Life for the villagers, Dom and Baman alike, is hard. They rise between four and five, before dawn when they drink tea. No food passes their lips until noon, when they may eat a little rice and vegetable curry with a sauce of chili and garlic. They eat once more about the time of sunset, a chapatti with some dry vegetables and thick, sweet tea. All the villagers use hashish, which they grow as a crop, harvesting its leaves and collecting its resin. Smuggling hashish into the cities provides them with a supplement to their tiny incomes. The drug provides these people with an escape from the harshness of their lives. Hashish, coupled with an extremely low-calorie diet, keeps them constantly in a state of near-hallucination, in which the supernatural world seems very close. Is that a dark man on the forest path? Careful! It may be the demon Khabish. Khabish is middle aged with a face disfigured by suppurating sores. He has only one arm, his left, and his body is continuously racked with spastic tremors. One must never go near him, for he passes on his illnesses to others.

A temple carving in hardwood of a goddess with horse's head. This form of the Great Goddess is very old among Indo-European peoples and gives rise to the word 'nightmare'.

Bhumiya is an earth spirit who protects the fields and punishes anyone who defiles them. He change into a snake and bites his victims, or steers them into the path of hungry wild animals. Airi is a vampire who must lick human blood to survive. He attacks villagers as they work in the fields, or walk through the forest. Runiya is an incubus who visits young women at night. He appears as a young man with an insatiable sexual appetite.

Shaitan is a bald old man with a drooling face, always on the look out for liquor and women. Those who have strayed sexually, he punishes with blisters, aches and pains. He is particularly severe with those who have committed the sin of incest. In Devagiri, Shaitan is a name given to a villager who has had sexual relations with his daughter.

Masaan haunts burning grounds, lonely ravines and remote forest pools. He looks like a half-burnt corpse and his body exudes a repulsive smell of charred flesh. Masaan was once a Tantric recluse who worshipped Siva by meditating on a dead body at the Bimandeshwar burning ground. One day Siva appeared to him and told him that the corpse on which he had been meditating had been alive when he took his seat on it, and had suffocated under his weight. Siva told Masaan never to return to the burning ground. But Masaan met a young girl who told him that the great god was jealous and fearful of his yogic powers and that if he went back once more, he would become a god. Masaan returned and went into a deep meditation. But some Devagiri villagers, thinking he was dead, began to burn his body. Masaan awoke in agony to find his body charred and burned. Siva and Parvati appeared before him and told him that he had been punished for his disobedience. Henceforth, he would have to be a guardian of the burning ground.

The most powerful of all Devagiri's deities is Mother Kalika, 'the black one', feared and revered by Dom and Baman alike. They believe that she once killed more than half the villagers for missing a single performance of her exorcism ceremony.

This exorcism is performed in a temple that stands on a lonely nine-thousand-foot peak two days' journey from Devagiri. The temple is dedicated to Siva and Kali. On three sides of it are precipitous falls, and to the east a steep path leads down to a second temple, about a hundred feet below. Here, over a seven day period, the exorcism is carried out by a group of specially chosen Baman men and women from the village. Two goats are ritually slaughtered, cooked and eaten, prayers and spells are chanted.

The whole of the first evening and night is passed lighting the sacred fire. Throughout the night hymns and songs are sung to Siva and Kali and the exorcist leaders narrate their legends. The men share a few pipes of hashish, while the women drink glasses of tea. The following day, the women clean the temples, while the men collect wood to build a 'worship hut' nearby. The next two days and nights are spent in prayer, with the worship hut being occupied each night by a different male-female couple, who can be uncle and niece, or brother and sister. Their task is to recite 'uccharana mantra', or spells, continuously, while the rest take turns to sleep.

A temple carving of a threatening demon, the stuff of nightmares.

On each of the last two mornings, a goat is slaughtered in the upper temple. An exorcist leads the goat to the idols and forces it to genuflect. A second man makes a red 'sandars' dot on its forehead and then decapitates it with a single slash of his curved 'khukri', or hill-knife. Two more men stand ready with a tray to catch the blood, which is then offered by the whole group to the deities. The goat is cooked, to the accompaniment of more spells and chants, in the lower temple and then eaten. On the final morning, sacred ash from the fires is collected and each member of the party is anointed with it. They ring the temple bells and then begin the long walk down the mountain back to Devagiri.

A few nights later, in the village, it is the turn of the Doms to perform a further exorcism. The ceremony starts with the smoking of a pipe of hashish. Then, to the accompaniment of drum and flute, sacred songs are sung. The singing is at first very quiet, because the goddess is to be awakened gradually. The dancers, too, begin quietly to foot it around the fire. As Kalika slowly awakens, so her power flows into their bodies and possesses them. Suddenly there is a loud laugh and the dancers seem to shiver. Kalika is awake. A fast drumbeat begins and the dancers become frenzied, the goddess within them shivering their limbs with ecstasy. Many cases of healing are reported during these rituals, at which fruit, vegetables and grain may be offered as sacrifices.

A Himalayan bronze dating from the sixteenth or seventeenth century, of a Tibetan godform, holding the sacred symbols of Tantric Buddhism, the conch, prayerwheel, lotus and vajra.

The goddess Kalika of Devagiri is, of course, none other than Kali, supreme goddess of the Tantric sects. The villagers know her both in her terrible Kali-aspect and as the lovely and benevolent Parvati, 'daughter of the mountain'. She is also honoured as Gauri, Durga and in the ancient form of Uma. The goddess and Siva are celebrated as the lingam-in-yoni and the women of Devagiri believe that worshipping the Siva-lingam will make them fertile.

Devagiri even tells the story of its own creation. Once, in the unimaginably-long-ago, the village was a paradise of the gods. But a quarrel arose about where to site the exorcist temple. One group of villagers said it should be in the centre of the village, another that it should be at the periphery. Kali and Siva were invited to settle the question. Kali said she worried that if the exorcist temple were not in the middle of things, the villagers would lose their sense of morality. But Siva disagreed. So Kali decreed that, as a test, a replica of heavenly Devagiri should be created on earth, complete with Doms, Bamans and deities. The exorcist temple in earthly Devagiri would be at the edge of the village.

It was done and, as Kali feared, the villagers began to steal, quarrel and commit all sorts of lecherous and immoral acts. Only certain of the incarnated gods remained pure and true to their ideals. They realised that, in order to save the village, they must perform a great exorcism. So, taking with them some sacred ashes from the exorcist temple, they travelled a long way until they came to the Trisuli mountain. A huge snake lay coiled around the peak. The snake instructed the gods as to how the exorcism should be performed.

The exorcisms performed today by the villagers in their remote mountain temple are repetitions of that first, divine, exorcism. The rituals are necessary to purge the village of the guilt of its moral failures. In Devagiri, as in other small, cut-off communities, there is a great deal of laxity in sexual matters. It is taken for granted that women will not be faithful to their husbands and that men will stray. But unless the laws of caste are flouted, men and women generally turn a blind eye to each others' peccadillos.

The legend of Shaitan indicates that even incest, although beyond the pale, is distressingly common. Once again, one is reminded of Karna's two-thousand year old diatribe against the hill-people. Although the material relating to Devagiri was collected in the mid-1980s, the outcaste Doms are the direct descendants of the aboriginal inhabitants of the land, the Nisada and Sabara hunter tribes.

In the Devagiri myth we encounter a mountain called 'Trisuli'. The name, of course, means 'trident', or 'three-pronged'. The story is similar to that in which the great serpent Vasuki wraps himself around 'trikuta', that other triple-mountain, and tears it away from

A greystone carving of a village deity from north India. *Fourteenth century.*

mount Meru. The trident is the sign of Siva, which explains why any triple-peaked mountain like Trisuli; or the Koh-e-Mor, alias Trikakud, alias Trikuta, alias Trsrnga; would have been sacred to Siva and the goddess.

The rituals practised in Devagiri, although they do not conform to the instructions of a particular text, and though they are not accompanied by a complex philosophy or by specific techniques of sexual yoga, are pure Tantric worship of the oldest kind. This is the real religion of the common folk, simple, crude, bloody, and just one step from superstition. The shadows that dance at the edge of light around the sacrificial fire are ghosts, evil spirits and demons.

The worship of Devagiri is still essentially a communal rite, performed for the benefit of all. The villagers do hope for 'moksa' or liberation from the torment of birth and rebirth, but the Tantric techniques for attaining gnosis are unknown to them. The only available enlightenment is that of the 'chillum', or hashish pipe. It is not, however, to be lightly dismissed. Before a villager lights his ritual 'chillum', he never fails to invoke Siva, who is patron deity of hashish, datura and all forms of intoxication. Sometimes, he is rewarded with a vision of the god. This is why the Bamans honour all wandering, hashish-smoking sadhus and offer them food and shelter. They can never be certain that one of these naked, unwashed, intoxicated scetics is not Siva himself, for in their imaginations the god still wanders these hills and haunted forests.

Chapter 5

The Lingam of Siva

A medieval greystone figure of Siva in his wrathful form as Bhairava.

If we could revisit the triple-mountain, at a period before the Nysaeans, before the forest sages composed the Upanisads, or their forefathers sang the Vedas, before even the baked-brick cities were built on the Indus flood plain, we would find a land not unlike Kumaon. A landscape of unbroken forests, rich in game, bounded to the north by towering ice-peaks, the abode of supernatural spirits. In these forests moved the dark peoples, with bows and arrows, simple grass and leaf shelters. Dressed in skins, they had no temples for their worship, only crude stones, which they daubed with the blood of animals (later with vermilion powder). The stones were sacred to the great Mother, 'amma' or 'ma', and the stone itself was symbolic too of the lingam of her consort, the horned god who might one day be called 'deva-nisa', and who would certainly be referred to as 'isa-deva' or 'THAT god'.

His name is not uttered, says the Aitareya Brahmana, it must not be mentioned, only indirectly may He be referred to. The name they would not speak was that of Rudra, who would one day be Siva. 'Rudra' means 'he who howls', or 'he who roars', but can also suggest 'ruddy' or 'red'. Rudra was a wild hunter, untameable by men or gods, defying all attempts of the sages and gods of the Aryas to bring him and his worship under control. As Rudra, he challengéd the great grandfather of the Vedic gods. Prajapati, the Creator, was in the forest one day with his daughter, Usha, the dawn, who was in the form of a deer. Filled with desire for her, the All-Father changed himself into a hart and was enjoying her when he saw Rudra among the trees, aiming his long arrow straight at him. In fear, Prajapati begged Rudra to spare his life, offering him as a reward the overlordship of the wild, and naming him 'Pasupati', Lord of Beasts. It is as Pasupati, surrounded by his animals: the rhinoceros, the tiger, the elephant, buffalo and antelopes, that his image appears on the Indus seals.

In the Matsya Purana, a king asks why Prajapati's incest with his daughter was not considered a fearful sin. The answer is that only human beings with mortal bodies can have such taboos, the gods are beyond them. The daughter with whom the Creator cohabited was a hypostasis of that Creator Himself. She was one with him before she was herself. In knowing her, he knew only himself. This is tantalising to those who recall the 'incestuous' injunctions of the Guhyasamaja and other Tantras and, indeed, there are at least three levels on which the answer may be understood.

First, there is the simple question of god and sin. He who has the mind of a god cannot sin, no matter what he does. This is a theme that recurs again and again in the Tantras, which shared it with the gnostics.

Next, there is the nature of divinity itself, united beyond all wordly division. To unite with this godhead is, symbolically, to know one's ultimate Mother, Sister, Daughter - Self. This is the yoga of gnosis, the deliberate unfolding, one after another, of the seven cakras of the spiritual body, until the worshipper is absorbed into the divine.

Third, there is the cosmology of it. 'Creation is an act of violence that infringes upon the Uncreate' says Stella Kramrisch in a memorable sentence from her fine book The Presence of Siva. After this initial act of violence, the inchoate darkness bleeds divinity, which flows down from one god-form to another, into all living things and all matter, organic and inorganic. The whole universe is alive with God, there is no part of it that is not God and not of God.

Rudra, letting fly at Prajapati, did not see it this way. He had not yet evolved into Siva and 'Ma', the grisly aboriginal goddess of blood sacrifice had not yet evolved into the immanent, transcendent Sakti who moves the universe.

Rudra, this earliest form of Siva, was a god of the dark hunters. Clothed in the skins of wild beasts like the tiger and the black antelope, he reeked of badly cured hides and was sarcastically referred to as 'the scented one'. The gods of the Aryas - the Vedic gods - loathed Rudra and would not admit him to their 'soma' sacrifice. Contemptuously, they offered for his sacrifice the leavings from the altars of other gods. He did not mind. For Rudra, a rice sacrifice was plenty. Even the foam from boiled rice was acceptable to him, though he was still partial to the blood of animal, and even human, victims.

The Vedic gods and their priests despised Rudra but because they also feared him, they attempted to appease him with a hymn and a sacrifice of 'a hundred oblations'. They left other offerings for him, at places deep in the forest, or at haunted crossroads. Rice cakes were left on the paths and hung in baskets from the trees. They implored Rudra to take the rice cakes and return to his home in the far north, beyond Munjavan. Munjavan, in the Himalayas, it almost goes without saying, is a multi-peaked mountain very like Meru. It is of course sacred to Siva, a place where he rambles for pleasure with his army of 'wild goblins', just like Dionysus with the maenads on Nysa:

> 'They looked like elephants, like mountains. They had the shape of dogs, boars and camels and the faces of horses, jackals, cows, bears, cats, tigers, panthers, crows, frogs and parrots. Some had the heads of mighty serpents, others those of different birds, tortoises, crocodiles, porpoises, whales and lions. Some had ears on their hands, a thousand eyes, no flesh, or no heads. They had blazing eyes and tongues and faces of fire. Some were like conches, had faces like conches, or ears like conches. Some wore garlands and girdles of conches, and the voices of some resembled the blare of conches. Some had matted locks and some were bald; some wore diadems. Some had beautiful faces, some had head ornaments of lotuses, some wore white waterlilies. They numbered hundreds and thousands. Some had weapons of various kinds. Some were covered in dust or smeared with mud; all were dressed in white. Some had dark blue limbs and others light red. The excited retinue played upon drums and conches. Some sang, some danced, some leapt and skipped, fleet and fierce, their hair waving in the wind. They were terrible, frightful. Some had large genitals. They were fearless, masters of speech, astonishing the Great God by their worship. They adored him in thought, word, and deed, and he protected them as his legitimate sons.'
> (Stella Kramrisch: The Presence of Siva)

A linga-yoni – the Siva lingam contained in the sacred yoni. Icons like this caused great offence to early European missionaries like the Abbé Dubois, who would have been astonished to learn that they would one day become a tourist gift item, like this one. *Polished soapstone, late twentieth century.*

If the magic mountain is one of the god's great icons, the lingam is the other. Stone lingams of Siva have been erected in the sanctuaries of Siva temples for two thousand years. The earliest sculptures that can definitely be identified as Siva-lingas are to be found in Guddimallam in South India and at Mathura. They are simple stone pillars with rounded tops carved into the shape of a glans, the shaft representing the erect phallus

> sivalingasthāpanasya māhātmyaṁ kiṁ bravīmi té | yatsthāpanānmahāpāpairmuktō yāti param padam || svarṇapūrṇamahīdānadvījimédhāyutārjanāt | nistōyé tōyakaraṇāt dīnārtaparitōśṇāt || yat phalaṁ labhaté martyastasmāt kōṭiguṇaṁ phalam | śivalingapratiśṭhayāṁ labhaté nātra sanśāyaḥ ||
> (Mahanirvana-tantra, XIV, 5,6)

The pale goddess: another of the exciting 'ritual' series of Tantric paintings. In this one, the goddess carries on her body emblems of the sacred yoni. On her cheeks are symbols of the sun and moon, which respectively identify the subtle channels through which kundalini energy travels in the body. The kundalini force, in the form of a snake, is just awakening from where it has lain asleep, coiled three and a half times around the Siva lingam, in the cakra at the base of the spine. (See also 15, 19, 44, 49.) *Eighteenth century.*

> "Without doubt, the man who erects a Siva-linga earns ten million times more merit than by giving away all his gold to the poor and sick, or by inviting ten thousand to a sacrifice, or by digging wells in a waterless country."

Siva's lingam is worshipped as 'svayambhuva' - 'self-created'. (It is fascinating to remember that the very first name in the pedigree of the Mauryan Emperor Chandragupta Maurya was that of 'Spatembas', said to have been the most bacchic of the companions of that 'Other-Siva', Dionysus. What else is 'spatembas' but a corruption of 'svayambhu'?)

From the stone age onwards, the lingam had signified the phallus of the god, his procreative power. It is still worshipped this way by the women of Devagiri. In later times, the erect penis was understood as signifying not the ejaculation, but the retention of semen. Brahma once asked Rudra to create beings who would age and die. But Rudra refused. He said he would not be responsible for creating suffering. Instead he stood quite still, his penis erect yet motionless, and pointing upward as a sign that he had not shed his seed, which was held, consumed or transubstantiated within the body.

The polarity of this erect penis is not that of life and death, but that of 'kama' or desire, and 'moksa', or release from the bondage of eternally recurring lives. As Stella Kramrisch perceptively says: 'Between these two poles stretches the path of yoga, of which he (Siva) is the lord.'

The transubstantiation of the sexual urge is the real meaning of the sacrament of 'maithuna' or sexual union, in Tantric worship. It contains a threefold answer to the question about Prajapati's sin: there is no sin if the mind is pure; the erect penis demonstrates the yoga of gnosis; the semen energy is transformed into spiritual force that drives the worshipper towards union with the divine.

In the sexual union which forms part of Tantric worship each partner worships the divine in the other.

According to another tradition, when Rudra was asked by Brahma to create living beings, he plunged himself into deep water to meditate, in the belief that such a creation could only be born from strict austerity. While he was meditating, Brahma lost patience with him and asked one Daksa to undertake the creation. Daksa set to work with all the haste of an inept sub-contractor and created living beings that were consumed with hunger and immediately ran to eat him, their creator. In fear, Daksa turned to Brahma, who created living plants for certain of the animals to feed on, and ordained hierarchies of predation for the rest. When Rudra arose from his meditation, he was mortified to discover that creation had taken place without him. Grasping his now, as he felt, useless phallus, he ripped it from his body, castrating himself, and flung it to the ground, where it was received by the good mother earth.

In yet another version of the legend, the god took the form of a young 'sadhu' or ascetic, and went into the deodar forest to beg. The wives and daughters of the sages who lived there were very struck by the appearance of this ash-smeared stranger. He seemed to them irresistibly handsome, yet in truth he was hideous, with large, painted teeth. According to the Bhagavat Purana, 'his penis and testicles were like red chalk, the tip ornamented with black and white chalk'. The women, previously virtuous, were driven wild with lust. Their hair in disorder, shedding their ornaments and clothes, they sported with the stranger who at times would sing and dance beautifully, but at other times roar, utterly naked, showing off his large penis, the hairs of his body standing on end. The forest sages were, understandably, so enraged that they tore off his phallus, or, by other accounts, uttered a curse that made it fall, or ordered him to castrate himself.

The linga fell and burned everything it touched. It broke through the earth into the underworld and out into the sky. It blazed with a great fire and lit the darkness of outer space. The gods Brahma and Visnu had been arguing about which of the two of them was the greater. Without warning, the light of Siva's lingam burst upon them. Brahma, assuming the form of a wild goose, flew upwards to see where the pillar ended. Visnu, in his form of the great boar, travelled downwards to find its base. But to the height and depth of the pillar there was no end and when the two gods returned exhausted, they saw Siva within the lingam and heard the thunder of his laughter. The sound that emanated from the shining lingam was the sacred syllable 'aum' which afficionados of classical ragas will recognise as the source and fount of all music. (Unlike the devil, who only has the best tunes, Siva has them all, for he is Lord of Music as well as of the Dance and all other forms of intoxication.)

These legends dimly recollect a past where the horned god was chased in a ritual hunt and torn to pieces. But they also reveal the gnostic meaning of castration, which is the conservation of semen and its transmutation into spiritual energy.

Why are the stone lingams set in yonis? When Siva's lingam fell, flaming, and burning everything it touched, the sages approached Brahma and asked him to do something, anything, to save creation. Brahma's advice was that they should ask Devi, the great goddess, to assume the form of 'yoni', the vulva, and grip Siva's raging phallus. Siva had himself said that no woman except Parvati, 'mountain-daugher', the great Mother goddess in her loveliest form, had the power to hold him. Thus the severed lingam of Siva came to stand in full yogic control in the yoni of Parvati.

Siva's earliest incarnation was that of a wild god of the forests that clothed the foothills of the Hindu Kush and the Himalayas. His rites, from time immemorial, had been associated with those giant snow-peaks, and particularly with three-peaked mountains, as we have seen. Who else could his goddess be but the 'daughter of the mountain', Parvati, third and youngest daughter of Parvata, King of Mountains, who was as old as the rocks and older than the Rg Veda? So lovely was she that the very thought of her drove poets to ecstasy:

A white stone columnar relief of the Goddess: Surprisingly, this is a lovely form of Durga, normally depicted as a terrible goddess. The statue represents the Indian ideal of feminine beauty with its narrow waist, broad arching hips and heavy breasts. The poem Saundaryalahari contains many fine lyrics praising the Goddess's physical beauty. *Gujarat, fourteenth century.*

gatairmaṇikyatvaṁ gaganamaṇibhiḥ sāndraghaṭitaṁ
kiriṭaṁ té haimaṁ himagirisuté kīrtayati yaḥ I
sa nīḍéyacchāyācchuraṇaśabalaṁ candraśakalaṁ
dhanuḥ śaunāsīraṁ kimiti na nibaghnāti dhiśṇām II
(Saundaryalahari, 42)

O daughter of the high ice-peaks, he who attempts to describe your crown of gold, studded with jewel- like suns, could be forgiven for mistaking that resplendent crescent moon, brilliant with the light of precious pebbles, for the bow of Indra himself.

arālaiḥ svābhāvyādalikalabhasasrībhiralakaiḥ parītaṁ
té vaktraṁ parihasati pankéruharucim I
darasméré yasmin daśanarucikiṇjalkaruciré sugandhau
mādyanti smaradahanacakśurmadhulihaḥ II (ibid, 45)

Your face, Lady, with its gentle smile, shames the shining lotus flower. Your dark curls are like swarms of little bees. Those lovely teeth that flash as you laugh and the honey of your breath have brought your bee-eyed Lord, the Slayer of Kama, to drink nectar from your mouth.

vipaṇjcyā gāyantī vividhamapadānaṁ pasupaté-
stvayārabdhé vaktuṁ calitaśirasā sādhuvacané I
tadīyairmādhuryairapalapitatantrīkalaravāṁ
nijāṁ vīṇāṁ vāṇī niculayati cōlén nibhrtam II
(ibid, 66)

When the goddess of music picks up the vina and sings the legend of the Lord of Beasts, your head begins to nod in time and words of pleasure escape your lips. But your voice is so much more musical than the vina that the goddess of music stills its trembling strings.

sthirō gangāvartaḥ stanamukularōmāvalilatā-
kalāvālaṁ kundam kusumaśaratéjōhutabhujaḥ I
ratérlīlāgāraṁ kimapi tava nābhirgirisuté
biladvāraṁ sidvérgiriśanayanānāṁ vijayaté II
(ibid, 78)

O mountain-daughter; this cave so deep that it could still the Ganga's torrents, this fire pit tended by Kama where Rati dances, this secret cleft which draws the eyes of your ascetic Lord, from whence this line of hair climbs like a creeper to bear your heavy breast-buds: Lady, is this your navel?

This is how the saint and Tantric poet Sankacarya described the gloriously beautiful Parvati. Because her skin was dark, her parents gave her an affectionate pet name, by which she is these days probably better known. They called her Kali, 'the dark one'.

When the gods decided that Parvati should be Siva's bride, Indra summoned Kama, god of love, and his wife Rati, the goddess of lust and bade them, as we say in India, do the needful. When Kama entered the grove near the mountain peak he found Siva seated in meditation upon the coils of Vasuki, the king of snakes. Siva's long, tangled hair reached the ground. In front of him stood a water pot and a human skull, which served as his food bowl.

A lion skin was about his shoulders. Fierce cobras with raised hoods guarded him. Nonetheless Kama, or desire, was able to strike through the asceticism of Siva. Kama entered Siva's mind through his ears and the great god awoke momentarily from his samadhi, his complete absorption. Instantly Siva, exercising his vast yogic control, returned to samadhi, expelling Kama. But the mischievous god strung his sugarcane bow with its string of humming bees with a lotus-tipped arrow and struck Siva to the heart. In anger, Siva opened his third eye, a great fire flashed forward, which burned Kama to ashes. Now Rati wailed and wept, but Siva had returned to his deep meditation and could not be disturbed further. This story, in the poetry of myth, conceals the answer to a conundrum we have already mentioned: that of the right relationship between the Tantra and Kama traditions.

A sandstone temple carving of rapturous lovers: her mouth is raised to his in a lifted kiss and her body clings to his in the posture known in the erotic manual Ananga Ranga as 'kirti' or 'fame' *Thirteenth century.*

Siva's next visitor was king Parvata himself, who brought with him the beautiful Parvati. Siva asked Parvata to go away and return without his daughter, whose beauty was distracting. What use, he asked, was a lovely woman to a celibate yogi? But Parvati answered him herself by pointing out that his asceticism was only sustained by his 'prakrti' or energy. Siva retorted that he burned up prakrti by his austerities. Nonsense, the goddess replied, everything is at all times sustained and bound together by prakrti, the primal energy that drives every atom of the universe. If you are greater than prakrti, she asked him, why do you practice austerities here on this mountain? 'I am Prakrti', she said, 'and you are Purusa'. With these wise words, Parvati enlightened Siva. She could have pointed out that her worship was older than his, her mysteries deeper, but she knew that this would be a false distinction. Between herself and Siva in the world beyond human understanding there had never been, nor ever could be, any distinction. Siva was herself, just as she was Siva. The goddess, young and lovely, demonstrated her wisdom to the naked, ash-smeared Siva and awakened him. In that enlightened moment, she won his admiration, his respect and his love.

Their love burned with a passion that had never before been felt in the universe and their lovemaking reached the innermost secrets of creation and shook them. A story is told of how Siva once teased Parvati about her dark skin: like Siva, she had originally been a divinity of the Nisadas, or 'dark people'. Parvati, or Kali, thinking that he did not find her beautiful, flew into a rage and stormed away to practise austerities on a lonely mountain peak. They missed each other horribly. When she returned, they threw themselves into one another's arms. Their lovemaking, which seemed to last the whole night, actually lasted a thousand heavenly years. The earth shook with their passion and the gods feared for the safety of the world:

śliśyantī gahanāmbaraṁ rahasi té śaktiḥ sarīraṁ vibhō
prémpraśvasiténa vāṁ vitanuté sarvatra gūḍāṁ sriyam |
sāndrānandakṛta yathā vapuśi vāṁ dharmāmbhisāṁ mālikā
vairiṇjcāṇḍaparamparā yata iyaṁ tārākṛtirnrtyati ||
(Ahnika Stava: Sri Kapali Sastriar)

She clings to the deep nightsky of his body,
    her harsh love-breaths send
a secret perfume stealing out across the world:
what else are the glittering stars that fill
    this dancing universe but
        pearls of sweat
            flung off
by the violence of their love-combat?

Throughout this most yogic and sublime of encounters, the door to the bedroom was guarded by Nandi, the divine bull. Overcome by the beauty and profundity of what he had, inevitably, witnessed, Nandi could not help but speak of it. The aphorisms that fell like flowers from his lips were collected and written down by one Svetaketu, son of the sage Uddalaka Aruni. Svetaketu's stanzas would pass down through many recensions until, mightily condensed, they formed the collection of sexual knowledge that would be called 'Kama Sutra'.

This luminous miniature shows royal lovers on a palace terrace, making love in the position which Vatsyayana in the Kama Sutra calls 'Indranika', named for Indrani, consort of the Vedic god Indra. The artist demonstrates great skill in the handling of the prince's diaphanous jama. *Jaipur, late eighteenth century.*

Chapter 6

The Severed Phallus

> There are two kinds of eunuchs: those who dress as men, and those who dress as women. A eunuch who assumes the feminine role should use all the tricks of the courtesan's trade: imitating her style of dress, her voice, her gait and the way she laughs, her delicacy, charm, hesitancy, helpfulness and, indeed, helplessness of manner. In this way, she can derive pleasure as well a living by practising Auparishtaka, or fellatio, with men. (Vatsyayana, Kama Sutra, II.ix.1-4)

The Gupta period, occupying roughly the first three centuries of the first millenium, was a time of efflorescence in the liberal arts, literature, music and dancing. Small wonder that it was in this era that the old collections of verses about erotics were dusted off, updated and simplified into the one comprehensive yet terse and witty text which we know as Kama Sutra.

Its author, the mysterious Mallanaga Vatsyayana, although by his training a traditionalist, had an eye for contemporary detail and a feisty disregard for established wisdom. He never hesitated to disagree even with holy scriptures to make a point about which he felt strongly.

This was the case when he argued the existence of a female orgasm, and mocked the arguments of his predecessors, including the forest sage Auddalaki, whose son Svetaketu had been the first to codify the erotic mumblings of the sacred bull Nandi, after he had spent ten-thousand years witnessing the lovemaking of Siva and Parvati. Vatsyayana easily demolished the argument expressed in Auddalaki's old verse:

> 'In swyving man the luste
> Of blisful woman doth abate,
> Yet ne kisse, love-drurye, ne thruste
> Of phallos doth her passioun sate,
> But knowliche of hire herte mate.'
> (ibid II.i.31)

A woman's pleasure, Auddalaki and his followers believed, did not come from orgasm or indeed any physical act of love, but from the joy of receiving and satisfying her partner. But if this is so, Vatsyayana retorts, kindly explain why her body is at first still and only gradually yields to the passion which in the end shakes her so violently. Is not woman's pleasure more like a potter's wheel, which spins slowly at first, gathering speed until at last it blurs in the mindless beauty of release? He quotes another old verse, this time by Babhravya, in support:

> 'His spasm is his pleasure's end,
> Whilst her fierce ardour knows no cease,
> For in love's battle both must spend
> And blend their seed ere she finds peace.'
> (ibid II.i.41)

A brown goddess: another in the great 'ritual' series of Tantric paintings. (Others in the series may be seen on pages 15, 19, 44, 49 and 61.) Here is evidence that castration was an extreme form of celibacy, and the Tantric idea of conserving semen within the body finds expression in the numerous floating lingams. The testicles of the central set of male organs are identified with the female breasts – both centres of psychic nourishment. *Eighteenth century.*

His conclusion, pleasingly modern, is that women's orgasms are not very different from men's, and that men should take the trouble to arouse their lovers properly during lovemaking.

Vatsyayana plunges once more into controversy when he writes about the practice of fellatio, customarily offered as a service to their customers by barber/masseurs and transvestite eunuchs who made a living from prostitution.

> Teachers advise against this practice on the grounds that it is forbidden in the shastras and is abhorrent and detestable to all decent citizens... Precisely, says Vatsyayana. The shastras apply to decent citizens and therefore, by definition, not to prostitutes and their patrons ...Besides which, the holy texts regard four mouths as pure. The mouth of the calf does not pollute the cow's udder, the mouth of the hunting dog does not pollute the deer, the bird's beak does not pollute the fruit it plucks from a tree, and the mouth of a woman does not pollute her lover. Admittedly, though, the texts are ambiguous and since no-one can agree on this matter, Vatsyayana says everyone should follow local custom and their own conscience. (ibid, II.ix.22-23, 29-30)

Vatsyayana then gives ten techniques of fellation, culminating in the celebrated 'amracusita' or 'sucking of a mango'. Similar services are still offered today in India by eunuchs, or 'hijras' who, like their Gupta predecessors, often dress in women's clothing and ape their manners. You may see them at night in the red light district of any large Indian city, singing, dancing and collecting alms in the street. They are particularly skilled at bandying 'gali' or abuse, which, as Kipling's Kim knew, has in India attained the status of a minor art form. For many hijras, prostitution is the only way to earn a living. Some have organised themselves into communities called 'deras', centred on a house run by a guru. From this house they go out into the streets to sing, dance, drum and beg for a living. If the 'dera' is also a brothel, they will receive male customers here, much as in the days of Vatsyayana. Today's 'hijras' are as downtrodden as their Gupta and Maurya predecessors were. Like the female prostitutes with whom they share the red-light districts, they are often rapaciously exploited by criminals who kidnap and castrate young boys and introduce them to a life of prostitution. In 1986, Mr. Khairati Lal Bhola, President of the All India Hijra Kalyan Sabha, the hijra's own welfare society, complained in a letter to the then Prime Minister, Rajiv Gandhi, that as many as 40,000 males, often young children, were being illegally castrated every year. One child, now an adult, reported:

> "I was lifted by four hijras (eunuchs) and put on a heap of ashes. They held me tight, while the rest kept on singing and dancing in the adjoining hall. The drumbeats now rose to a frenzy. The old hijra came to me and seized my genitals with his left hand, and with his right hand, slit the bamboo-cane in the centre, running it down quite close to my pubis. The slit firmly held my genitals at the root. The burly hijra ran down his sharp razor along the face of the cane and removed my penis, testicles and scrotum in one swoop, leaving a large bleeding wound. Soon another hijra poured boiling oil to stanch the bleeding. The wound was covered with a rag soaked in warm oil." (Reported in the Illustrated Weekly of India, 8 August 1976)

Hijras come from all classes and regions and religions. Any child born hermaphrodite, or with missing or damaged genitals, is considered by the hijras to be theirs by right - 'a hijra belongs to hijras' - and they insist on exercising that right. In many cases even parents who were unwilling to part with a child had eventually to give them up. One eunuch related how, when he was eleven years old, a group of hijras had come to his home.

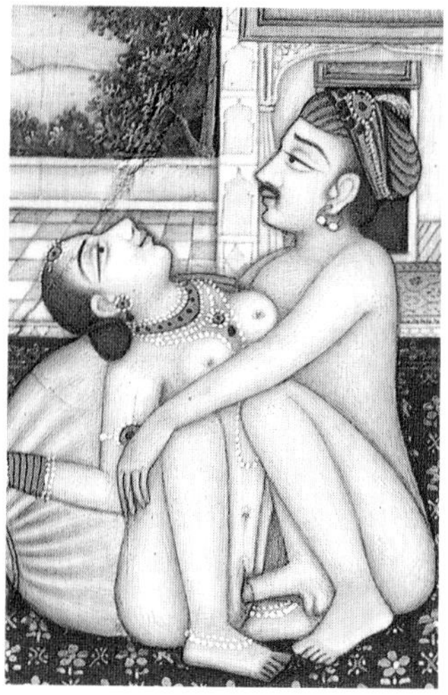

An erotic scene on an ivory comb, used by a high class prostitute or as a 'beard comb' by her wealthy patron. *Late nineteenth century.*

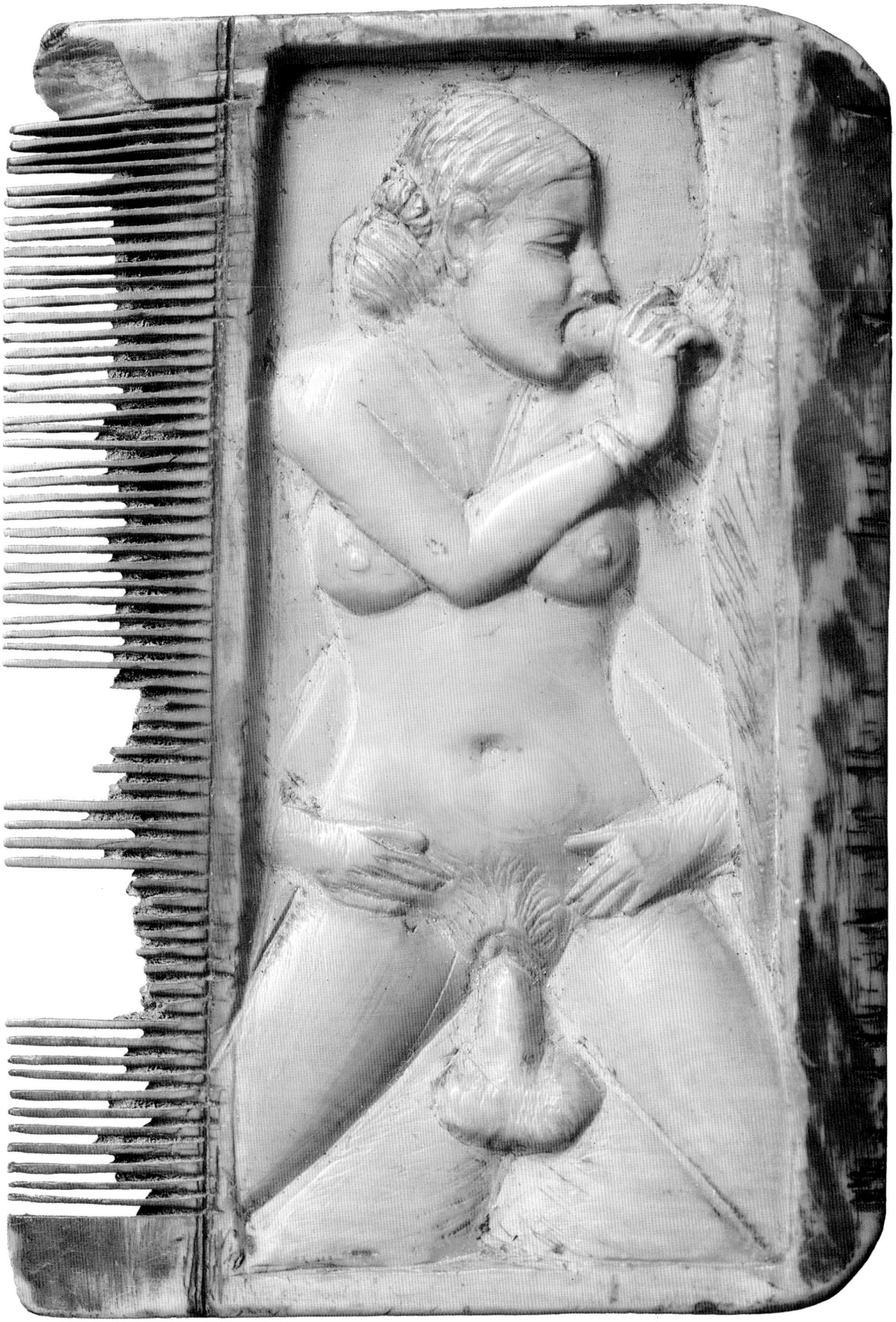

> 'On seeing them my parents asked me to hide myself in the adjoining room. I immediately did so. The hijras were requesting my parents to hand me over to them. But my parents would not... After fifteen- twenty minutes exchange of arguments, both the parties started shouting loudly. The hijras said that I being of neither sex belonged to them only. It was a custom upheld for centuries. My mother cried helplessly. My father tried to scare them away with threats... But all that went in vain. Finally, I had to leave the house.'
> (Case study collected by S.K. Sharma in the 1980s.)

The Hindu hijras virtually constitute a closed religious sect. Their chief patroness is the goddess Bahuchara Devi, whose temple stands near Ahmedabad in Gujerat. One eunuch related that he set aside five percent of his daily earnings for the goddess, whom he called 'murgewali', or 'cockerel-goddess', after a year distributing the collected money as alms to the poor. Bahuchara Devi was worshipped in the form of the vulva, a fact which immediately identifies her as the great Mother goddess, consort of Siva and the embodiment of Sakti. In her form as Kali, according to the Nirutarra-tantra, she was worshipped with an offering called 'kukkutodabhava', which is probably the flesh of a cockerel. In Nepal also, offerings of cockerel's meat and hen's eggs are made to Kali. In their worship of the goddess and their organisation under gurus who command complete obedience, the hijras in some respects are like an order of Tantric sadhus.

This is not such a farfetched notion. Like the naked, ash- smeared sadhus, hijras have a religious charisma in rural India. They are regarded by the superstitious villagers as having been marked by god and are given the respect due to representatives of divinity. Are not Siva and Sakti, when united, one being who is neither male nor female, but 'Ardhanaresvara', 'the divine- half-man-half-woman'? The eunuchs also deserve reverence for they are, in a sense, Sivas-of-the-severed-lingam: beings made magically powerful by the fact that they do not eject and spend their semen. These modern hijras are part of a mysterious tradition that stretches back beyond Vatsyayana and outside India.

The cults of the goddesses Astarte and Cybele, respectively the great Mothers of Syria and Phrygia, were so similar to one another that in ancient Rome the priests of one cult were frequently taken for those of the other. Numerous ancient historians have recorded how the young men, inspired to frenzy at the festival of the goddess, intoxicated with religious fervour, would dance before the altar, finally rushing forward to seize one of the razor edged swords left there for the purpose and with one stroke severe their genitals. In the temples of Cybele, these bloody organs were flung triumphantly onto the altar itself. In the cult of Astarte it appears that the new eunuch, bleeding freely, ran through the town holding his severed genitals, finally flinging them into the open doorway of the house of his choice, which then had to furnish him with the female dress he would wear in his new role as priest of the goddess.

What was the meaning of such a castration? It seems, on the face of it, a barbarously cruel thing to do - whether to oneself or someone else. Yet, paradoxically, the custom may have had its origins not in the goddess's malice, but in her mercy. In the far off days of the bacchic chase, the anointed priest of the horned god was torn to pieces after being ritually hunted: his organs of generation were presented as a sacrifice to the goddess. There must have come a time when the man and his clan did not wish to give his life. How could the offering still be made? By allowing the sacred victim to keep his life - if he voluntarily surrendered his manhood. It was the generative power, the potency of the man, which had always been given to ensure fertility - that and his red life-blood which replenished the Mother's own energies. The goddess could not be denied the life-restoring blood, so, baulked of human blood, she chose instead the largest and most magnificent of domesticated animals, the bull. The life she had spared - that of the newly castrated male - remained hers, however. It must not be rendered in any way impure. What remained of it must be spent wholly in her service.

If castration was an alternative to violent death, we may perhaps see celibacy as an alternative to castration. Priests of the goddess would have been entitled to remain 'entire', as the animal breeders say, provided that they never used their sexual organs, specifically that they never shed their seed. Instead of the vow demonstrated with the sword on the altar of Astarte or Cybele, we have the vow lived out in a lifetime of asceticism and penance. This is where the custom of priestly chastity must have arisen and the crucial point was to avoid shedding seed.

Were there sacred castrati in India? In Vatsyayana's time eunuchs worked as masseurs and some found employment as harem guards. Kautilya in his Arthasastra some three centuries earlier says that Maurya kings stationed 'varsadhara', or eunuch guards wearing helmets and turbans, outside their bedrooms although not, it would seem, in their harems. But did eunuchs ever play religious roles?

If we go back to the passage in the Mahabharata where Karna is abusing the Madra tribe, we find the following enigmatic verse:

> "The mlecchas are the dirt of mankind. The oilmen are the dirt of the mlecchas. The eunuchs are the dirt of the oilmen. Those who use ksatriya-priests in their sacrifices are the dirt of the eunuchs." (Karna Parva, 45)

What can this mean? Is it simply confirmation of what we already know: that eunuchs had very low status in the community. Or is Karna's choice of words so specific that we must look for a deeper meaning?

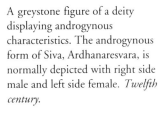

A greystone figure of a deity displaying androgynous characteristics. The androgynous form of Siva, Ardhanaresvara, is normally depicted with right side male and left side female. *Twelfth century.*

In the long passage from which this verse is taken, Karna is not just talking about deviations from sexual and social norms but, crucially, from religious orthodoxy. In some sects, the duties traditionally done by brahmins had been usurped by 'ksatriyas', men of the warrior caste. He mentions kings who pour their own libations and are their own sacrificer and priest. Karna's comparison of this sin, as he sees it, with the activities of the 'oilmen' and the 'eunuchs' has little force unless the 'oilmen' and the 'eunuchs' were themselves practitioners of some sort of depraved, non-Arya, priestcraft.

The 'mlecchas', as we have seen, were Aryas who were outside the main Vedic religious fold. The term may have originated in the name given to the dwellers of the Indus valley, which was known by the name of Meluhha. From their customs it appears that they were devotees of the Mother goddess, whom they may have worshipped with drunken and orgiastic rites. According to some authorities, the 'pumscalis' or sacred prostitutes associated with other outcaste Aryas, the Vratyas, were clearly connected with bacchantic, orgiastic rites. Thus, when Karna excoriates the 'mlecchas' he may well have in mind the temple-harlots who officiated over their wilder religious festivals.

What of the mysterious 'oilmen'? The word used by Karna in the Mahabharata is 'tailakah', which simply means 'oil-pressers', the oil in question being crushed from sesame seeds. Such oil had a variety of everyday uses, as well as possessing magical and ritual significance. That it had sexual connotations can be seen from the fact that oil-of-sesamum was also known as 'sneh' or 'love' and was highly regarded as a virility food. The 'oilman' was thus connected with potency and fertility.

An interesting suggestion as to the meaning of Karna's remarks was offered to me by the author and broadcaster Sreeram Vidyarthi, who speculated that the term 'oilmen' may have been applied to people of the barber caste, who had usurped some of the priestly duties of brahmins; and whose descendents today actually refer to themselves as 'nau-brahmins' or 'barber-priests' and specialise in the rites connected with marriage. It has become their function to pour oil - itself as we have seen a symbol of lechery - over the threshold of the house before the newly married couple enter. 'Open sesame' is not just a fairytale mantra. It is clearly a rite to ease, in every sense, the anxieties of the newlyweds. As such, it represents another significant contact between the Kama and Tantra traditions.

Other evidence identifies certain 'oilmen' as priests of the Mother goddess. The 'tailotsava' is an 'oil-festival' still celebrated in the south Indian town of Madurai in honour of the goddess Minakshi. Her temple is full of wonders, like the famous hall of a thousand pillars; other 'musical pillars' which play notes when they are struck; and the great temple bell, which, oddly enough, was made in America. The main festivities last for three days in April and commemorate Minakshi's marriage to Siva, a liaison which instantly identifies her as a form of Parvati-Kali, the great Mother Goddess.

'Madurai': the very name is a promise of religious festivals. In Tamil, the name means 'sweet place'. In Sanskrit the meaning is not so different. The Sanskrit root 'mada' signifies 'hilarity', 'joy', 'lust', 'intoxication', 'honey-wine', 'honey'. (The Greek root 'mel', 'honey', has much the same set of meanings.) 'Mada' is the root of the Tantric wine-sacrament of 'madya', and the name 'Madra'. The Madras, as we have seen from Karna's diatribe against them in the epic Mahabharata, were a people much given to wine and hilarity. 'Mada', like oil, has sexual connotations. It is the name given to the oily fluid that flows from the temples of an elephant in rut: a familiar metaphor in Sanskrit erotic poetry.

In a second poetic metaphor lies another connection: the names of the goddess of Madurai, whether Sanskrit 'mina-akshi' or Tamil 'an-kayal-kanni', mean the same thing: 'with-the-eyes-of-a-fish'. In both Tamil and Sanskrit poetry, this metaphor was used to describe the large, lustrous eyes of a beautiful woman. It was a sign of beauty and the images of the goddess have exaggeratedly large, round eyes. In Meluhha, the terracotta goddess-

An eighteenth-century greystone stele of Siva and Parvati.

Blue Siva: part of the fine 'ritual' series of Tantric paintings published for the first time in this book. (For others, see pages 15, 19, 44, 49, 61 and 67.) From his mouth ascends a stalk which blossoms into a red lotus at the level of the sahasrara, or crown, cakra. He is attended by four strangely sexless priests, perhaps representing the four divisions of mankind. The artist who painted this magnificent series was never lost for ideas. The 'halloween pumpkin' at the foot of the page and the magnificent Bhairava eyes that command us from the top of the painting, both have startling toothpaste grins. *Eighteenth century.*

images were given similarly striking eyes, probably as a consequence of the sculptors' mass-production methods. After being roughly shaped into a torso with head, swelling breasts, hips and thighs, the figurines' faces were pinched to fashion a nose. Small clay discs were pressed on for eyes, and then outlined with a thinly- rolled thread of clay. These little statuettes are almost indistinguishable from those of Syrian Astarte, the great Mother of Hierapolis, who was also known as Atargatis, a fish goddess, and whose rites were attended by orgies, sacred prostitution and ritual castration.

The connection between 'oilmen' and 'eunuchs' is straightforward. Sesamum-oil was scented and used in massage, an art which often had sexual overtones. Kama Sutra says that massage culminating in fellatio was one of the services offered by eunuchs and masseurs. On this reading, if the 'oilmen' were priests of the goddess, the 'eunuchs' would have been special priests of their number who had undergone castration for religious reasons.

The belief in the magical potency of semen lived on and was as crucial to the gnostics in the West as to the Tantrics in India. People continued to believe in the magical efficacy of celibacy. But celibacy is difficult. In India, the 'brahmacaryas', or celibate sadhus, practised fearful austerities, torturing the body to bring the mind under control. Mahatma Gandhi tried and failed for years to rid himself of all sexual feelings. To strengthen and test his self-control he hit upon the risky stratagem of sleeping in the same bed as his attractive nineteen year old grandniece, Manu. But this chaste experiment was inevitably misunderstood and Gandhiji had to give it up. He had proved a great deal more successful, however, than the early Church Father, Origen, who found celibacy so difficult that the only way he could guarantee it was to have himself castrated, pointing to the words of Jesus to his disciples:

> There are some eunuchs, which were born so from their mother's womb: and there are some eunuchs which were made eunuchs of men: and there be eunuchs which have made themselves eunuchs for the kingdom of heaven's sake. He that is able to receive it, let him receive it. (Matthew, 19.12)

But even being castrated does not protect against desire. A present day Punjabi 'hijra' describes his torment:

> eh gal sade dimag wich jadon asin aapne pind which hunde han tan nahin aundi. kyonki ethe tan sab sade bhai-behan ne. par jadon asin kise dusri jagah jande han tan lokan noon dekhke asi sochde han je asin bhi aadmi-jan aurat hunde taan asi bhi shadi karde te bache jamde. par eh gal da saade dimag which aana tan toofan aan wali gal hai. eh taan oh aag hai jehri jwani which lagdi hai te ant which saadi chita jalan te bujdhi hai.

> 'When we're in our own place, thoughts of sex don't occur to us, because everyone is our brother and sister. But when we're out and about and see other people, then we think: if we had also been men or women, then we too would have got married and had children. This thought blasts my mind with the force of a hurricane. This thing is a fire that flares up when we are young and which is extinguished only on our funeral-pyre.' ('Hijras: The Labelled Deviants')

To the Tantric adept, the celibacy of the monk and the celibacy of the eunuch alike are crude and desperate attempts to solve the problem of desire. The male adept follows the example of Siva, the teacher of the sexual art, who is also a celibate ascetic. In Tantrism, the apparent contradiction vanishes when sexual yoga is practised. If preserving the semen is the objective of celibacy, then there is a kind of celibacy in having sexual intercourse without ejaculating. In this way the adept is able to rouse and channel the vast psychic energies released during intercourse and yet retain his seminal purity. This is why Tantric sex places such emphasis on prolonging lovemaking without orgasm. It is one of the unwritten secrets of what we may call the 'yugma' tradition - the practice that spans the huge gap between the elementary teachings of the kama-shastras and the mastery of the Tantras. As a final refinement of celibacy, Tantric adepts have perfected the 'amaroli mudra'. After long lovemaking they permit themselves to ejaculate into their partner's vagina, but then, after allowing the semen to mix with the woman's secretions, they draw the mixture back into their bodies. 'Amaroli mudra' is impossible to learn except by long and difficult practice, and can be dangerous when wrongly performed.

We can now begin to trace the evolution of the sacrament of sex in worship. For the male it developed from simple ritual copulation in mimicry of prey animals; to a sacred chase in which the victim died and was torn to pieces; to an offering of the severed sexual organs; to the practice of celibacy; to the Tantric practice of indefinitely prolonged intercourse; finally to the virtuoso feat of the 'amaroli mudra'. This is still only an outward description of a process which, having begun as simple fertility magic, at some point kindled into gnosis.

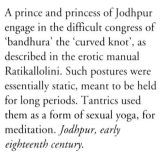

A prince and princess of Jodhpur engage in the difficult congress of 'bandhura' the 'curved knot', as described in the erotic manual Ratikallolini. Such postures were essentially static, meant to be held for long periods. Tantrics used them as a form of sexual yoga, for meditation. *Jodhpur, early eighteenth century.*

Chapter 7

WHORES OF BABYLON AND BOMBAY

> 'The old, rickety, ramshackle buildings jutting out into the narrow and irregular streets, strewn with stinking garbage; shoddy hotels perpetually filled with loud and jazzy film music and the lingering smells of stale onion and oil smoke; pedhis (shops) of rapacious marwaris and the ever-busy paan shops; hideous looking eunuchs in saris, carrying their brass gods and goddesses on the head and calling for alms in their incongruous male voices; large numbers of young and middle-aged men leisurely rambling on the streets and lustfully staring at the women of pleasure; the prostitutes, cheaply dressed in tight clothes and invariably chewing paan, sitting in voluptuous postures and indulging in unashamed and pitiably professional coquetry... In the nights, life here is highly exaggerated. The gloomy streets with their dark alleys and the dim and diffused lights casting ill-defined, sinister shadows, fire one's imagination with disquieting thoughts. In other parts the place looks as if a fair is on, brightly lit and thronged with people —- the prostitutes soliciting in colourful clothes and heavily made-up faces and men of all ages brazenly bargaining and settling terms with them; groups of people squatting on mid-streets in circles and gambling on card games, heedless of the law or the police; the hotel boys rushing hither and thither with packets of snacks and cups of steaming tea; pedlars hawking their fancy merchandise, from bleating balloons to hush hush contraceptives; music from all sides played louder than ever, the resultant discord menacingly assailing the eardrums.'
> (Punekar & Rao, A Study of Prostitutes in Bombay)

The mistress: an oil painting betraying British influence, probably commissioned by a rich man for his private collection. The girl had probably been a prostitute. Even today, girls dedicated as devadasis, or temple prostitutes, are expected to look for rich patrons. *Early twentieth century.*

This is a description of Bombay's Falkland and Foras Roads as they are today. But many details could have come directly from a Gupta city. India does not change. In these streets we encounter three themes connected with Tantrism in India: castration, religious prostitution and mind-altering drugs. Here are the street corner paan-wallahs whose inventory of pleasures includes 'charas-ki- goliyaan', balls of hashish spiced with opium; and the famous 'palang-tod' or 'bed-breaker' paan, whose ingredients are said to include cocaine. Here, side by side, are female and transvestite brothels. Many of the transvestites are eunuchs. Some were born hermaphrodite, but most have had their genitals razored off. Of the female prostitutes, a large number are 'devadasis' or 'temple- slaves', in some cases, dedicated by their parents from birth to the service of a particular goddess.

As recently as the 1960s, about a third of the prostitutes in the 'cages' of the Falkland and Foras Roads were 'devadasis'. Of 113 girls interviewed in a field study, just over two-thirds were dedicated to the goddess Yellamma of Soundatti, four were dedicated to Khandoba of Jenjuri, four to Bhawani of Tuljapur, two to Hanuman, one to Manjunath of Dharmasthal and one to Hulegavva, sister of Yellamma.

Secular prostitution in India dates back to Vedic times. Even in those far-off days, the 'ganika' had an assured status and function in society. Kautilya's Arthasastra has a section on the regulation of prostitutes and defines several different kinds of public women, including the 'rupajiva' or woman who lives on her beauty and who may have been an actress or a society courtesan, rather than a common whore. At important social gatherings and religious festivals prostitutes entertained guests with singing, dancing and elegant conversation. Kama Sutra lists sixty four arts and crafts in which the educated ganika should be expert, in addition to the sixty four sexual techniques indispensible to her profession. In the Mahabharata, we encounter the 'deva-vesya', a 'harlot of the gods', who may have been attached to a temple. As we shall see, women also called 'deva-vesya' played a central role in certain Tantric rites.

Prostitutes were regarded as 'lucky'. The Vishnu Samhita stated authoritatively that to circumambulate a prostitute was an auspicious practice. Matsya Purana said that meeting a 'veshya' at the start of a journey was a sign of great good fortune. In many places of Southern India, the Mangalasutram of a newly wed bride was and still is, made by the hands of a prostitute. While in northeastern India a handful of earth from the threshold of a strumpet's house is still required in making a holy image of the goddess Durga.

The custom of dedicating a girl as a temple-slave was recommended in the Puranas and widely practised from the third century AD onwards. The seventh-century Chinese traveller Huien Tsang saw a large number of temple-dancers in the sun temple of Multan. The spread of temple-prostitution was directly linked to the medieval explosion of temple building. In roughly the same period that the stonemasons of western Europe were erecting the great cathedrals with their rich stone pageants and their gnostic and alchemical secrets, the stonemasons of India were employed by rajas to erect temples that honoured the gods and assured that their own names would not be forgotten.

At Khajuraho in central India, magnificent stone temples covered with erotic figures began to be erected by Chandella kings at the end of the first millenium. The temple of the Sun at Konarak, built in the thirteenth century was also decorated with erotic carvings.

Part of a frieze from a Khajuraho temple depicting every imaginable sort of sexual activity. Like the much later miniature on page 10, these acts often involved holy men, demonstrating that they had a spiritual dimension and were not intended to be taken literally.

Figures engaged in every possible kind of sexual activity crawled, hopped, walked and skipped across its stone flanks. At Khajuraho we find: men making love with two women; copulating men touching the yonis of female attendants; several couples making love together; couples making love standing up or with the woman astride; women fellating ascetics; women kneeling before men and sucking their organs; nude men and women exposing their private parts; an ascetic enjoying a woman from behind; aristocratic couples helped by attendants to make love in acrobatic head-down postures; attendants masturbating as they watch; even a man mating with a mare can be seen on the Lakshmana and Visvanath temples. Inside the Matangeshvara temple is a huge Siva-linga, over eight feet high and four feet across, to which devotees have thronged now for nearly a thousand years. Villagers travel for days to reach the temples and camp outside them: families, large parties of all ages, eating their simple meals and sleeping in the open air. At every moment of the day and starlit night, the light on the temples changes and, ceaselessly, the figures dance.

Donations of gold and silver and grants of land turned many temples into rich institutions. Their priests became, in effect, landlords and the temples became cultural and commercial centres around which priests, musicians, dancers, garland-makers, temple-girls and barbers settled. An inscription on the Brhadesvara temple at Tanjore, built by the Chola king Rajaraja at the beginning of the second millenium, lists the endowments the king made to the temple: 226 kg of gold, 272 kg of silver, the income from several villages, 400 'devadasis' or temple-girls and 212 male servants, including a dance master, musicians, drummers and tailors.

Medieval temple managements opened shops and hotels for pilgrims and collected rents. Even the state benefited, by imposing a tourist tax on the large numbers of pilgrims attracted by the fame of the temples. Part of that attraction was, of course, the temple girls. Their original duties had included cleaning the temple and its precinct, lighting the oil lamps and fanning the image of the deity. But their main function had always been to sing and dance at temple ceremonies. From literary evidence and from certain of the carved figures that adorn the temples themselves, we know that temple priests often enjoyed the temple girls themselves. The carved facades of many temples must have served as inventories of the pleasures available to the tired pilgrim for, of course, a fee that went straight to the temple treasury. Temple-girls could be expensive. In the 1930s a typical fee was reported to have been between ten and forty US dollars. A Nizam of Hyderabad was once said to have offered a thousand pounds sterling for three nights. Girls - preferably of good family, good looking and healthy - were in demand. Rich temples were able to create a financial incentive for poor villagers to part with their daughters, by rewarding girls with gifts of land and cash.

A loving couple, their rapture preserved in the stone facade of a Khajuraho temple.

The temples of the goddess Yellamma have to this day a strong hold on the villagers of north Karnataka and southern Maharashtra. Nearly half of the devadasis interviewed in Bombay's red light district had been dedicated to a temple because of a longstanding family commitment that one daughter must become a 'jogti' or 'devadasi'. The vast majority of these families were Yellamma worshippers who believed it was their duty "to keep the light of Yellamma burning". In some cases, villagers seem to have looked for the flimsiest pretext to dedicate a child to Yellamma, as the sad story of Yellu, whose parents were so devout that they even named her after the goddess, illustrates:

> 'When Yellu was a little girl, she accompanied her grandmother to the temple of Yellamma. The old woman, a stauch devotee of this goddess, asked Yellu to bow to Yellamma. But she refused and said, 'I don't see Yellamma or anyone there and I won't bow to a stone'. The outraged grandparent beseeched the goddess to forgive the ignorant brat and forced Yellu to bow to her. After a day or two the girl got a sty in her eye and it did not subside for a week. It then dawned on her grandmother that the

The nobleman with his harem: in this exceptionally fine modern painting, great care has been taken with details like the inlaid flowers of semi-precious stone set into the palace's marble panelling. Powerfully erotic, the work gains its impact by the soft modelling of bodies, using light to sculpt forms in a manner not found in earlier miniature painting. *Twentieth century.*

sty was a punishment inflicted on Yellu for her impudent behaviour at the temple and that the goddess might even make her blind. So the old woman ardently prayed to Yellamma again and implored her to pardon the child. She took a vow that if the goddess cured Yellu of her sty and spared her eyesight, she should be made a jogti'. (Punekar & Rao: A Study of Prostitutes in Bombay)

The temple in which this child's fate was sealed was one of many built in Yellama's honour during the tenth century, when medieval Tantrism was spreading across India like a fire out of control. Her largest and most famous shrine was at Soundatti, which was even mentioned as one of the great 'saktisthanas' or centres of Tantric sakti-worship in the Devi-bhagavata, a text on Mother worship which considered by many to be more sacred even than the Puranas. But this goddess, who was identified with Adi Shakti, or the great primaeval Kali herself, had begun her life long, long ago, as Ellamma, a village divinity whose only homes were the rough unhewn stones marked with vermilion powder to which the village women brought flowers and over which the village men cut the throats of cockerels. Yellu, taken unwilling to the temple of Yellamma, did not see great Kali, only the stone. Of course, the ancient power that dwells in the stone is Kali herself in her most ancient form: consort of a god who must die. Her story as told by her devadasis, has become blended with that of Renuka, who was the virtuous wife of the sage Jamadagni. Renuka herself was an incarnation of Durga, who is also Kali. The tale of Yellama-Renuka is remarkable in that it simultaneously obscures and reveals the origin of her cult.

Renukaraja, king of Kashmir, was fortunate in all things except children. Neither his wife Bhogavati, eldest daughter of the king of Kasi (Benares or Varanasi), nor any of the twenty other lovely princesses he had married, could give him an heir. Grief-stricken, he entrusted the affairs of state to his brother-in-law Candrakant and with Bhogavati went on a pilgrimage to consult their guru, the sage Agastya. He instructed the king and his wife to perform the the 'putrakamesti yajna', or sacrifice for the birth of a child, under his directions at a sacred festival at the confluence of the Ganga and Yamuna rivers, and promised: 'You will be blessed with a daughter who will be the Great Mother herself'.

The holy festival was well attended by sages, ascetics, royalty and gods. When the king, guided by Agastya, poured the final offerings onto the sacrificial fire, a tiny form appeared in the flames. Out from the fire, before the onlookers' astonished eyes, came a baby girl of divine beauty, dressed in lovely clothes and rich jewels. At the moment of her birth, the gods rained flowers on the child. With great rejoicing they took her home and named her Renukadevi. The child soon captivated all in the palace except her jealous step-mothers, who bribed a snake charmer to loose a cobra in her bedroom. But no sooner had the snake slithered onto the child's cradle than a sword flashed out of the empty air and the snake fell back in two pieces. That evening, in the temple of Durga, the king noticed that the sword of the great goddess was bright with blood.

Renuka grew up into a charming young woman. At the age of eight, her father decided it was time to find her a husband. His ministers began a tour of foreign capitals in search of a suitable groom, but returned unsuccessful. The king then consulted Agastya, who announced that the only possible husband for Renuka was the sage Jamadagni, who was an incarnation of the god Siva. They were duly married and Renuka left the palace of her childhood and began a new life of austerity as the wife of the great ascetic sage. Such was his fame that holy men and even gods came to stay at the ashram. Renuka was a devoted wife and excellent hostess. Indra, king of the gods, came to visit, and on his departure made Jamadagni and Renuka a gift of the wish-fulfilling cow Kamadhenu. But possession of the magical cow brought its own problems.

There was a powerful and arrogant king called Kartiviryarjuna, a friend of the arch-demon Ravana (of Ramayana fame). They had once had a fight in which Ravana came off worse and ended chained in a dungeon. It must have been a fight to watch: Kartiviryarjuna's thousand arms against Ravana's ten heads. This powerful king and his men went hunting in the forest of Ramasrnga. The terrified birds and beasts sought refuge in Jamadagni's ashram. The king and his men followed them there and were hospitably received by the sage and Renukadevi. Kartiviryarjuna was astonished that so simple a hermitage could feed his entire hunting party and asked how it was done. Jamadagni told him that he had only to wish for something and his magic cow would produce it. Kartiviryarjuna was possessed by a lust to own the cow. He offered to give five million cows for it, but Jamadagni refused. He then offered even half his kingdom but Jamadagni would not part with Kamadhenu. The wicked king ordered his men to seize her, but Kamadhenu turned into a huge herd of wild cows which kicked all Kartiviryarjuna's men to death. The king now grabbed the noseband of the magic cow and, followed by Jamadagni, began to lead her away into the forest. But she slipped from his grasp and melted away up into the sky. The sage laughed and, enraged beyond restraint, the king beat him to death.

Krishna and Radha find bliss in each other's body, mind and spirit. Their lovemaking, which was illicit, is a parable of the soul's love of the divine: the same metaphor that we find in the Biblical Song of Solomon.

Renuka waited a long time for her husband to come back from the forest. At last she went in search of him. She found his body lying in the pool of blood where Kartiviryarjuna had left it. Renuka fell to the ground, wailing and beating her breast and mourned her husband. At last she arose silently, wiped the red marriage-dot from her brow and broke her bangles. Their sons built a funeral pyre and laid their father's body on it. For a month the body lay unburned and did not corrupt, while Renuka and her sons sent word to their old mentor Agastya rishi. At last out of the forest came Agastya, bringing with him the parents of Jamadagni, the sage Rucika and his wife Satyavati. As always, Agastya knew what to do. Under his instructions, Rucika performed the rite of 'sanjivani', sprinking his son's dead body with the magic elixir of life. Jamadagni stirred and the breath returned to his body.

In the temples of Yellama-Renuka, this story is acted out each year. The devadasis identify completely with the grief stricken Mother Goddess. When the glass bangles of her idol are smashed, they too smash their bangles. When the kumkum dot is wiped off the brow of the idol, the girls wipe the kumkum from their own brows and beat their breasts in

The terrific Mahishasuramardini – a form of the Mother Goddess Durga, in whose mouths boar-tusks gleam like crescent moons – slays a buffalo demon. Both demons and deities could be depicted in many-headed, many-armed forms, which denote omniscience and omnipotence.

mourning for Jamadagni. For a month they grieve and they only put on their bangles and kumkum again when he has been brought magically back to life.

Elsewhere in the world we find stories of a great Mother Goddess, weeping for her consort who has been cruelly killed, mourning for a month and rejoicing when he returns miraculously to life. Astarte mourns Tammuz, and Cybele mourns Attis. Both these goddesses were served by a castrated priesthood and by temple prostitutes. The legend told by the temple-prostitutes of Yellama not only identifies her as the great Adi Shakti of the Tantrics, but with the great Mother Goddess who was known elsewhere as Astarte and Cybele.

How did such customs first arise? Sacred prostitution is linked in the worship of Astarte and Cybele with the castration of male priests. This is probably no coincidence.

In the very earliest sacrifices, a man was killed in order that his potency could ensure the fertility of crops and herds, and that his life-energy, or 'prana', could flow to restore and rejuvenate the Mother principle by replacing the life-energy lost during menstruation, defloration and childbirth. At a very much later date, the life of the male victim was spared, provided that he gave up his potency to the service of the goddess by castrating himself at her altar. The institution of living priests would in turn have enabled the cult to grow at a faster rate, spreading to new regions, attracting more converts. A system that starts growing wants to keep growing. But there were limits. The sacrifice by a man of his procreative power, symbolised and contained in his genital organs, could not be expected of every male in the community. Hence it is likely that circumcision was first introduced as a token castration, to widen the sacrifice to all males in the community and to mark them as worshippers of the goddess.

Circumcision was a sacrifice made by the male worshipper. What sacrifice could be expected of the female? Female circumcision was not unknown and in Arabia is traditionally believed to predate male circumcision. The form still practised in the Sudan involves cutting away the whole of the clitoris and clitoral hood together with the inner and outer labia. The Sudanese call this vile practice the 'Pharaonic circumcision', which indicates its origin. Moses is said to have got the idea of circumcising boys from the same source. Two factors weigh strongly against the circumcision of women as a sacrifice. First, it is a desecration of the yoni, the sacred womb of the Mother. Second, since women menstruate monthly, there is no need to ask them for a further blood sacrifice. What women could and were asked to give was their sexual power, their sakti.

Herodotus recorded how, once in her lifetime, every woman born in Chaldea had to enter the enclosure of Aphrodite, sit within the temple walls and offer herself to a stranger. Many of the wealthy were too proud to mix with the hoi-polloi and took closed chariots to the temple. But most seated themselves in long lines along the sacred pavement to wait in hope for someone tall, dark and handsome, because once a woman had taken her place there, she could not go home again until a stranger had thrown her a silver coin and led her out of the temple enclosure with the words: 'May the goddess Mylitta make you happy'. (It is interesting to note that the Sumerian name of the Indus Valley culture was Meluhha, also written as Mi-la-kkha. Was there a link?)

In India, the aboriginal Santal tribe, the present-day equivalents of the Nisadas and the Sabaras, until recently observed the custom that all girls at Telkupi Ghat were obliged publicly to prostitute themselves at least once in their lives. In some places a variant evolved. Instead of each woman offering herself once to the goddess, each family was obliged to dedicate one daughter to her service. This remains the case among worshippers of Yellamma to this day.

The villagers fear the goddess as much as ever their ancestors did. A vow taken before her can never be revoked, even when it involves the life of one's own child.

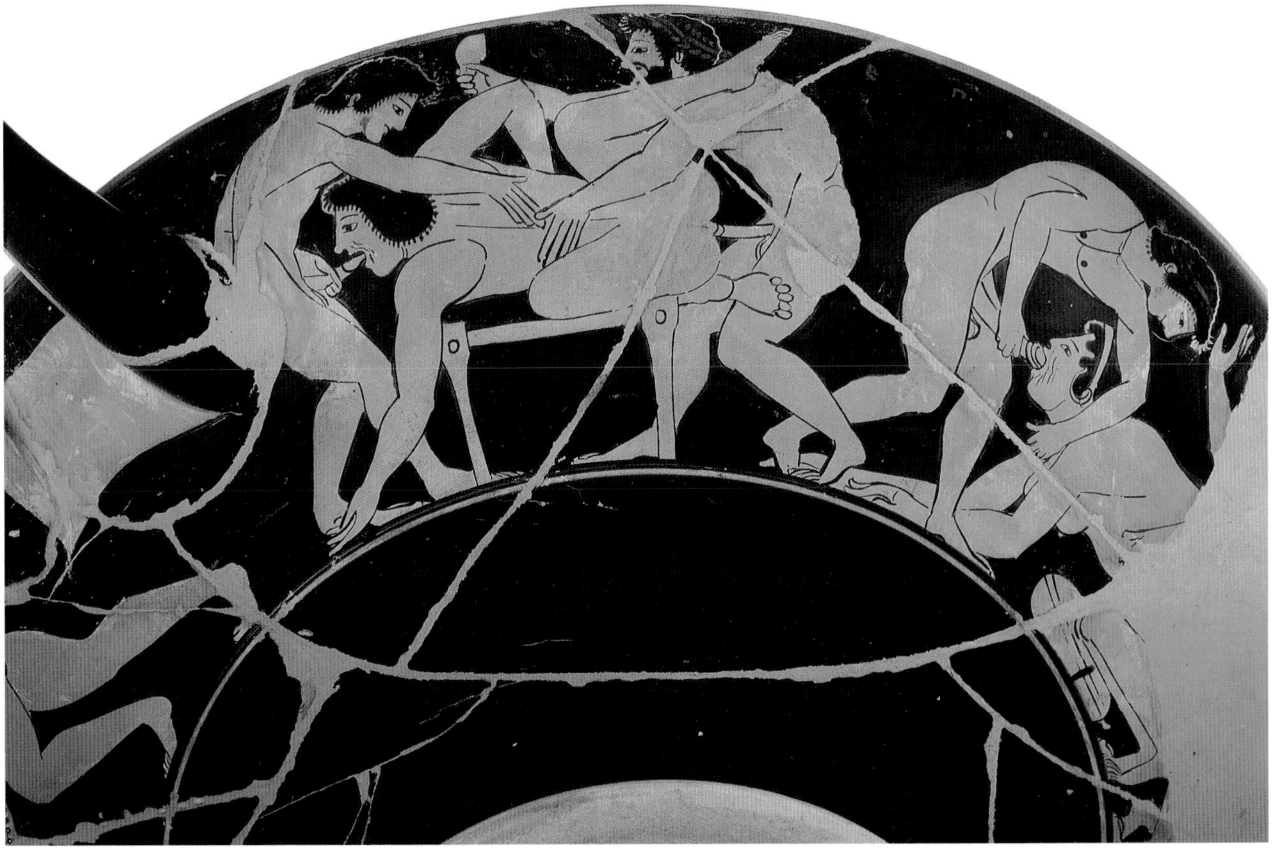

Attic red figure cup, probably intended for use at symposia, or wine-drinking parties. *Late sixth century BC.*

'Shantava fell ill when she was a girl of seven. Her father had gone to the neighbouring village on some work. Her mother and grandmother in a state of desperation prayed to Yellamma and said to her that if she saved the life of little Shanta, the girl shall be made her jogti. Shanta recovered and when her father returned he was told about what had happened in his absence. He became indignant and said that he would not ruin his daughter's life by making her a devadasi. When Shanta attained puberty the women-folk made preparations for presenting her to Yellamma with due ceremonies. The father had planned to get her married. So there was a big quarrel in the house and all including the neighbours insisting that a girl promised to Yellamma must be given to her, if not the wrath of the goddess would bring ruin upon the family. Defeated and helpless, Shanta's father left the village because he could not bear to see his daughter "being sacrificed".'
(ibid)

Shantava's father was right. His daughter had been sacrificed in a tradition so old that its origins were forgotten. If, at this time of writing, Shanta is still alive, she must be an old woman, perhaps by now one of the gharwalis or madams who sit in the front rooms of the houses in Falkland Road and train girls in the art of pleasing men.

Chapter 8

A Gnostic Journey

> 'Young wenches have a wanton sport which they call moulding of Cockle-bread, viz, they get up on a table-board, and then gather up their knees and their coates with their hands as high as they can, and then they wabble to and fro, as if they were kneading of dough, and say these words, viz:
>
> "My dame is sick and gone to bed,
> And I'le go mould my Cockle-bread."
>
> I did imagine nothing to have been in this but meer wantonnesse of youth. But I find in Burchardus, in his 'Methodus Confitendi'...one of the Articles (on the VII Commandment) of interrogating a young woman is, "If she did ever, subigere panem clunibus, and then bake it, and give it to one she loved to eate, ut in majorem modum exardesceret amor". So here I find it to be a relique of naturall magick - an unlawful philtrum.'
> (John Aubrey, Lansdowne MS No 231)

John Aubrey, that peerless raconteur and collector of oddities, was merely amused by this game of bread 'cockling' until he discerned in it traces of the old fertility religion which, in seventeenth-century 'merry Englande', was still finding dozens of ways to express itself. Was it an unlawful philtrum? Or a half-forgotten sacrament?

For an answer, we must return to the temple of Yellama, where the child Shantava is being dedicated as a temple-prostitute. Her father, saddened and angered by this 'sacrifice' of his daughter, is not present. He cannot bear to watch. He understands that what Shantava is giving to the goddess was more than just her youthful energy, more even than a lifetime of service. She is giving up something priceless in a sacrifice that a eunuch priest would well understand. Remember the words of the Punjabi hijra:

> asin bhi aadmi-jan aurat hunde taan asi bhi shadi karde te bache jamde. par eh gal da saade dimag which aana tan toofan aan wali gal hai.
>
> '...if we had also been men or women, then we too would have got married and had children. This thought blasts my mind with the force of a hurricane.'
> ('Hijras')

The temple-harlots are denied the most fundamental and magical of female experiences: motherhood. Once-in-a-lifetime prostitution may correspond to circumcision, a sign that one belongs. But in its most archaic form, the sacrifice of the temple-prostitute corresponds to that of the eunuch, the ascetic sage bound by vows, and the celibate nun. She has to dedicate her whole life entirely to the goddess. She may not be a mother.

This explains another oddity in the diatribe, to which we have repeatedly returned, of

A red goddess: one of the unique 'ritual' series of Tantric paintings. (For others, see pages 15, 19, 44, 49, 61 and 67.) Elsewhere in this series, the painter has symbolically linked the lingam with other parts of the body, here it becomes the nose of Siva. *Eighteenth century.*

Karna against the Madra women, when he accuses them of destroying the embryos in their wombs by procuring miscarriage. Karna's revulsion reflects the fact that children were regarded as such a blessing that it was considered sinful for a husband to avoid his wife's bed during her 'rtu', that part of her menstrual cycle when she was most likely to conceive:

> tīrthōparōdhō hi dharmavadha
> (Kautilya, Arthasastra 3,iv,36)
>
> 'To flout the rtu is to murder dharma.'

It is inconceivable that any woman would voluntarily destroy her own pregnancy, unless for an overwhelming reason. Considerations of paternity would hardly arise in a country where women were permitted to be as promiscuous as Karna claims the Madra women were. But suppose they were priestesses, to whom motherhood was forbidden?

Never to bear a child is a kind of virginity. It would not be surprising to find that the term 'virgin' was often applied, not to women who had yet to be penetrated by a phallus, but to women who had not yet given birth. This is certainly the case with certain Tantric sex rituals, which had to be performed by a 'vesya kumarika' or 'virgin whore', an experienced woman who had not yet borne a child. Sacred virginity has, in the end, nothing to do with lack of sexual experience. It is the power of the womb to keep producing, month after month, a flow of menstrual blood.

Something of the sort is suggested by Robert Graves apropos the Roman Vestal Virgins. They are supposed to have been strictly celibate, but Graves argues that there was a time when they were not:

> 'Now, as to the proof that the Virgins were once permitted occasional erotic delights: in the first place the novice, when initiated by the Chief Pontiff on behalf of the God, is addressed as "Amata", beloved one, and given a head-dress bordered with pure purple, a white woollen fillet and a white linen vestment — the royal marriage garments of the bride of the God.' (The White Goddess)

He adds that it seems to have been Tarquin the Elder who first prescribed for the Vestals what amounts to perpetual virginity, his object being to prevent them breeding claimants to the throne. But even if they were denied the pleasures of motherhood, these temple-women, whether harlot or virgin, were permitted to bring into the world other children, just as magical and miraculous.

The toilet of Aphrodite. *Dutch, seventeenth century.*

> Circling the circlings of their fish,
> Nuns walk in white and pray;
> For he is as chaste as they....

These words, coming unbidden from nowhere, set Robert Graves exploring the poetry of myth and led him to compile his extraordinary White Goddess. He had, he says, a sudden vision of white-clad Vestal Virgins in their temple grounds devoutly circling the fish-pool which the sacred fish were also mystically circling. The poetic metaphor translates back into history when we remember that the fish was sacred to the goddess Astarte and swam in her temple pools at Hierapolis. As the Canaanite fertility goddess Atargatis, she was worshipped in a fish-tailed form. In her fish-tailed form, she was sometimes also Aphrodite, 'risen from sea-foam'. Her temples stood by the sea shore and tunny, sturgeon, scallops and periwinkles, all sacred to her, were used as aphrodisiacs.

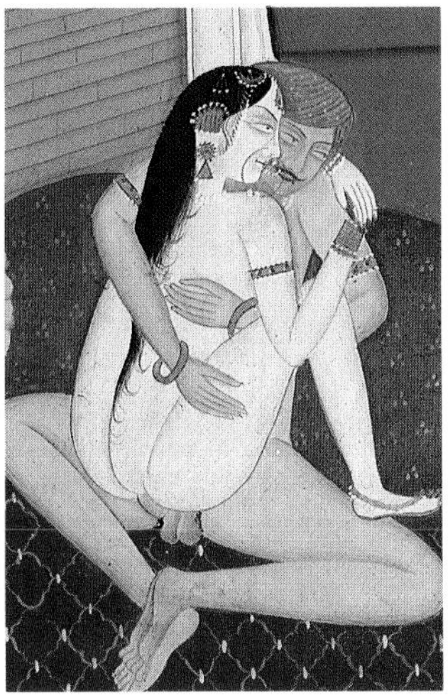

The fish is a magical child of the goddess. Jesus himself was such a miracle child, a fish plucked from a holy pool by a sacred virgin. 'The mighty and stainless Fish from the Fountain whom a pure virgin grasped', Aviricius, the second-century bishop of the Phrygian Pentapolis, called him. At four weeks, the embryos of humans and fish are indistinguishable. Their destinies then diverge, the human passing through 440 million years of evolution in nine months, bathed in the waters of an internal sea: a fish swimming in a sacred pool. We may recall, now, Coleridge's 'sunless sea'. Woman carries the primaeval sea within her body and the smell of fish is the clean smell of her yoni.

There was another kind of magical child which could be born to a virgin in a sublime alchemical process. The pure seed of the father must be taken and churned in an analogue of the act of love, and mixed with the juices of the mother, thence placed in a hot retort to grow to term. This process is called making bread. The grain is the pure seed of the father, which must be crushed to flour. The ancient symbols of pestle and mortar are the lingam and yoni and their crushing and churning is the act of love. The water, oil or milk that moisten the dough are the fluids of the female and the hot oven is the mother's womb. Within the oven the dough rises and swells, a child growing in the womb. Is it coincidence that we talk of 'a bun in the oven'? What about 'loaves and fishes'? 'Cockle-bread', bread kneaded with the yoni, is doubly magical.

If this seems fanciful, we may recollect that in Greece and Rome and even in medieval Europe, mills and bakeries were often connected with brothels. Other reminders of this context are the 'fair miller girl' and the 'wanton seed' of folksong. The Vestals themselves were priestesses of Vesta, goddess of the hearth, whose temple in the Roman forum was a round, oven-shaped brick building. In ancient Greece, vulva-shaped cakes called 'mylloi' were baked in honour of Aphrodite and eaten smeared with honey.

A passage from The Needle, a story by the Czech writer Capek shows that these mysteries can still be experienced:

> 'You wouldn't believe what a fine job it is, to bake rolls, and especially to bake bread. My poor old dad had a bakery, so I know all about it. You see, in making bread, you've got two or three important secrets which are practically holy. The first secret is how to make the yeast; you have to leave it in the trough and then there's a sort of mysterious change takes place under the lid; you have to wait until the flour and water turn into live yeast. Then the dough is made and mixed with what they call a mash-ladle; and that's a job that looks like a religious dance or something of that sort. Then they cover it with a cloth and let the dough rise; that's another mysterious change, when the dough grandly rises and bulges, and you mustn't lift the cloth to peep underneath — I tell you, it's as fine and strange as the process of birth. I've always had a feeling that there was something of the woman about that trough. And the third secret is the actual baking, the thing that happens to the soft and pale dough in the oven. Ye gods, when you take out the loaf, all golden and russet, and it smells more delicious than a baby, it's such a marvel — why, I think that when these three changes are going on, they ought to ring a bell in the bakeries, the same as they do in church at the elevation of the host.'

Bread too, is a sort of sacrifice. It may be offered in place of flesh, especially in place of living human flesh. The loaf of bread is metaphorically a human body and may be broken and offered instead of a human sacrifice. When Jesus said, 'this is my body', it was perfectly true. The sacred loaf evolved from the blood sacrifice. The god was no longer hunted and torn to pieces, nor castrated with the curved knife, but cut with a sickle and crushed and beaten and baked. The clearest possible indication of this changeover is in the rites of Cybele

herself. Attis, her lover, is said to have emasculated himself on a Day of Blood. During the period of mourning for Attis, worshippers fasted from bread. Just so, the worshippers of Ishtar, while they wept for Tammuz, would not eat anything ground in a mill. To eat bread or anything made from flour at such a time would have been to profane the bruised and broken body of the god.

> But after night had fallen, the sorrow of the worshippers was turned to joy. For suddenly a light shone in darkness: the tomb was opened: the god had risen from the dead; and as the priest touched the lips of the weeping mourners with balm, he softly whispered in their ears the tidings of salvation.
> (Goldberg, The Sacred Fire)

The risen god here is not Jesus, but Tammuz. It could also have been Attis, and the rejoicing goddess may be called Cybele, or Astarte, or Yellamma, who is Kali of the Tantrics.

The light that shines in darkness is the light of knowledge in the darkness of ignorance. The Greeks called it 'gnosis', the Tantrics call it 'jnana': two very similar words from the same Indo-European root. To accept the substitute, to make the magical identification of one essence with another, is the beginning of gnosis, the beginning of alchemy - and the beginning of Tantra.

Transubstantiation, as sceptics never tire of pointing out, has no effect on the physical plane. Bread remains bread, wine is still wine. But the transformation we should look for is not of the outward substance, but a change that takes place in the mind of the communicant. Let us add three more sacraments to these two familiar Christian ones: the same holds true. Meat is still meat and fish still fish. The lingam in the yoni is still a lingam in a yoni. But in the midnight darkness of the adept's mind, a light has blazed.

At last we can begin to draw together the threads of our theme. We have seen how the five sacraments of Tantrism arise out of the immemorial worship of the great Mother; and how in each case, the sacrificial offering always, in reality, represents one thing: the vital energy of creation. The meat is the flesh of the sacrificial victim who gives his potency for the good of all; the bread is his magical body of grain that grew out of his first sacrifice; the wine is the cup of his blood; the fish is the magical child that swims nine months in the hidden sea; the sexual union of lingam-in-yoni is the final transformation of the energy of creation into the light of gnosis.

Of these, the fish and the bread are feminine mysteries, brought to the sacred table by the woman. The meat and the wine are male mysteries, brought to the sacred table by the male. The man and the woman themselves are the final mystery.

In visiting the origins of these sacraments we have made a pilgrimage that began in the stone age and witnessed the ritual hunt, the ecstasy of the bacchantes, the castrated priests and temple harlots, the rearing of cattle and corn and fruit, the baking of sacred loaves and the transformation of blood into wine. The work of Tantra, like alchemy, is the return journey. The gnostic journey back to our true nature.

In the Mahabharata there is a whole section devoted to nothing but pilgrimages. The poet mentions a holy place called 'Yoni'. By following the route given here, we shall make our gnostic journey:

> 'By arriving at Bhadratunga with sanctified soul and purity of conduct, one acquireth the region of Brahma and a high state of blessedness...Then there is the tirth of the Kumarikas of Indra, that is much resorted to by the Siddhas... In Kumarika there is another tirtha called Renuka, which is also resorted to by the Siddhas. O best of men, by bathing there, one obtaineth the region of Indra... Proceeding next to the tirtha

called the Panchananda, with controlled sense and regulated diet, one obtaineth the fruit of the five sacrifices that have been mentioned one after another in the scriptures. Then, O King, one should go to the excellent region of Bhima. O best of Bharatas, by bathing in the tirtha there, that is called Yoni, a man in his next birth becometh, O king, the son of a goddess, bearing ear-rings decked with pearls, and obtaineth also the merit of the gift of a hundred thousand cattle.'
(Vana Parva, 82. translator: Kisari Mohan Ganguli)

The first place on the route is Bhadratunga, for which we may read the Tungabhadra river in Karnataka. Here is our first 'tirtha'. The word, which means literally 'river ford', can also be applied to a mountain or any sacred spot that becomes a focus for pilgrimage. The journey itself is undertaken as an act of devotion. At the tirtha, the usual practice is to bathe, 'snana'; circle the temple or holy spot, 'pradaksina'; make an offering, or carry out a rite such as the 'sraddha' ceremony, performed in honour of one's ancestors. The pilgim may also have his or her name recorded by 'pandas', priests who make their living from thus building up meticulous and labyrinthine genealogical records. In the evening, if staying at the tirtha, the pilgrim may listen to performances of music, dance, or expositions of the scriptures.

The Tungabhadra river flows through the state of Karnataka, whence the temple-priestesses of Yellama come from to this day. An apt place to reflect on the ephemerality of human life would be the ruined city of Vijayanagar. Here, huge ruined temples dominate a landscape that has been slowly returning to jungle for four hundred years. Where better to bathe than in the river itself and then, for a general view of the ruins, cross the Tungabhadra in a circular basket boat of the type used on the Tigris and Euphrates for 2,500 years.

From here, one proceeds to the region called 'Kumarika', or 'the region of virgins, resorted to by the adepts'. The tirtha here is of Renuka, whom we have already met. She is called Yellama and her chief temple is at Soundatti, which is thought to be her original place of worship. Inside the temple, if the experience of poor Yellu is anything to go by, we shall not see the goddess, just an old, rough-hewn stone. But this goddess is Adi-Kali, the great Mother Goddess, supreme being and first principle. She is the darkness of space-time in which the bright energy of creation manifests and shines. This is a place resorted to by the Siddhas, spiritually advanced adepts of great powers. What did the Siddha do in the 'place of the virgin'?

Further south, as far south as you can go, the Indian peninsula narrows to a tip of land which the British called Cape Comorin, but which since independence has reverted to its old Sanskrit name of 'Kanyakumari', 'the place of the sacred child-virgin'. There is a famous temple here, which derived its name from the fact that it specialised in Tantric 'child-virgin' worship.

The rituals are described in many Tantric texts and exhibit great variation. In some, the child-virgins worshipped could be as young as two years old. They were called 'kumarika'. In this system, a three-year old girl was called 'trimurti', a four-year old 'kalyani', a five-year old 'rohini', a six-year old 'kali', a seven-year old 'candika', an eight-year old 'sambhavi', a nine- year old 'durga', and a ten-year old 'subhadra'. They should be free from blemish, some texts demonstrating a curious pedantry in demanding that they should not be ulcerous, leprous or similarly afflicted. Depending upon the objective of the puja, or ritual worship, a child of any of the four castes could be adored. The child, richly clothed and garlanded with flowers, was treated as a manifestation of the goddess, a living idol. Over the several days of the puja, she would hear prayers, be bathed, dressed, fed and adored. The devotees would make presents of money and rich clothes to her parents and offer feasts in her honour.

The Mahabharata passage is full of Tantric language. 'Siddhas' are adepts who have attained the Tantric 'siddhis', or powers. The name 'panchananda', or 'five-fold bliss', is reminiscient of the five-fold Tantric sacrament usually called 'panchamakara' or 'panchatattva', which consists of meat, wine, fish, grain and sexual union. Are these what is indicated by 'controlled sense and regulated diet'? The subsequent reference to the 'five sacrifices' could refer to the five sacred sacrifices expounded one after another in the Brhadaranyaka Upanisad, the fifth of which is 'maithuna' or sexual union. This is, of course, the famous description of the woman as sacrificial fire, often quoted in works about Tantra and Indian sexuality and, inevitably, out of context.

> yōśā vā agnigautama tasyā upastha eva samit lōmāni dhūmaḥ yōnirarchiḥ yadantaḥ karōti té angārāḥ abhinandā visphūlingāḥ tasminnétasminnagnau dévā rétō juhvati tasyā āhutyai puruśaḥ saṁbhavati sa jīvati yāvajjīvati atha yadā mriyaté ||
> (Brhadaranyaka Upanisad, VI,ii,13)
>
> Woman in truth is the sacred fire, O Gautama, her lower limbs are the fuel, the hairs of her body the smoke, her vulva itself is the flame, the act of entering is the kindling, the blaze of pleasure is the sparks that fly up: in this fire the gods offer up the seed of humanity. From this sacred offering man is born. He lives for as long as he is destined to live. And then he dies.

The five sacrificial fires that burn in this beautiful Upanisad are, in order: the heavenly world; Parjanya the god of rain; the earthly world; man; and woman. In each fire an offering is made and from each a gift is obtained. The gift from one fire becomes the offering made to the next. Thus in the heavenly realm, faith is offered and the gift is 'soma', the divine ambrosia. In the next fire, soma is offered to Parjanya, who produces life-giving rain. In the third fire, the rain is offered to the earth and the earth produces all kinds of food. In the fourth fire, food is offered to man, and man's well nourished body creates the gift of human seed. In the fifth fire, human seed is offered and the gift is a new human life. The ultimate offering is man himself, on the funeral pyre that will disassociate his body and return his soul to the heavenly realm. It is possible to see in the Tantric fivefold sacrament of meat, grain, fish, wine and sexual union, a metaphor for the five offerings of the sacred fires, which is itself a description of the descent of spirit into flesh. The offering of semen creates flesh, 'mamsa', the body; the offering of food, 'mudra, corresponds to sacred bread; the watery offering of rain corresponds to 'matsya', the fish; the offering of 'soma' corresponds to 'madya', the wine, itself a metaphor for the blood of the early sacrifice; the offering of faith is 'maithuna', the union beyond polarity. The work of Tantra is now laid before us: to transubstantiate the coarse flesh of the human body back to the One from which it originally came and to which it eternally belongs. This takes the fire of death. Or, the Tantrics would say, of gnosis.

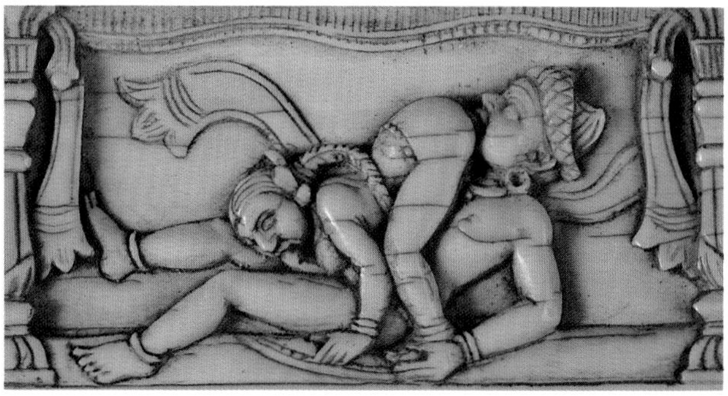

PART II

The Rites of Gnosis

Kama, god of love, rides forth on a mare composed of women.

Chapter 9

PROPOSITION 7.0

In the beginning there was nothing. Not even nothingness. There was no air, no sky beyond. What bounded this emptiness? Where was it? Was there water, deep beyond imagining? Death did not exist, for there was no life, nor any torch of day in that night, in which One breathed, without breath, alone. Alone in darkness robed in darkness, that One awoke, awakened by the power of heat, and desire, the primal mind-born seed, arose, in the beginning. Sages who search their hearts for wisdom know that what is, is is next of kin to what is not. Let them dissect the void, separate above from below; speak of first causes, huge forces, strength down here, spirit above: who really knows what happened? Who can say how it was born, whence came this world? Even the gods are younger than creation, so who can tell how it arose? Only he knows; that One with whom creation started, who now sits in high heaven and surveys the world; he knows if he made it, or if he did not make it. He knows. Or maybe he does not.

This, with apologies to the poet of the Rg Veda, is how for three thousand years brahmanical Hindus have told the story of creation. The hymn, with its poetry of darkness and deep waters is strongly reminiscient of the beautiful opening words, the 'berashith ruach alhim...', of Genesis.

The Arya sages and priests who composed the Vedas and Upanisads spent a great deal of time pondering the origin of the world, and came up with a variety of answers, of which the magnificent 'Hymn of Creation' is only one. The very opening verse of the great Brhadaranyaka Upanisad proposes that the universe should be conceived of as a cosmic sacrifice:

> ōm. uśā vā aśvasya médhyasya siraḥ. sūryaścakśuḥ, vātaḥ prāṇaḥ vyāttamagnivaiśvānaraḥ, saṁvatsar ātmāśvasya médhyasya. dyau prśṭham, antarikśamuram, prthvī pājyasyam, diśaḥ pārśvé, avāntaradiśaḥ parśavaḥ, rtvō-angāni, māsāścārdhamāsāśca parvāṇi, ahōrātrāṇi pratiśṭhāḥ, nakśatrāṇyasthīni, nabhō maṁsāni. ūvardhya sikatāḥ, sindhvō gudāḥ, yakrcca klōmānasca parvatāḥ, auśdhayasca vanaspatayasca lōmāni, udyan pūrvādhiḥ, nimlōcaṇjaghanārdhaḥ yadvijrmbhaté tadvidyōtaté, yadvidhūnuté tatstanayati yanméhati tadvarśati, vāgévāsya vāk. (Brhdaranyaka Upanisad, 1.i.1)
>
> Om. Dawn is the head of the sacrificial horse; the sun its eye; air its breath; the fire of sacrifice its mouth; the year is the body of the sacrificial horse, heaven its back, the sky its belly, earth its hoof, the directions its flanks and ribs; the seasons are the legs of the sacrificial horse, months and fortnights its joints, days and nights its feet; the stars are the bones of the sacrificial horse, clouds its flesh, desert sand its half-digested food, rivers its arteries, mountains its liver and lungs; the herbs and trees are the horse's hairs; its forefoot is the rising of the sun, its hindquarters the sunset. Lightning flashes when this horse yawns, when it kicks the thunder rolls; when it makes water, down comes the rain: all sounds are the sound of its neighing.

A silk mounted thanga, or meditation painting, depicting peaceful Buddhist deities. *Tibetan.*

A gilt bronze Buddha with a third-eye of turquoise. *Nepal, eighteenth century.*

The Brhadaranyaka Upanisad opens with this sacrifice and closes with the sacrifice-of-five-fires, which we have already encountered. Between these two sacrifices, the two ends of the Upanisad, there is a crucial development. Both are meditations, but the first is as an exploration of 'bhakti' or faith and the second is an exploration of 'jnana' or gnosis. The horse- sacrifice belongs to that early stage of religious experience which dealt in metaphor and mimetic magic. The five fires, with their chronicling of the descent of spirit into flesh, hold out at least the possibly of the reverse climb. And since spirit manifests itself in a succession of symbolic ejaculations of seed, there is, perhaps, in the notion of retaining rather than spending one's seed, the beginning of a technology of gnosis.

The process of thought, speculation and psychic experiment that bridges the gap between the beginning and end of the Brhadaranyaka Upanisad was vigorous and chaotic. In the seventh and sixth centuries BC India was full of masters who thought they had solved both the secret of the universe and of the nature, status and prospects of the human soul. According to these theorists, the world began variously as water, fire, wind or ether. Fate, time, nature and even chaos were invoked as primary causes. Some philosophers rejected the possibility of ever attaining any certain knowledge. There were atheists who denied the existence of a human soul, exchanging the Vedas for Carvaka's ironies:

> 'The atheists are fond of saying that the fruits of sacrifice, meant to sustain us in a future life, may very well prove inedible... 'Better a pigeon today than a peacock tomorrow, a copper in the pocket than a promise of gold.'
> (Kama Sutra I,ii,25-30)

Some madmen even said the world was made of tiny, indivisible and eternal particles of matter, formed from the primal, imperishable mind of god. The astro-physicists who have detected cosmic strings and listened to the dying echoes of the Big Bang are in essence no nearer to solving the problem than these descendants of the simple herdsmen of three millenia ago. The physicist who writes E = mcc is stating the speed of light in terms of a time whose nature he does not comprehend. The equation explains nothing, it is merely useful. The mathematician who, in asserting that 'time has inertia', claims that:

> 'E = mcc [Einstein] must be replaced by E = m(0) exp(-At) [Abian]'

is excoriated by physicists for writing unquantified, unverifiable nonsense, but they are unable to say what time is.

Voices separated by twenty-seven centuries agree on the futility of trying to apply scientific logic to fundamental questions. The Buddha urged his students not to waste time speculating about first causes. In the twentieth century Wittgenstein, influenced by Schopenhauer who had studied eastern philosophy, composed his Tractatus Logico-Philosophicus to map the logical geography of what can truly be said. Only by a process of inexorable and ascetic logic can we climb up to a point from where we can see what the really important things are - things like aesthetics, ethics and mysticism, which cannot be said, only shown. At this point, we have no option but to throw away the ladder of logic, but in doing so we are no longer able to speak of our experiences. Wittgenstein numbered his propositions to mark the degree to which each grew out of its predecessor. Many of them are wonderfully epigrammatical: 'When the answer cannot be put into words, neither can the question'. Some have even been set to music! Wittgenstein's final proposition was the famous 7.0:

> '7.00 : What we cannot speak about, we must pass over in silence.'

A sandstone head of the Buddha from the post-Gupta period.

Those who recognised the justice of this in their own experience turned to the higher knowledge, or 'jnana' that was beyond both the clumsy mythological and the hopeless scientific attempts to find answers to questions which, in Wittgenstein's terms, could not even be meaningfully asked. 'Jnana' is 'gnosis': two ways of pronouncing the same idea. Gnosis is experience that transforms, and which by definition cannot be explained. It is the great secret of the Eleusinian Mysteries, which could be shouted from the rooftops without a soul recognising it.

Poets and mystics have always known the wisdom of silence, but priests have generally felt obliged by their office to explain the inexplicable; and thereby inevitably utter the unspeakable. The dogmas of the early Church are an excellent example. In its literal insistence that the sacred host was the actual body of Christ and the cup of wine actually his blood, the Church missed the profundity of Christ's sacrifice. Instead of understanding him gnostically, it metaphorically hung him on the cross wearing horns and dressed in animal skins. But religion likes to have all the answers. And if the answers were, as they often were, unacceptable by virtue of absurdity, illegality, immorality or obscenity, they became classified and were called Mysteries. This is why, with any religion, its Mystery tradition is the only place worth looking if we are seeking real religious experience: experience that can be called gnostic. A story which combines absurdity, illegality, immorality and obscenity, is the old Arya myth we encountered in the forests that clothed the three-horned mountain. Prajapati the Creator couples with his daughter Usa, the dawn. His daughter was his own mind-born child, she was One with him before they were Two. The One divided itself into Two. The Two coupled and brought forth Three, Four, Many. In the story of Prajapati and Usa we have a gnostic theorem, with an unacceptable, unnatural and illegal sexual act as its primary equation. How creation then unfolded from One to Many - and we are talking about events that take place within the human psyche - may be seen from the way counting itself began:

1 = urapon
2 = ukasar
3 = ukasar-urapon
4 = ukasar-ukasar
5 = ukasar-ukasar-urapon
6 = ukasar-ukasar-ukasar
7 = ukasar-ukasar-ukasar-urapon

This is the counting of the Australian aboriginal group, the Gumulgal. Compare it with the counting that framed the greatest of all Tantric meditation symbols: the Sri Yantra or Sri Cakra.

Yantras are meditational diagrams which represent in abstract schematic form the universe or particular aspects of it. They are mind-maps which guide the adept as he explores the unknown topography of his subconscious. By meditating on a given yantra, the adept experiences an awakening and unfolding of the knowledge, or gnosis, which is symbolically present in the coloured lines and and triangles and dots of the yantra. This seems bizarre until we remember that the cartographical map which guided us from the Tungabhadra river to Yellama's shrine at Soundatti and thence to the yoni-pitha of Kanyakumari is also nothing more than coloured lines, squiggles and dots on a piece of paper.

There are an infinite number of possible yantras. The Tantraraja-tantra speaks of 960 of them which were used in Tantric meditations. They may be painted on paper, or card, or wood; or carved in stone; or engraved on metal. Often, a devout worshipper will invest in having his or her favourite yantra engraved onto a small gold plate, which can be hung from

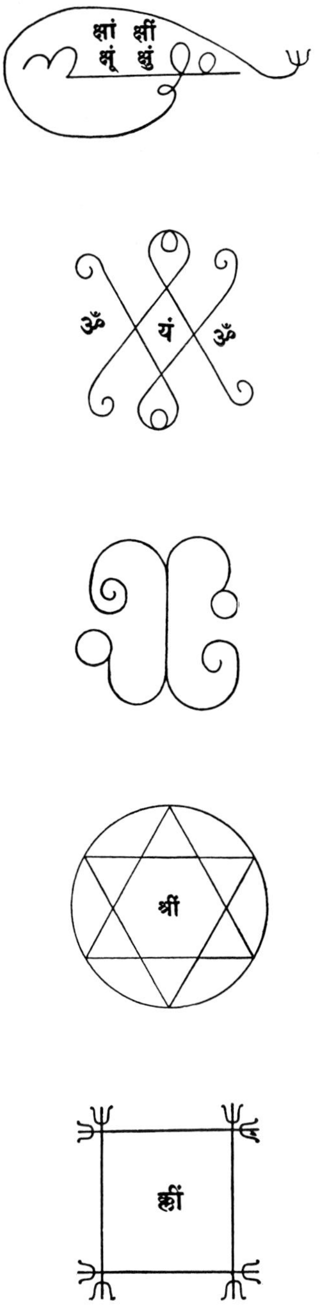

Some yantras of Saundaryalahari verses.

a chain or a thread and worn round the neck. There are yantras also for almost every purpose. Tantric 'bij-mantras' or 'seed-spells' may be engraved within a yantra on an amulet or talisman. Particular verses from scripture, for example from the Rg Veda, may be inscribed on a yantra. Spells from the Atharva Veda are commonly used in this way. Devotional poems too, were thought to possess spiritual powers, which resided in the verses and the letters and sounds of the verses, which could be rendered in symbolic form as yantras. For example the hundred verses of the lyrical Saundaryalahari each have their own yantra. The devotee would meditate on the yantra while repeating its related verse a set number of times. We have encountered a number of these verses already - here are the relevant yantras:

The most complex and important of all yantras is unquestionably the Sri Yantra or Sri Cakra. How old this yantra is, we do not know, but Saundaryalahari, written in the eighth century, contains a somewhat Euclidean description, which we may take the liberty of reading in a way that preserves its lyrical feeling:

caturbhiḥ srīkaṇṭhaiḥ śivayuvatibhiḥ paṇjcbhirapi
prabhinnābhiḥ śaṁbhōr navabhirapi mūlaprakrtibhiḥ |
catuscatvārinśadvasudalakalāsratrivalaya-
trirékhabiḥ sārdha tava śaraṇakōnāḥ pariṇatāḥ ||
(Saundaryalahari 11)

Forty-four times blessed your home,
O beloved of Siva:
shining angles thrice-girdled in beauty,
revealing nine roots
of all being, unfolding the eight
and sixteen petals
of the lotus wherein you dwell.

The yantra is a metaphor for the descent of spirit into matter: the manifestation of the universe out of the primordial darkness of the uncreate. Although in speaking of it, we should be careful about using words like 'emptiness', 'nothingness', 'chaos' and 'darkness', because as we saw in the great Rg Vedic hymn, the condition of things at this point is unknowable.

At the very centre of this yantra is the bindu - the dimensionless point. Around it are interlaced nine triangles. Five of these, representing Sakti, point downwards; and four, representing Siva, point upward. The triangles themselves are called 'yoni' and thus the yantra also has the name 'navayoni cakra'.

yadā sā paramā śaktiḥ: svécchyā visvarūpiṇīṁ |
sphurattāmātmanaḥ pasyét tadā cakrasya sambhavaḥ ||
(Yogini-hrdaya I.9-10)

When the Supreme Sakti, of her own will assumes every form in the universe,
in that one quivering instant the Cakra comes into being.

Out of absolute nothingness shining creation manifests: first a spasm of desire, 'kamakala', creates a throb, 'spanda', which vibrates as sound, 'nada'. This primal sound is depicted in the Sri Yantra as the central 'bindu', the dimensionless point. In the first moments of its manifestation the point is called 'parabindu' and it contains everything that will, or can, or may be, or have the possibility of being or becoming. 'Parabindu' is a point of intensely concentrated energy that contains within itself the potentiality for Siva and Sakti, but at this point they are still undifferentiated One.

In the next phase of creation, the 'parabindu' unfolds into 'Aparabindu' and two more points spring into existence to form the 'mula-trikona' or downward-pointing 'root triangle'. Each point of the triangle vibrates with its own sound and the combination of the three sounds is the primal sound of the universe. The triangle symbolises the female principle, the Sakti, while the fiercely compacted energies of the vibrating point, the 'parabindu', represent the male principle. From the interaction between point and triangle, many more points and lines now spring into existence as the interplay of static and active energies brings the world in all of its complexity into existence.

A fine, turquoise-studded gilt bronze of the Buddha Maitreya. *Tibetan, eighteenth century.*

> Proposition 6.4312: ...The solution of the riddle of life in space and time lies outside space and time. (Wittgenstein, Tractatus Logico-Philosophicus)

The 'parabindu' is the point at which the Supreme Creator touches space-time. It is a circle without radius, a triangle without area in which all three points occupy the same space. When 'parabindu' shivers into 'aparabindu' and 'aparabindu' throbs and separates, we now have three bindus, the 'misrabindu', in which Siva and Sakti are united, the static 'sivabindu' and the energy-filled 'saktibindu'. These are the three points of the 'mula trikona', the root triangle.

The 'root triangle', the primordial glyph of the Sakti, maps her three major aspects and functions. As triple goddess, her work is bringing into being, 'srsti'; maintaining, 'sthiti; and destroying 'samhara'. Her destructive aspect, although it has been singled out and its fierce energies channelled into sorcery, is in essence a benign activity, the function of death and winter, disassembling moribund structures in order to create new growth.

The yantra is not merely a glyph intended to illustrate a lecture on cosmology. It is a 'machine', a device for meditation, a psychic tool. Within its depths the interlocking triangles shine, inviting the adept to climb their lattice-work and ascend from the realms of matter into that of spirit. But the yantra is grounded in the real world. It is here and now. The earthly world is its square periphery, pierced by four gates. The ground of this is yellow and is known as 'bhupura' the 'wide-earth'. Within, three concentric circles or girdles, called 'trivalya', enclose the centre of the yantra. The region between these circles and the edges of the square is the 'trailokyamohana cakra', the realm of Circe, 'enchantress of the triple-world'. In meditating on Sri Yantra, the aspirant will encounter temptations, desires and ambitions. Perhaps thoughts of power, aggrandisement, wealth: all will come and tempt him from his meditation. They are wraiths from the world of illusion, meaningless and worthless phantasms, but they will seem real, full of life and excitement. He must get past them.

Once past the zone of enchantment, the adept enters further into the yantra and encounters two rings of lotus petals. The outer, with fourteen blue petals, is called 'Sarvasaparipura cakra', or 'the fulfiller of all desires' and the inner, with eight red petals, is 'Sarvasankshobhana cakra', 'agitator of all things'.

Beyond these lotus petals we enter into the centre of the yantra where the interlacing of five downward and four upward pointing triangles has produced a latticework of forty-three triangles which can be grouped in four rings.

The outermost ring of fourteen blue triangles is named 'sarva saubhagyada cakra' or 'the bringer of all good fortune'. Within this is a ring of ten red triangles called 'sarvartha sadhaka cakra' or 'the accomplisher of all purposes'. Deeper into the yantra is another ten-triangle ring, these blue, which is known as 'sarva raksakara cakra', 'the protector against all evils'.

The Sri Yantra.

We are now in the very heart of Sri Yantra. The innermost ring of eight red triangles is 'sarva rogahara cakra', 'the remover of all diseases'. Within this nestles a single inverted triangle, a harmonic of the primal 'mula trikona'. This triangle is called 'sarva siddhipradada cakra', 'the bestower of all accomplishments'. Finally, at the very centre of the yantra is the 'bindu' which is given the name of 'sarvanandamaya cakra', 'the all-blissful'.

Given this mind-map, how can we interpret it? The postulant begins his journey in the real, phenomenal, world. At the outset of his journey, he is swayed by the ego, dazzled by the illusions it holds up before him. This is the realm of Circe. He cannot help but hear the siren voices, but like Odysseus, he must tie himself to the mast of his yoga and ignore distractions. The story is told of the young zen student who went to see his master in a state of high excitement. 'Roshi! Roshi!' he cried, 'last night I was sitting in zazen and revolving my koan over and over. Mu! Mu! I was forcing myself to confront Mu! and nothing but Mu! Suddenly, a great light appeared and within it stood a shining figure in the shape of the Buddha Maitreya and he smiled at me and spoke some words so profound that their beauty

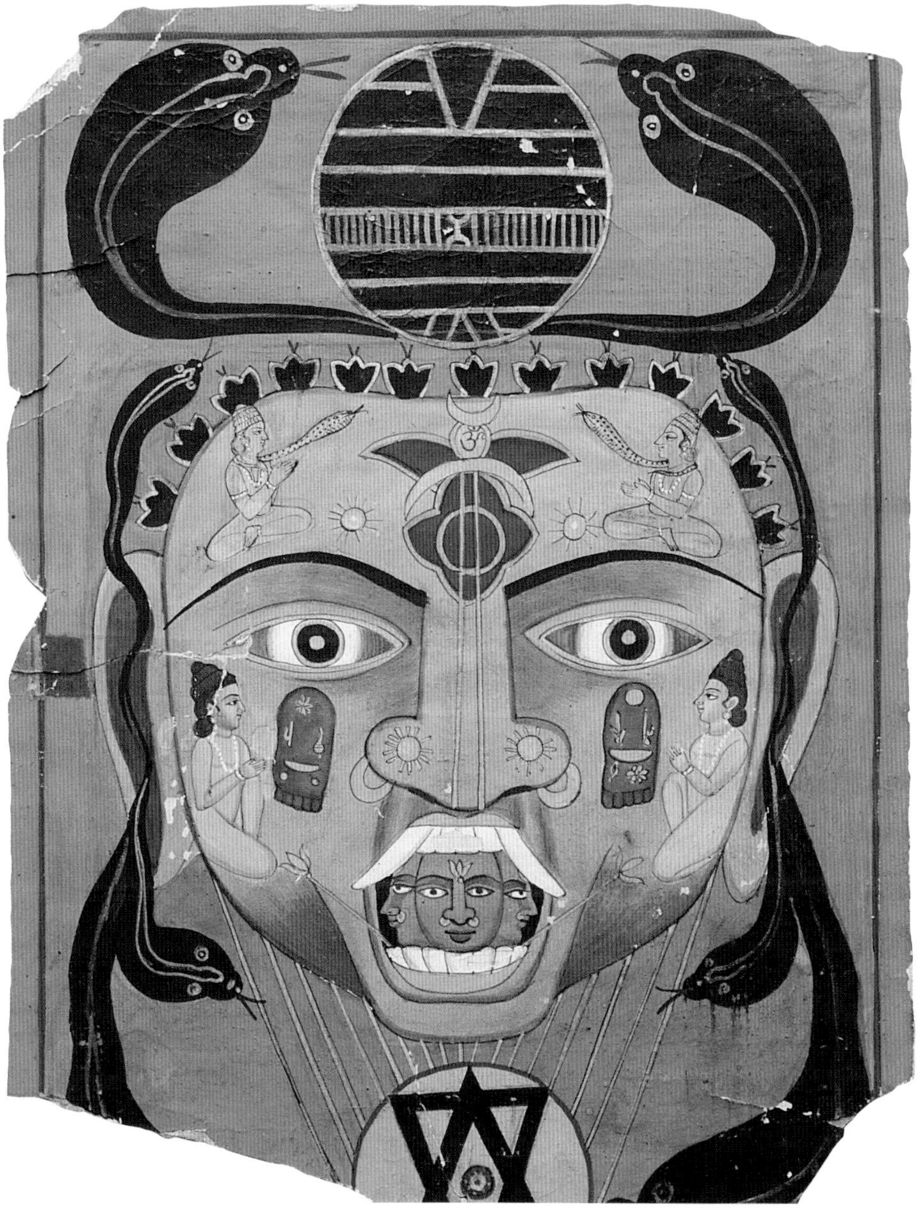

The blue head: perhaps the most striking of all the 'ritual' series of Tantric paintings. The writhing snakes of kundalini-energy, familiar to us from others in the series (see also pages 15, 19, 44, 49, 61, 67 and 85) here are reminiscent of an Egyptian uraeus. At first glance curiously modern and un-Indian, it is nonetheless a portrait of the god, Siva, whose third eye carries the sacred syllable 'Om'. *Eighteenth century.*

caụsed me to weep!' The master replied, 'Don't worry. If it happens again, just ignore it and it will go away'. How fortunate a ṣtudent, the story concludes, to have so compassionate a master.

Unusual Himalayan bronze of a standing Siva with serpent and staff.

> vandé vāṇjcchitalābhāya karma kiṁ tanna kathyaté I
> kiṁ dampatimiti brūyāmutāhō dampatī iti II
> (Nilakantha Dikshita)
>
> For my prayer to be granted, I bow down - to whom?
> Is 'the couple' singular or plural?

In the Sri Yantra, which is the universe, Siva and Sakti cannot be separated. Although we may speak of a triangle being Sakti, or a point being Siva, and of static and active energies, in fact these energies are aspects of one another. The icon of Kali dancing on the corpse of Siva is not the dance of Kali alone, Siva is dancing within her limbs, and when Siva flings his hat in the air and dances the 'tandava' that destroys the world, Kali is dancing within his limbs. Siva is eternally in Sakti and Sakti in Siva. To the Tantric worshipper, this is no more philosophical abstraction. It is their living experience. For devotees of the 'samaya' tradition, their highest spiritual aim is by meditation to experience the blissful unity of Siva and Sakti in the thousand petalled lotus of the 'Sahasrara Cakra' in the crown of the head. Bearing this in mind - that Siva and Sakti are ultimately inseparable - we may approach a central mystery of the Sri Yantra.

> tvamagsṛngāmaṁsamédō-stidhātavaḥ śaktimūlakāḥ I
> majjāśuklaprāṇajīvadhātavaḥ śivamūlakāḥ II
> (Sri Kapali Sastriar, Ahnika stava)
>
> Skin, blood, flesh, fat, bone:
> these are the gifts of Sakti.
> Marrow, semen, life and self:
> these are the gifts of Siva.

The Sri Cakra is microcosm as well as macrocosm. Of the nine elements that form the human body, five are produced by the five Sakti triangles and four by the four Siva triangles. They are produced by the intimate interaction of the Siva-Sakti energies, for the whole Cakra represents the divine pair in union, indeed, in that same passionate, blissful union on the mountain-top in the dawn of the world. To see how the worshipper can emulate and use the body created for him by Siva-Sakti, we have to turn from the Tantric system of 'yantra' to the Tantric system of 'cakra'. The two, at first glance, appear to have little in common. In order to understand how they relate to one another, it will be easiest to turn to a parallel tradition outside India, which posseses a glyph in which the 'yantra' and 'cakra' of the Tantras are unified.

A parallel of the 'yantra' worship of Indian Tantrics is found in the qabalistic meditations of the Jewish Hasidim. As in Tantra, the qabalist conceives the universe as a series of emanations of the divine, starting from primal unknowable One (beyond the 'bindu' through which divinity enters space-time.) Three veils of divine light before even the first instant of creation: the 'ain', 'ain sof', and 'ain sof aur'; corresponding to the three light-infused grounds-of-pure-being in Buddhist Tantrism, which are called 'dharmakaya', 'sambhogakaya' and 'nirmankaya'.

In the qabalistic conception, divinity manifests in ten stages or emanations, called

The union of Siva and Sakti: Sakti, here depicted as Kali, the wrathful form of the lovely goddess Parvati, rides upon a Siva whose hair is whitened with ash from the funeral pyre. This work perfectly represents the paradox of Siva, who is simultaneously master-ascetic and first teacher of the sexual arts.

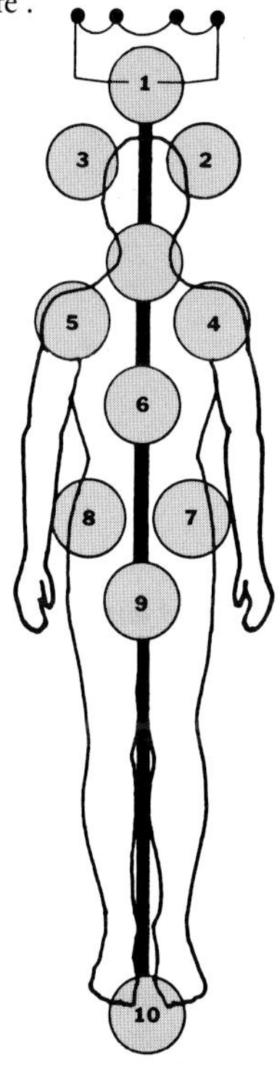

The qabalistic Otz Ch'im or 'Tree of Life'.

'sefiroth'. First from the unmanifest into the light-filled 'Kether' or Crown. 'Kether' trembles and spills into 'Chokmah' which then overflows into 'Binah'. These three form the first and highest triad of creation: they are depicted as an upward facing triangle with 'Kether' at the apex and 'Chokmah' on the right as we face it. 'Chokmah' represents the All-Father and 'Binah' is the sphere of the Great Mother. From here now, as in the Sri Cakra, further configurations, shining spheres, triangles and pillars evolve and arrange themselves.

Like the Sri Cakra, the qabalistic Otz Ch'im or Tree of Life is a glyph designed for meditation, and represents the entire universe of matter and spirit. 'Malkuth', the tenth and last 'sefira' is the world of matter. Above it hangs 'Yesod', the moon 'sefira', the world of psychic phenomena. Above and to the left is 'Hod' which pertains to the active intellect, the mind of the magician. Opposite is 'Netzach', 'victory', a centre of the emotions. In the middle of the mandala hangs the luminous sphere of 'Tifareth', 'beauty'. This is the heart centre of the glpyh, a sphere of love. In the modern western mystery tradition, 'Tifareth' is the sphere of the love-sacrifice, and of Jesus.

It will be seen that correspondences emerge between the 'sefiroth' and different parts of the body. Thus 'Malkuth' is the feet, 'Yesod' the genital centre, 'Tifareth' the heart, 'Daath' the throat and 'Kether' hovering over the crown of the head. These are the 'sefiroth' of the central pillar of the Tree. The study of qabalah is as vast and intricate a subject as Tantra and we can go no further than to point out that the central pillar of 'sefiroth' is cognate with the other great Tantric system, that of the 'cakras'. These are not the same 'cakras' as the triangle- and lotus-petal 'cakras' of the Sri Yantra. They are the seven 'cakras' of the human body, the Jacob's Ladder up which we must climb on our gnostic journey.

Chapter 10

KUNDALINI

tasyōrdhvé visatantu sōdhara lasat sūksmā jaganmōhinī brahmadvāramukhaṁ
mukhéna madhuraṁ sācchādayantīsvayaṁ śankhāvarta nibhā navīna capalāmālā
vilāsāspadā suptā sarpasamā śivōpari lasāt sārdha trivrttākrtiḥ

kūjantī kulakuṇdalīnī ca madhuraṁ mattalimālā sphuṭaṁ vācāḥ komala kāvya
bandha racanā bédhāti bhéda kramaiḥ śvāsōcchvāsa vibhaṇjanéna jagatāṁ jīvō
yayā dhāryaté sā mūlāṁbuja gahvare vilasati prōddāma dīptāvaliḥ
(Satcakra-nirupana, 11-12)

Like a cobra which has cast its coils
spiralling conch-like three-times-
and-a-half round Siva, her mouth
laid on that other mouth
which leads to bliss,
the enchantress
of the world,
slender as a lotus stem,
bright as a lightning-flash,
lies sleeping,
breathing softly out and in,
murmuring poems
in sweetest metres,
humming like a drunken bee
in the petals of
the muladhara lotus,
how brightly her light shines.

With poetry like this, no wonder the Satcakra-nirupana, which started life as a mere chapter in the larger Sritattvacintamani, gained a life of its own. This lovely metaphor, simultaneously of a woman resting on her lover between bouts of passionate lovemaking, and a serpent-force of beauty and awesome power, is the poet's way of describing kundalini, the dazzling life- energy that lies coiled within each of us, waiting to be awoken. Kundalini is the energy of Sakti herself, the primal energy that created the cosmos. It is the sexual energy that arouses and uplifts us, generates love and the desire for children. It is the driving force of evolution, the mating instinct, the libido of Freud and Jung's vision of the 'other face of God'. For the Tantric yogi, the objective of all ritual work, whether it be via the medium of yantra, mantra, or sacramental sex, is to awaken the kundalini energy where it lies coiled at the base of the spine in the muladhara cakra, lowest of the seven cakras or psychic nodes; and to draw it up into the sahasrara cakra at the crown of the skull. Such an undertaking is neither easy - it can take a lifetime - or particularly safe. Kundalini is dangerous. In the daily

Siva with horned serpents: a very fine painting from the 'ritual' series, whose artist yet again succeeds in surprising us. Here, a gilt 'shako' contains a meditating yogi with an erect phallus, the classic symbol of Tantric yogic control, but one possibly last seen in Indian art in the famous Mohenjodaro 'Pasupati seal'. The goddess, in her benevolent form, glows in Siva's heart cakra. Snakes of kundalini energy coil between them. *Eighteenth century.*

newspaper harvest of sexual assaults and murders, we see the evidence of the destructive power of kundalini. Before beginning a programme of Tantric meditation the mind and body must be thoroughly purified. It is not wise to undertake any Tantric practice, except under the guidance of an experienced and respectable teacher.

Satcakra-nirupana, the eighty-five verse Tantra from which our description comes, means simply 'a description of the six cakras'. The cakras are psychic centres that do not physically exist in the body, although some Tantric masters who have studied allopathic medicine have found links between the cakras and the functions of various glands and nerve complexes. However, the Tantras themselves say that the cakras have their existence in the subtler bodies that surround, permeate and penetrate the gross material body.

The Tantras recognise five bodies. Annamaya, 'made of food': the body in which our waking consciousness dwells, with which we work, play and make love. Pranamaya is the body of our vital life energy. Kirlian photography has recorded that all living things radiate a field around themselves that can be recorded on a photographic plate. This energy, given off by living things, surrounds us like a halo and is our second body.

The third body is manomaya, the mental body, a body constructed of thought-stuff. The concept will be familiar to occultists as the 'astral' or 'etheric' body. There can be little doubt that out-of-the-body experiences have been had by thousands of people, usually after an accident or at a moment of near death. Typically, the person finds her or himself standing or floating outside the flesh and blood body, able to observe the most disturbing scenes with quiet dispassion. These out-of-body experiences, we may speculate, are made possible by the mental body.

Still more rarified is the vijnanamaya, the spiritual body, which is composed of prayer and fortified by meditation. In such a body the great masters of Hindu and Buddhist tradition are said to be able to live for centuries. Or they can assume it at will, leaving the bliss of union with the divine to return to earth to help others. Even more ineffable is the body called anandamaya, the body of the joy of union with god which, for the Tantric adept, means with the primordial Adi-Sakti. These five bodies, it will be seen, correspond to the five fires- of-sacrifice of the Brhadaranyaka Upanisad and thus to the five sacraments of Tantric worship.

According to the Bhutasuddhi-tantra, the body contains some 72,000 'nadis'. A nadi is a subtle channel through which the vital life energy, or prana-sakti, flows from cell to cell. Nadis are often misleadingly described as 'arteries' or 'veins', but they do not correspond to the blood vessels of allopathic medicine. If the work of the nadis is carried out at the cellular level, then it is difficult to see how a mere 72,000 would suffice. Indeed, the Prapancasara-tantra increased this number to 300,000 and the Siva-samhita speaks of 350,000, but even this would not be enough. We are talking about subtle currents that pass osmotically from cell to cell at level detectable only by powerful microscopes. Perhaps, when we consider that the function of the main nadis is to carry kundalini energy to stimulate the brain cakras, we would need a vastly more powerful microscope than most major hospitals possess. Within the brain, after all, information is passed from neuron to neuron along synapses that function at molecular level.

> 'Triggered by the dance of the retinene molecules, the nerve cells, or neurons, respond. First in the eye and then in the brain. One neuron has just gone into action. Protein molecules on its surface suddenly change their shape, blocking the flow of positively charged sodium atoms from the surrounding body fluid. This change in flow of electrically charged atoms produces a change in voltage that shudders through the cell. After a distance of a fraction of an inch, the electrical signal reaches the end of the neuron, altering the release of specific molecules, which migrate a distance of a

Cosmic goddess: the yantras or meditational diagrams symbolise the emanation of the universe from the body of the primaeval goddess. Snakes of kundalini energy coil around this fine example from the 'ritual' series of Tantric paintings. The painting was used in ritual worship as can be seen by the red colouring, symbolic of blood, that has been spattered across it. (See also pages 15, 19, 44, 49, 61, 67, 85 and 97.) *Eighteenth century.*

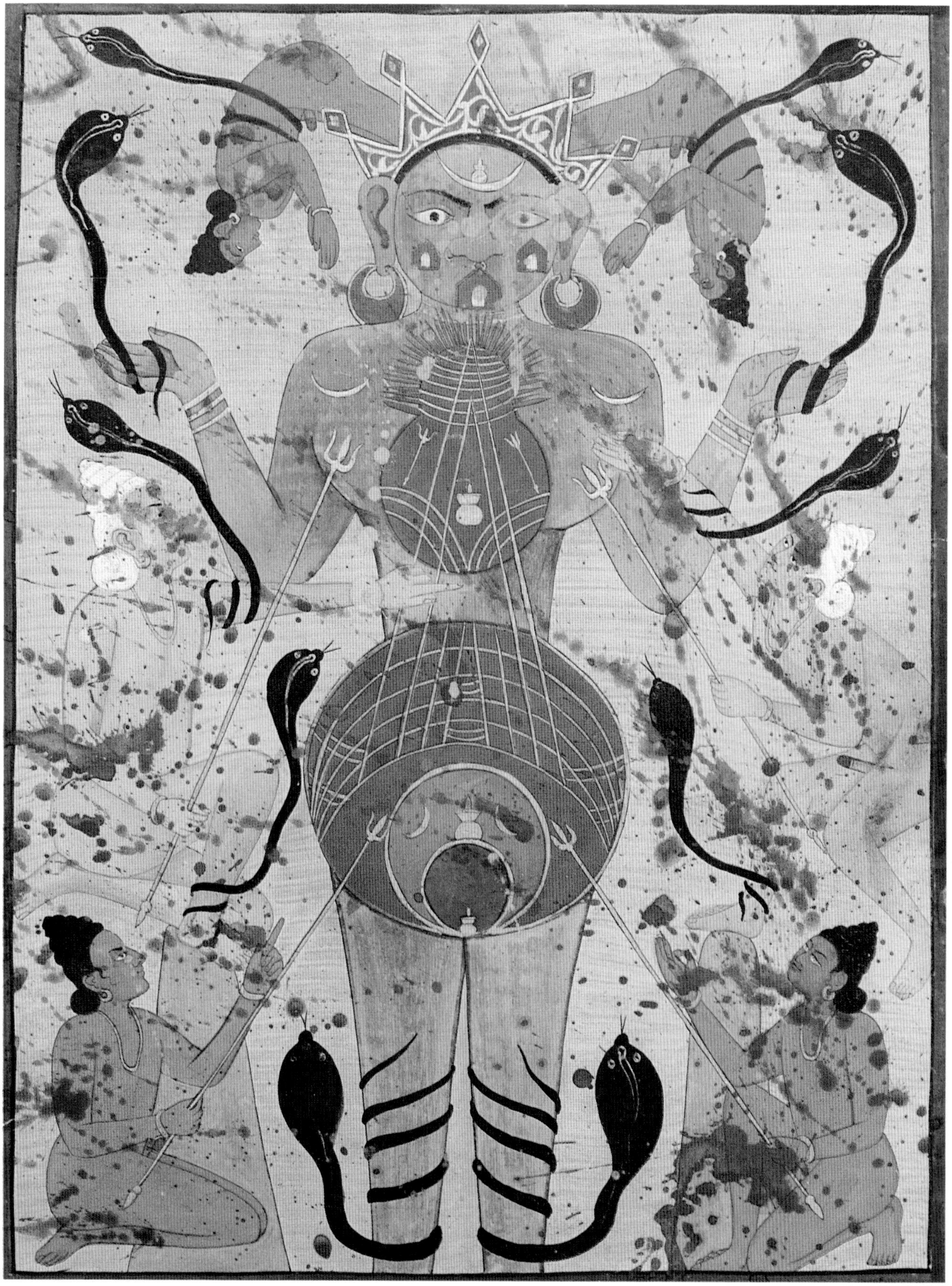

A demon ties a man and a woman to a stake in another of the 'deadly sin' paintings. *Eighteenth century.*

> hundred-thousandth of an inch, until they reach the next neuron, passing on the news. The impulses race to the primary visual cortex, a highly folded layer of tissue about a 10th of an inch thick and two square inches in area, containing 100 million neurons in half-a-dozen layers. The fourth layer receives the input first, does a preliminary analysis, and transfers the information to neurons in other layers. At every stage, each neuron may receive signals from a thousand other neurons, combine the signals - some of which cancel each other out - and dispatch the computed result to a thousand-odd other neurons.'
> (Alan Lightman, Smile)

This complex description of the brain in action comes from a story whose entire plot consists of the fact that a man sees a woman and smiles at her. If the information channels of the brain are to be involved in the work of the nadis then the estimate in the Satcakra-nirupana, that the body contains some thirty five million nadis, may be conservative.

Thirty five million nadis there may be, but the Tantras recognise only seventy-two major ones. Of these, the three most important are susumna, ida and pingala.

The susumna nadi is route by which the kundalini, or sakti-energy, in the body travels upward from cakra to cakra. The susumna nadi rises in the muladhara, the lowest of the cakras, and ascends to the highest cakra, sahasrara. The raising of kundalini is the mission of the Tantric yogi. Therefore the susumna nadi, the path which the energy will follow, is also known as brahamanadi, 'the brahma-channel', and moksamarga, 'the road to release', for when the energy of kundalini enters the sahasrara cakra, the yogi is united in bliss with the divine couple Siva and Sakti, and there is no more rebirth. As children in India, we were told of yogis who, after piously meditating for years, were found dead because kundalini had reached the top of the head and burst out into the sahasrara, killing the meditator. Such a death was enviable. It was, to borrow the fine Shakespearean phrase, a consummation devoutly to be wished. The susumna nadi, which delivers this awesome force, is believed to contain the entire universe. Its place in the physical body is in the interior of the cerebro-spinal axis, the merudanda, or spinal column.

The ida nadi has its origin in the right testicle or ovary and runs up the left side of the spinal column and eventually exits in the left nostril. Ida is feminine, pale, ruled by the moon and represents the divine nectar, amrta vigraha, over which the gods and asuras fought in the unimaginably distant past. The pingala nadi arises in the left ovary or testicle and runs up the right side of the spinal column, eventually exiting in the right nostril. It is masculine, red, ruled by the sun and partakes of the nature of Rudra. These three nadis, susumna, ida and pingala are also given the names of the three most sacred rivers of India, the Ganga, Yamuna and the mythological Saraswati. These three flow together in the muladhara cakra, then separate to come together again in the ajna cakra. Then they part company again, the susumna heading upwards for the crown cakra and ida and pingala dropping downwards into the top of the nose. The psychic physiology of these nadis, it will be seen, is structured precisely on the spinal column. Along this column, from the base to the top of the head, are located the six cakras of importance to the Tantric yogi.

At the base of the spinal column, in the centre of the body, is the muladhara or 'root' cakra. Its exact location is the perineum, although we must remember that it is a psychic and not a physical centre. The yantra, meditational symbol, of the muladhara is of a lotus with four crimson petals on which are four golden Sanskrit letters which are the seed-mantras of the cakra. In the centre of the lotus is an inverted, or female, triangle which represents the yoni and in it is the self-born lingam of Siva, around which lies coiled the sleeping kundalini, just as described in the poem. She has her body coiled three and a half turns around the linga of Siva and her head hides the door of Brahmadhvaja, which is the opening into the

Golden Sakti from the 'ritual' series of Tantric paintings. (For others, see pages 15, 19, 44, 49, 61, 67, 85, 97, 101 and 103.) The goddess's gold-outlined body connects different aspects of the primaeval sakti-energy of creation, symbolising the descent of spirit into matter. At the highest level, Siva and Sakti are united in the crown cakra. At a lower level, he thrusts his arm into her womb to assist in the birth of the world. At the lowest level he catches the blood flowing from her breasts, a metaphor for sacrifice, out of which matter begins its return journey into spirit. *Eighteenth century.*

susumna nadi. Serpent, linga and yoni-triangle are in turn carried on the back of the divine elephant Airavata. The muladhara is also the centre of the prthvi, or earth, element in the body. This is symbolised by a yellow square and the seed-syllable 'la'.

Halfway between muladhara and the navel, still in the line of the spinal column, is the svadisthana cakra, so-called because it is the genital centre and the site of the param lingam, or supreme lingam. The yantra is a vermilion lotus of six petals adorned with 'letters like lightning'. The element of the cakra is water, which is symbolised by a white ground and a crescent moon. The seed-syllable is 'vam'.

Within the navel itself is the manipura cakra, sometimes called nabhi, 'navel', cakra. It is a ten-petalled lotus, lustrous as a gem, and the region of the fire element, which is symbolised by a red triangle carrying three svastikas. The seed-syllable is 'ram' and the ram, by a completely meaningless coincidence, is its sacred animal. In this centre the image of Rudra the wild hunter, smeared with ashes, is to be found, along with the goddess Lakini, who is said to be 'fond of animal flesh and whose breasts are red with the blood and fat which drip from her mouth'. Lakini is a very ancient form of the goddess, corresponding to the same period in the archaeology of religion as the old Sabara and Nisada hunter god. It would be a mistake to see her as primitive, however. She dwells within us. Like all the god forms of the lower cakras, she is a living, contemporary aspect of ourselves.

In the region of the heart we find the anahata cakra, which is red as a bandhuka flower and is named for the 'unstruck' sound, which is the first note of all music, without which no raga would have any meaning; the sound of 'one hand clapping'. Anahata is 'the great cakra in the heart of all beings.' A twelve petalled lotus of vermilion is the yantra. In the middle of the lotus is the symbol of the element vayu, or air. Two smoky brown triangles interlaced in the classic star of David. The sacred animal is the black antelope and the seed-syllable is 'yam'. The visuddha, or bharati, cakra is situated in the throat. The cakra is consecrated to 'isa-deva', whom we may recall from the three-horned mountain. The goddess is Kakini, garlanded with human bones, whose 'heart is softened by the drinking of nectar'.

The visuddha cakra is situated on the spinal axis at the base of the throat. Its lotus has sixteen petals of smoky purple on which are inscribed in golden letters the sixteen nasal vowels. The symbol in the heart of the lotus is the white cirle of the element ether and the seed-syllable is 'ham'. The presiding deity of the cakra is Siva in his androgyne form as Ardhanaresvara, the half- man-half-woman and the corresponding goddess-form is Sakini, the white Sakti whose form is light. The sacred animal is an elephant.

The ajna cakra occupies the space between the eyebrows and is a lotus of two white petals on which are the golden letters 'ham' and 'ksham'. It is a centre of the subtle elements of mind and prakrti, or nature. In the centre of the ajna lotus is the sacred syllable 'Om'. The deities are Siva in the form of Hamsa, and the goddess Siddha-kali, 'elated by draughts of ambrosia'. This cakra, along with muladhara and anahata, is the site of a sacred linga. As the mental centre, it is brightly illuminated by the soul's own light and shines on the whole kundalini path from the muladhara upwards. It is a centre of far-seeing, which is particularly interesting in light of the fact that the ajna occupies the place traditionally ascribed to the pineal gland, or third-eye.

A great deal of interesting work on the possible physiological basis of the cakra system has been done by Swami Satyananda Saraswati, who finds that the ultimate seat of kundalini is in the cerebral cortex. He conceives of the cakras as being switching centres for neurochemical activity, each monitoring, modifying and regulating the activities of the others. His ideas have been developed by Serena Roney-Dougal, in whose intelligent and thought-provoking book Where Magic and Science Meet we find the cakras identified with physical organs as follows: the ajna with the pineal gland, the visuddha with the thyroid gland, the anahata with the mammary glands; the manipura with the solar plexus; the svadhisthana with the ovaries and prostate; and the muladhara with the uterus and testes.

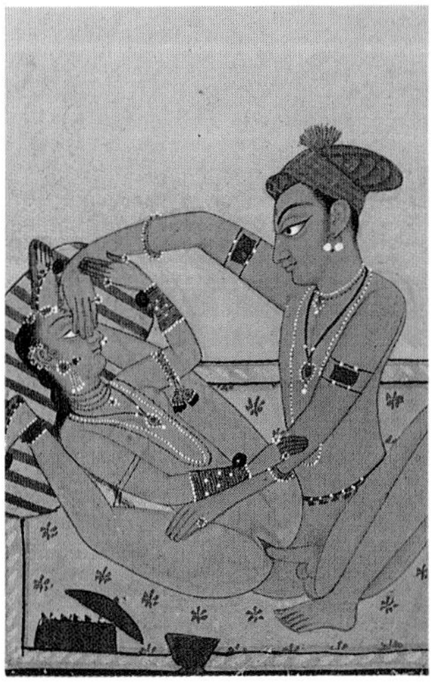

The psychic events associated with the raising of kundalini through the cakras are, in the Roney-Dougal system, facilitated by complex neurochemical transactions. The lynch-pin of her thesis is that the pineal gland, the so-called 'third eye' in the ajna cakra produces powerful natural hallucinogens called beta-carbolines, similar to the natural alkaloid hallucinogens that are found in the Amazonian shaman-vine, the Ayahuasca. The suggestion is that it is these hallucinogens which produce the blissful experience of kundalini pouring like sweet silver into the brain and dissolving it in delight.

What happens in the sahasrara cakra? It is shown as a brilliant white lotus of a thousand

Sacrifice: the goddess with the heads of animals offered to her to restore her creative energies. For the same reason, her hands hold severed lingams. The painting, one of the 'ritual' series, is to be read metaphorically, the severed lingam standing for immaculate yogic control of the senses. Siva, lord of ascetics and teacher of sexual science, is enshrined in her heart. *Eighteenth century.*

petals inverted above the crown of the head, so that the flower is worn like a hat. This is the abode of the Supreme Deity, Siva-Sakti conjoined, and it is the home of the realised kundalini. Whoever fully realises and knows this cakra is liberated from the bonds of samsara and the pain of rebirth. He gains all siddhis, or powers, and becomes a liberated soul, or jivanmukta, while still alive. Moksa, the final freedom, becomes his on death. At the apex of the sahasrara cakra is the dimensionless point called bindu, through which divinity manifests in the first moments of creation. Both the parabindu of the active Sakti principle and the primal bindu are present: allowing us finally to make the connection between the cakra system and the system of the Sri Yantra. We have to project the yantra

A man and woman caught in the bonds of sensual pleasures are led away by a sage. Snakes, symbolic both of torment and of wisdom, attack them and hang from their bodies.

from two into three dimensions. If we return to the Sri Yantra and imagine that the bindu in its centre is the peak of a mountain; that the mountain is built up in tiers, each tier being one of the circles of triangles or lotus petals, with the outermost square representing ground level; and if we now imagine a vertical spine down the centre of the mountain, then at each point that the spine and a tier intersect, there is a cakra. The peak represents Mount Meru, abode of the gods. It's a long way from Nysa.

The mastery of kundalini yoga can take a lifetime and is not to be practised without a guru. It is dangerous to read things in books and try them without proper preparation. In normal practice, a candidate for Tantric sadhana, or spiritual discipline, has to be accepted by a guru. The formal initiation, called diksa, is a ceremonial meeting between guru and pupil, in which the guru gives the aspiring sadhaka a personal mantra. A fuller description of the sadhaka's training will be given in the next chapter. For this yoga, the body and mind must be purified, involving a daily regime of yoga to keep the body fit, meditation to calm and balance the mind, and diet. The Ayurvedic system of dosas, or humours, can be used to determine which foods should be taken and which avoided. The kundalini yoga itself should be practised in a regular, disciplined way. Before starting the daily meditation, the devotee must quiet the mind and purify her or himself and the room in which she or he is sitting with incense and prayers to Siva and Sakti. Processes such as nadisodana, the cleansing of the nadis using breathing techniques, may be performed. The basic yoga posture used is padmasana, the lotus posture, but others may be used as appropriate to the specific part of the task being undertaken. Particular bandhas, or knots, involving considerable muscular control, and breathing techniques are also used. If following a particular text, for example the Satcakra Nirupana, the instructions are given for each stage of the process. In any case, the meditation should be done under the guru's guidance.

Let us return to the question, posed and then abandoned, of what happens in the sahasrara cakra when the kundalini pours into it. It may never happen. Or it may take years.

The experience, when it comes, seems to be unexpected and overwhelming. Those who have known it say that it dissolves duality, the sense of self and other, and is a complete and limitless union with god. Whether we attribute it to mystical or endocrinological causes, it remains the blissful end of the gnostic road, the return journey of matter into spirit, the great work which began in the ordinary world of matter and body and every physical form in the universe, the Sri Yantra, the muladhara cakra, the physical world of which Wittgenstein said:

> 'Proposition 1.00: The world is everything that is the case.'

If Wittgenstein's 'Proposition 1' is a perfect mantra for the first cakra, the only possible mantra for the seventh cakra is his 'Proposition 7':

> 'Proposition 7.00: What we cannot speak about, we must pass over in silence.'

Words fail us, but no words can come closer to the experience than those of a person who has heard the blissful roaring of kundalini pouring into her ancient home.

> 'I sat steadily, unmoving and erect, my thoughts uninterruptedly centred on the shining lotus, intent on keeping my attention from wandering and bringing it back again and again whenever it moved in any other direction... My whole being was so engrossed in the contemplation of the lotus that for several minutes at a time I lost touch with my body and surroundings. During such intervals I used to feel as if I were poised in midair, without any feeling of a body around them.
>
> During one such spell of meditation I suddenly felt a strange sensation below the spine, at the place touching the seat, while I sat cross-legged on a folded blanket spread on the floor. The sensation was so extraordinary and so pleasing that my attention was forcibly drawn toward it. The moment my attention was thus unexpectedly withdrawn from the point on which it was focused, the sensation ceased... After a while I grew composed and was soon deep in meditation as before. When completely immersed I again experienced the sensation, but this time, instead of allowing my mind to leave the point where I had fixed it, I maintained a rigidity of attention throughout. The sensation again extended upward, growing in intensity, and I felt myself wavering; but with a great effort I kept my attention centered around the lotus. Suddenly, with a roar like that of a waterfall, I felt a stream of liquid light entering my brain through the spinal chord.
>
> Entirely unprepared for such a development, I was completely taken by surprise; but regaining self-control instantaneously; I remained sitting in the same posture, keeping my mind on the point of concentration. The illumination grew brighter and brighter, the roaring louder, I experienced a rocking sensation and then felt myself slipping out of my body, entirely enveloped in a halo of light. It is impossible to describe the experience accurately. I felt the point of consciousness that was myself growing wider, surrounded by waves of light. It grew wider and wider, spreading outward while the body, normally the immediate object of its perception, appeared to have receded into the distance until I became entirely unconscious of it. I was now all consciousnes without any outline, without any idea of a corporeal appendage, without any feeling or sensation coming from the senses, immersed in a sea of light simultaneously conscious and aware of every point, spread out, as it were, in all directions without any barrier or material obstruction.
>
> I was no longer myself, or to be more accurate, no longer as I knew myself to be, a small point of light and in a state of awareness confined in a body, but instead was a vast circle of consciousness in which the body was but a point, bathed in light and in a state of exaltation and happiness impossible to describe.'
>
> (Gopi Krishna, Kundalini: The Evolutionary Energy in Man)

Chapter 11

'The Thunder, Perfect Mind'

I am the first and the last. I am the honoured one and the scorned one.
I am the whore and the holy one. I am the wife and the virgin.
I am the mother and the daughter. I am the members of my mother.
I am the barren one
and many are her sons.
I am she whose wedding is great,
and I have not taken a husband.
I am the midwife and she who does not bear.
I am the solace of my labour pains.
I am the bride and the bridegroom,
and it is my husband who begot me.
('The Thunder, Perfect Mind', Nag Hammadi papyrus, translator George W. MacRae)

In December 1945, near Naj Hammadi in Upper Egypt, two brothers, Muhammad and Khalifah Ali, were taking camel loads of fertilizers to their fields. They had just hobbled their camels by a huge boulder, when underneath it they saw a tall earthen jar. The lid was sealed and at first Muhammad Ali was afraid that there was a djinn inside. When he finally broke it open, golden flakes of papyrus flew out into the sunlight. In the jar were twelve books, papyrus rolls covered with Coptic writing. Disappointed that he had not found a treasure, Muhammad Ali took the books home to use as firelighters. His wife burned one of them and the rest would have met the same fate had Muhammad not become involved in a blood feud which, six months earlier, had killed his father. Soon after the discovery of the books, a man was pointed out to Muhammad as his father's killer. He and his seven brothers attacked the man, hacked his limbs off, ripped out his heart and ate it as an act of blood revenge. Knowing that the police would come to search his house, and not wanting to be accused of stealing the papyrii, he gave them for safekeeping to a priest who realised their value.

One of the texts rediscovered in this macabre fashion was a poem called 'The Thunder, Perfect Mind'. It has puzzled scholars, for it contained no traces of the Jewish, Christian or Gnostic themes found in the other texts. The poem is a revelation given by a female power, or goddess, great beyond human comprehension, whose being is an unfathomable mystery. Did it refer to Isis, upon the pedestal of whose statue, in her temple at Sais in the Nile Delta, the inscription read:

> 'I am everything that was, and is, and shall be, nor has any mortal ever uncovered my veil.'

A fragment of this poem is found in another Nag Hammadi text which tells a creation story strikingly similar to the unfolding of the cosmos into the Sri Yantra of Sakti and Siva.

A sandstone stele of the goddess Laxmi. *Fourteenth century.*

A unique husband and wife in white marble, inscribed with devanagiri Prakrit characters. On his face is what may be a stylised beard and moustache. Could it be the gauze face mask worn by devout Jains, who had a horror of taking life, as a precaution against breathing in and thus killing tiny creatures? *Thirteenth or fourteenth century.*

In this second text, scholars have detected Sethian, Valentinian and Manichean motifs; Jewish and Christian ideas; Hellenistic magical, philosophical, mythological and astrological themes; and pieces of Egyptian lore. In such a melange, why not Indian ideas too?

> I am the mother of my father
> and the sister of my husband,
> and he is my offspring.
> ('The Thunder, Perfect Mind')

This is the theme of Siva and Sakti. Each begets the other. One becomes Two and Two become One in order to create the universe. Did Indian thought influence the 'The Thunder, Perfect Mind', Or was it the other way round? The first Tantric texts were not composed in India until the Gupta period, at the very earliest, and the early Buddhist Tantras date back to around the time that the Nag Hammadi books were being buried in their jar. Both the Hindu and Buddhist Tantras demonstrate distinct gnostic ideas, for instance that ignorance, avidya, is the root of all evil. Benjamin Walker in his book, Gnosticism, gives many more such examples.

There was certainly vigorous commerce between India and the Roman world during this whole period. Dion Chrysostom met Indian merchants in Alexandria. In about 20 BC the Emperor Augustus met, in Athens, an embassy sent from Madurai by a Pandya king. The diplomats had brought with them an ascetic whom the Greeks called Zarmanochegas, possibly Sanskrit Sramanacarya, who publicly burned himself to death. An ivory statuette of an Indian goddess was found in the ruins of Herculaneum. Elephants, lions, tigers, monkeys, parrots and peacocks were in demand. We read of Indian fortune-tellers, conjurors, mahouts and prostitutes in Rome.

Both mahouts and prostitutes were among those named by Vatsyayana in Kama Sutra as indulging in the low practice of fellatio, and especially soixante-neuf, which he called 'the lovemaking of the crow' and which was the particular speciality of eunuchs.

In the works of Pliny the Elder, Martial and Juvenal, we encounter the odd idea that crows and ravens mate with their beaks. Thus a man or woman who practised fellatio was said to be 'acting the crow'. The fact that the Romans had a reason, albeit fallacious, for naming the practice after the crow, plus the fact that these poets predated Kama Sutra by at least two centuries, suggest that the name came to India from the west. On the other hand, Vatśyayana was working in a tradition already several hundred years old. Might not a predecessor of Kama Sutra have reached Rome? Unlikely, for Ovid, who included some lovemaking postures in his Ars Amatoria, shows no sign of any Indian influence. However a flow of ideas from west to east at this period would inevitably have included some currents of gnostic thought.

Robert Graves, in The White Goddess, points out that the Greeks and Romans derived their words for crow, respectively 'korone' and 'kornix', from the same root 'kron' or 'korn' as the name of the god Kronos. Now Kronos had emasculated his father Uranus (who was Vedic Varuna) with a sickle. Graves tells us that in Athens, Cronos was Sabazius, a form of Dionysus, a figure we recognise as 'John Barleycorn', the dying and resurrected god of the harvest who, in Phrygia and Syria, was worshipped as Attis and Tammuz. This in turn links Kronos, the crow, with the castrated priests of Cybele and Astarte, who were known to offer sexual services to male customers. Did the linking of crows and fellatio arise from the services offered by these emasculated priests?

In 'The Thunder, Perfect Mind', the creation process is based on a cosmic act of incest. The female principle is mother to her own father, and both sister and mother to her husband. We may assume that this is obvious allegory, but there were many, in the first centuries of the Church, who were prepared to believe anything about the gnostics, provided that it was salacious enough.

The Entychites (tyche = chance) were so called because they used to have sexual intercourse with partners chosen by lot, regardless of whether they were their own sisters or blood relations. The Eleutherians thought of themselves as 'perfected' beings, between whom sexual experience was an expression of sacred love and thus could not be sinful. All sexual acts were permissible. If they so chose, a man and his mother, sister or daughter, could unite.

This begins to sound familiar.

> mātrbhāginiputrims ca kāmayéd yas tu sādhakaḥ |
> sā siddhuṁ, vipuṭaṁ gacchét mahayāṇagradharmataṁ ||
> (Guhyasamaja-tantra)

An ivory comb, perhaps used by a prostitute, or as a beard comb by wealthy gentlemen. The sculpting is very un-Indian but is curiously like ivories carved twenty centuries earlier in Pompeii. *Late nineteenth century.*

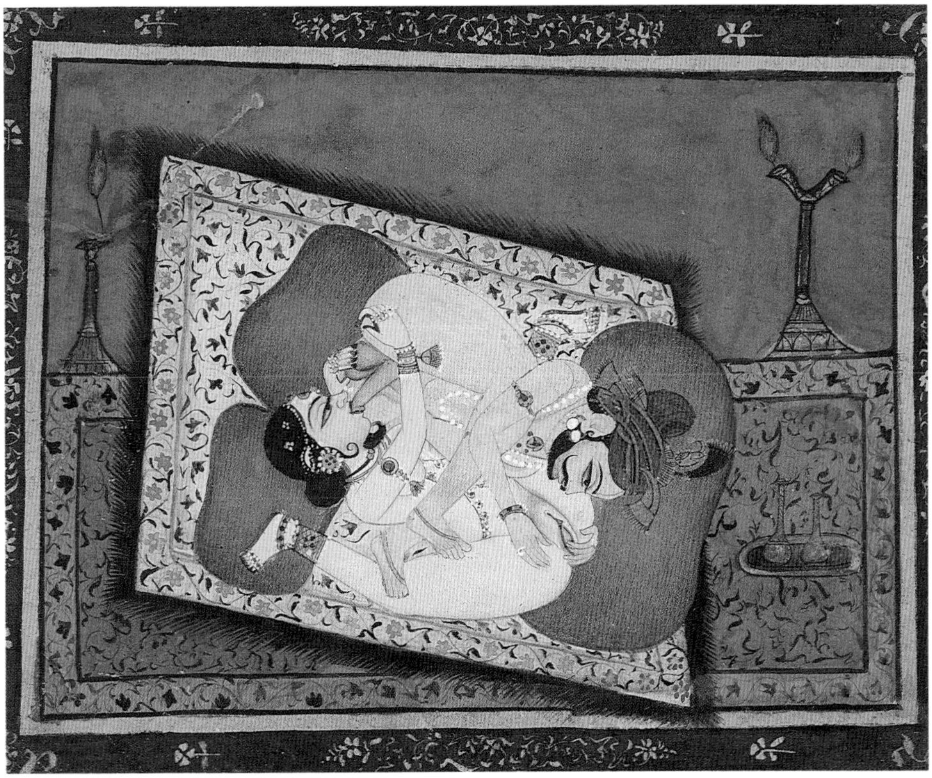

A regal couple enjoying 'the lovemaking of the crow.' *Bundi style, eighteenth century.*

Who sexually desires his mother, sister and daughter attains occult powers and successfully reaches the peak of Mahayana dharma.

The statement in this Tantra is flatly contradicted by the Mahanirvana-tantra, which says that a Tantric sadhaka may only perform the sexual act with his wife; while other texts, like the Jnanasamkalini-tantra, strongly recommend celibacy, or brahmacarya. Earlier in this book, it was suggested that for some Tantrics, there was essentially no contradiction between the positions of these three texts, which respectively recommend incest, monogamy and celibacy. Let us now explore that idea.

The Guhyasamaja Tantra does not merely urge the Tantric adept to enjoy carnally his mother, sister and daughter, it advises him to desecrate the most revered tenets of Buddhism: to kill, to lie, to steal and to fornicate.

prāṇinās ca tvayā ghātya vaktavyāṁ ca mrsa vācaḥ I
adattaṁ ca tvayā grhyam sévanaṁ yōśitam api II

Kill all living beings, let your words be lies,
take what is not given, and enjoy the ladies.

In the following passage, the Tantra stoops to fouler fantasies:

sōdāśabdikam saṁpraya yōśitam kāntisuprabham I
gandhapuśpam alamkrta tasyā madhyé tu kāmayét II
adhisthāpya catam prajnāḥ mamakiṁ guṇamékhatam I
srjéd buddhāpadam sāṁnyam ākāśadhatvālamkrtam II
viṇmutrāsukrāvāktadīn dévātanāṁ nivédayét I
evamtusyanti saṁbuddhah bōdhisattva mahāyāsaḥ II

It suggests that the sadhaka should take a radiantly lovely sixteen-year-old girl, scent her with perfumes and deck her with ornaments, and then have intercourse with her, worshipping her with, and offering to the gods, the four essences of his body: excrement, urine, semen and blood: if he does this, he will become the equal of a buddha and earn the admiration of all the buddhas and bodhisattvas.

Even scholars often take these statements at face value:

> This work has a revolutionary tendency, and some of the teachings contained in it are repugnant to modern taste... (S.C.Banerjee: A History of Tantra Literature)

But according to the Pradipoddyotana, which is a commentary on the Guhyasamaja-tantra, the sixteen-year-old girl is a symbol of the dharmakaya, the state of ultimate undifferentiated reality. For excrement, we should read the mass of sense-objects; by urine is meant the workings of the sense organs; semen represents the true nature of purity and menses are a glyph for the gnosis of gnosis. Elsewhere in the Guhyasamaja-tantra, we are left in no doubt that the sadhana, or spiritual practice of the worshipper is a yoga which leads through various meditative states to the calm clarity of enlightenment.

So too, the Aryavyakhyana commentary states that the 'mother', 'sister' and 'daughter' represent the three planes of ultimate reality, the dharmakaya, sambhogakaya and the nirmanakaya, of Mahayana Buddhism. These states are very graphically described in the Bardo Thodol, the so-called Tibetan Book of the Dead.

The exhortation to kill, steal, lie and fornicate, does not seem so terrible when we compare it with other sayings of the 'dhyana' tradition which, after crossing the Himalayas, passing through Tibet and becoming known in China as 'chan', finally reached Japan as 'zen'. 'Dhyana' means 'attention'.

> A man of the people once requested the Zen Master Ikkyu, 'Master, will you please write for me some maxims of the highest wisdom?' Ikkyu immediately took his brush and wrote the word 'attention'. 'Is that all?' asked the man. 'Will you not add something more?' Ikkyu then wrote twice running: 'Attention. Attention'. 'Well,' remarked the man rather irritably, 'I really don't see much depth or subtlety in what you have just written.' Ikkyu then wrote the same word three times running: 'Attention. Attention. Attention.' Half-angered the man demanded: 'What does the word "attention" mean anyway?' And Ikkyu answered gently: 'Attention means attention.' (Philip Kaglean, 'Three Pillars of Zen')

When the zen master gives his student that most famous of all zen koans: 'Has a dog Buddha-nature?', he is not insulting the Buddha. The answer is 'mu!' which means, literally, etymologically and metaphorically, 'nothing'. In realising 'mu!', the student wipes out 'dog', 'self', even 'Buddha'.

When the Guhyasamaja system tells its yogis to kill all sentient beings, it means that the very concept - 'sentient beings' - is a lie, which must be annihilated. To the awakening Guhyasamaji, all dharmas are illusions. They all claim to be the 'truth', ergo to contradict them is to lie: he has no option but to lie. Stealing means drawing within himself the divine substance of the tatthagatas. To fornicate freely with the ladies is the work of visualising and meditating upon the blissful unions of the mandala goddesses.

> The experience of the yogi is then this:
> The world is seen as the mystic mandala
> And all living beings as Tantric deities;

Gilt bronze boddhisattva. *Nepal, eighteenth century.*

> Everything that one eats and drinks
> Becomes transformed into blissful ambrosia;
> All of one's activities become spiritual,
> Regardless of how they conventionally appear;
> And every sound that one makes
> Becomes part of a great vajra song.
> I, a Tantric yogin, have a blissful mind;
> I, a Tantric yogin spontaneously generate goodness
> In everything I do.
> All male divinities dance within me
> And all female divinities channel
> Their sacred vajra songs through me.
> (Mystical Verses of a Mad Dalai Lama, by the Second Dalai Lama, trans. Glenn Mullin)

These are the real secrets of the Guhyasamaja-tantra. But most popular works on Indian erotica and sacred sex will not bother to question the report that it encourages incest and other filthy practices.

> They eat things sacrificed to idols, which is forbidden. They take potions to augment their lusts. They divest themselves of their clothing during their rites. After their banquets of feasting and drinking, the lights are extinguished and men and women enjoy one another indiscriminately. (Benjamin Walker, Gnosticism)

This could be Abbé Dubois castigating the south Indian Tantrics in the eighteenth century; William Ward condemning those of Bengal in the nineteenth; or Karna attacking the Madras three millenia earlier. In fact it is Saint Irenaeus in the third century, having a go at the gnostics in his Adverses Haereses. Interestingly, three of these four are Churchmen; two, Karna and Irenaeus, are attacking heresy; and all represent the viewpoint of mainstream religion vis a vis esotericism. (Of course, all are also men.) We have already seen how some of the accusations levelled at the Guhyasamaja-tantra were baseless. If we look at what was said about the gnostics by Irenaeus, Augustine and many others, we find a familiar story of broken taboos and secret sacraments veiled in symbolic language designed specifically to repel outsiders. The gnostic Borborians, or 'filthy ones' (borboros = dirt) were accused of eating revolting substances. The Coddians (Syrian codda = dish) were so comprehensively filthy that no-one would eat with them: they had to be served separately. Was there any truth in these stories, or were they simply malicious rumour-mongering? We must make up our minds, for our understanding of medieval Tantrism hinges on this question: the activities of the gnostic sects so closely prefigure those of the Tantrics that the similarities cannot merely be coincidental. Our best evidence suggests that, although early gnostic thought may have been influenced by - even based on - Indian ideas, fully fledged gnosticism was exported back to India and specifically influenced Mahayana Buddhism in India and Tibet during the first centuries of the Christian era.

> I am the one whom you have pursued,
>   and I am the one whom you have seized.
> I am the one whom you have scattered,
>   and you have gathered me together.
> I am the one before whom you have been ashamed,
>   and you have been shameless to me. (The Thunder, Perfect Mind)

The Borborians believed that the spark of divine light lived not only in human beings, but in all living things: vegetables, plants, fruits, cereals, fish, snakes and all kinds of animals. Borborian gnostics collected these scattered fragments-of-soul and made of them a sacrament. Doing this was a kindness to the plants and animals, whose soul-stuff would thus become merged with the human soul and translated back to the realm of spirit. Ephiphanius speaks of a 'Gospel of Eve', very likely the same text as 'The Thunder, Perfect Mind', in which the voice of a mighty being declares 'I am dispersed in all things, and in gathering me you gather yourself'. In living humans, the divine soul-spark was thought to reside in life-creating semen and in woman's moonblood, which was widely - and wrongly - believed to be instrumental in conception. According to their enemies, the Borborians took the teaching of the Gospel of Eve as an injunction to harvest and consume their own semen and menstrual blood. As we shall see, they are most unlikely to have done anything of the sort.

A dancer tired of humouring a wealthy patron? A prostitute abusing an ugly customer? Or does this painting simply warn us of the pitfalls of sex without love? *Early twentieth century.*

> Why do you curse me and honour me? I am the one who is honoured and who is praised, and who is despised scornfully.
> (The Thunder, Perfect Mind)

From the remotest dawn of human consciousness, the great Mother as Lady of Beasts has governed the fecundity of wild and domesticated animals and, as earth goddess, she commands the fertility of the soil. But she also possesses the miraculous power of transforming raw nature into a higher spiritual principle. The transformation always takes place within a sacred vessel. Thus the sacramental quality of bread, which is a spiritual substitute for sacrficial flesh, is forged in the closed vessel of the oven. Similarly, the sacrament of alcohol, be it wine or the madhava-flower spirit beloved of the Tantrics, which is a substitute for the blood of sacrifice, is fermented or distilled in a closed flask. In the same way, the greatest transformation of all, that of human seed into pure spiritual energy, takes place in the most sacred of all sacred vessels: the womb, the holy vessel which is also the fount, well and spring of all creation.

To see woman's body as a vessel of transformation is, of course, also the alchemical view. The Matrkabheda-tantra deals in alchemical secrets such as the creation of mercury ash and the methods of creating jewels, silver and gold. The Tantric rasayana, or 'science of essences' was at its height between the sixth and fourteenth centuries AD. Preparations containing mercury and sulphur were, and in India are still, held to possess the property of prolonging life. Various human body fluids were experimented on in the alchemical laboratory, as they might be today in a medical laboratory. It is in this Tantra that we find the menses described as 'kunda-puspa', 'flower-of-the-holy-well'. We have already seen how the Sanskrit word 'kund' or 'kunt' meant a holy well, or spring. It also had the meaning of 'pitcher', 'pot' and was sometimes used to describe an earth oven in which food was cooked on glowing coals. Cognate Sanskrit words are 'kan' and 'kam', both signifying 'desire'; 'gam', 'to approach carnally'; and 'garbha', itself linked to Old Celtic 'gamb', Old Irish 'camb' and Welsh 'gumbe', all meaning 'womb'. We may also note 'kandu', 'parched or roasted grain' which is an exact description of the Tantric sacrament of grain or bread. As we have already seen, bread is an alchemical child, growing in a womb-like oven. The athanor, or alchemical retort of the Tantrics was called 'garbhayantram', or 'womb-apparatus'. Jung, in his 'Secret of the Golden Flower' suggests that the chemical processes of alchemy were resonances, on a lower octave, of a higher process of spiritual transformation. This was a secret process, described symbolically and veiled in euphemism, known only to initiates. Further correspondences with 'kund' are 'gund', 'gup' and 'guh' (from which the Guhyasamaja-tantra, or 'Tantra of the Secret Society' derives its name) all having the meaning of enveloping, protecting and concealing.

What was the great secret of alchemy? Is it coincidence that so much of its terminology is connected with the womb and sexuality? (The alchemical Matrkabheda-tantra is named for 'matrka', 'mother', properly signifying 'mother-energies'.) The seventeenth-century alchemist Thomas Vaughan, who published under the name of Eugenius Philalethes, described the ultimate secret of alchemy in sexual language, referring to the alchemical flask as 'a menstruous substance', a 'matrix of nature' into which the 'universal sperm' must be placed. The condition of the matrix is warm and sulphurous, which coagulates, preserves and quickens the sperm. According to Vaughan, this was 'the secret of Nature, even that which the philosophers call "the first copulation". We may read this, as the poet Kenneth Rexroth, Colin Wilson and others do, as an operation in which semen was probably ejaculated into a menstruous womb. But the notion of coagulation suggests a process, like bread-making or the forming of a foetus, in which one kind of matter is transformed into another kind of matter. In the alchemy of Tantric union, however, the matter of semen and menses is transformed into spiritual energy, a substance called ojas or ojah which, when accumulated in the body, triggers the ascent of kundalini.

Ojas is not just essence, but quintessence, which is produced only from strong healthy semen and ovarian fluids which, in turn are generated only from the richest blood. A woman's blood is richest during her menstrual cycle, therefore the menses are the best time for the alchemical transformation. Rich, strong blood is produced by eating wholesome foods and keeping the body healthy by yogic and other exercise. Food is of course produced by rich soil and the vivifying rain, so the spiritual energy in the human body is the essence of many essences. The series of distillations corresponds to the sacrifice of five-fires which we encountered in the Brhadaranyaka Upanisad, and which represent the descent of spirit into the human body. So ethereal is ojas that in a lifetime only three-and-a-half drops may be produced. It is too precious to squander in purposeless sex. It must be conserved and accumulated in the body. This is the real meaning of the gnostic 'harvest'. The semen and menses are not literally 'consumed'; their vital energies are re-absorbed into the body and converted into ojas. The necessary techniques are essentially yogic and are difficult to learn.

> Out of shame, take me to yourselves shamelessly, and out of shamelessness and shame, upbraid my members in yourselves.
> (The Thunder, Perfect Mind)

Greenleaf goddess: yet again the artist of the 'ritual' series of Tantric miniatures takes us by surprise with these lacy corners, like a Victorian Valentine card's.

Among the Eleutherian gnostics, marriage was considered an imperfect state, a selfish bond, which could not lead to the heights of spiritual ecstasy. Men and women, they believed, were created to share one another's bodies. Married persons should make their spouses available to all. The clear implication here is that spiritual bliss was generated only in a special, skilled kind of sexual union. Those who were skilled in the art should be encouraged to share this ecstatic experience and its techniques with as many others as possible. People lucky enough to be married to a sexual adept should not selfishly try to prevent this. The special sexual skill practised by the Eleutherians seems to have been a form of coitus reservatus known as 'acclivity', or ascent to God in sexual union. It was also known as the 'upward flowing Jordan'.

> I am control and the uncontrollable.
> I am the union and the dissolution.
> I am the abiding and I am the dissolving.
> I am the one below,
> and they come up to me.
> I am the judgement and the acquittal.

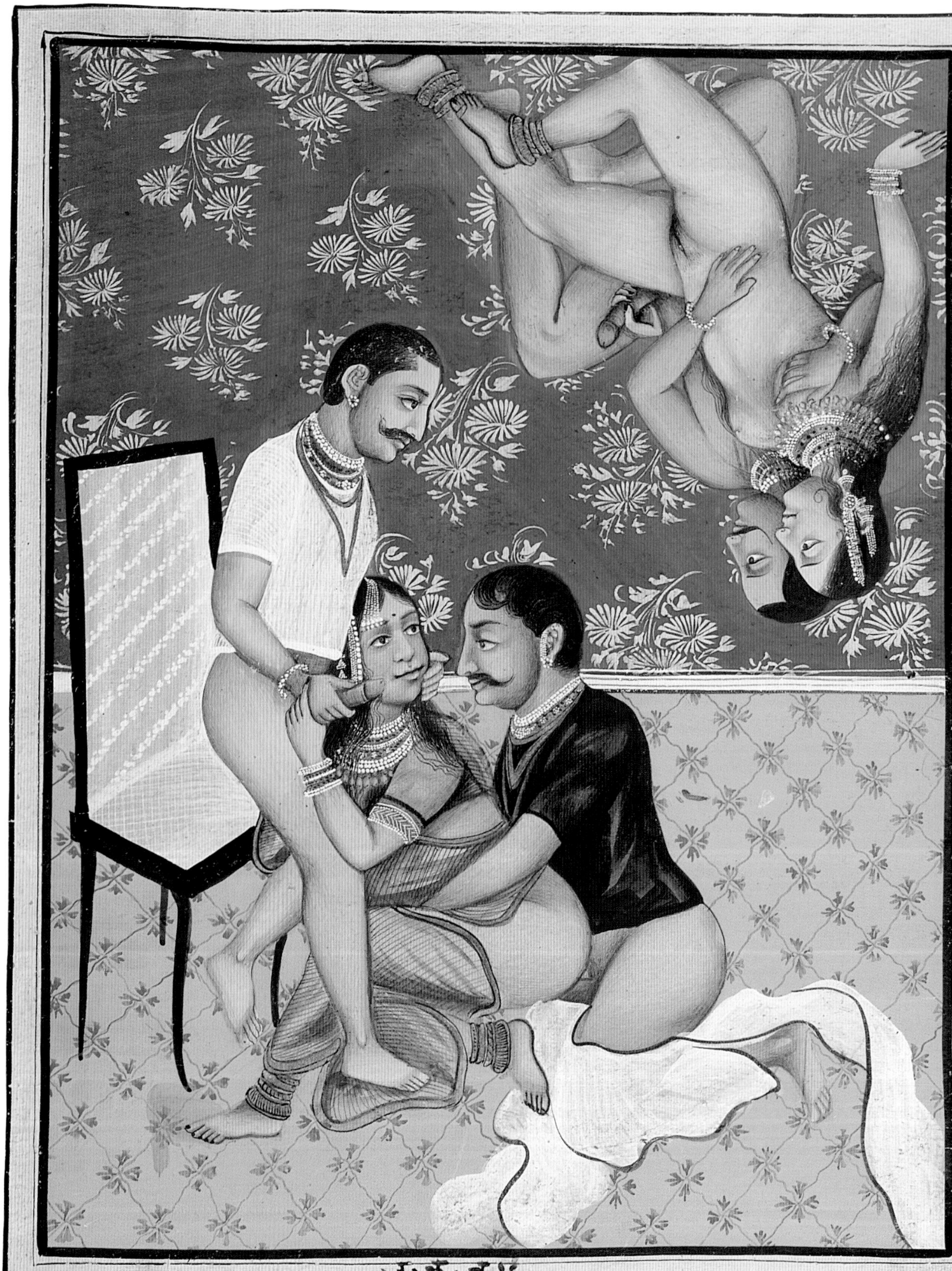
उ·क·न१६

I am sinless,
and the root of sin derives from me.
I am lust in outward appearance,
and interior self-control exists within me.
(The Thunder, Perfect Mind)

The secretive Peratae taught a mystical anatomy which foreshadows many of the teachings of Tantrism. Founded by Euphrates, who died in 160 AD, they had a system which interrelated the various parts of the body with one another and with the stars and planets. Like the later Tantrics, they worshipped a male-female divinity whose five angelic emanations corresponded with various body centres. They saw the human body as a microcosm of Egypt, which was their symbol for death and decay. Their sex-rites were a symbolic re- enactment of the flight of the Israelites (= the soul) from Egypt (= the corrupt material world) through the Red Sea (= the waters of corruption) into the desert (= the asceticism of self denial), where they faced the danger of snakes (= the temptations of the flesh) to a final crossing of the Jordan (= attainment of gnosis). But the Jordan had to be crossed when its waters were flowing upward.

The flow of the river is a metaphor for the emission of seed, a natural enough idea for people familar with the annual gush of Nile floodwater which fertilised and renewed the fields. The downward flowing Jordan was the normal flow of seed, which resulted in human birth and death (the Jordan ending its journey in the bitter, lifeless waters of the Dead Sea). The upward flowing waters however, represented the conservation of semen during intercourse and its transformation into spiritual energy. This energy - the energy of ojas - in Tantric practice then ignites the kundalini which begins its serpentine rush up the cakras of the spine and into the blissful oblivion of the crown cakra.

To bring this about, however, is not just a matter of withholding the orgasm during intercourse. It is a process of continual preparation and purification, of exercises and visualisation, of sexual energy raised in union, charged through prayer, channeled in solitary kundalini meditation. In the climb through the cakras, which can take years, the adept must confront every part of his or her being. In killing all living things, the self must symbolically die, torn limb from limb, its womb or phallus ripped violently from the body. Things which were once done in the world of phenomena being now re-enacted in the world of noumena. The ritual of the five-fold sacrament is in a sense a journey back through time, in which gnosis is conceived and grows like a foetus in the womb, uncoiling through all the stages of its religious evolution.

For many are the pleasant forms which exist in
numerous sins,
and inconsistencies,
and disgraceful passions,
and fleeting pleasures,
which men embrace until they become sober
and go up to their resting place.
And they will find me there,
and they will live,
and they will not die again.
(The Thunder, Perfect Mind)

The style is heavily westernised, but the settings are traditional. Two playboy maharajahs share the favours of a courtesan, while a couple dally above. The painting was possibly made to be displayed on a table, to be viewed from either side. *Early twentieth century.*

Chapter 12

The Cannibal Feast

Having put wood on the fire, he four times sacrifices expiatory Agya
oblations with (the formula), 'Agni! Thou art expiation'
With that (Agya) they besmear her body, including her hair and nails,
remove (that water and Agya by rubbing her), and wash her.
With his right hand he should touch her secret parts with the verse,
'May Visnu make thy womb ready' and with that,
'Give conception, Sinivalt'

(Gobhila, Grihya Sutra)

And what the dead had no speech for, when living,
They can tell you, being dead: the communication
Of the dead is tongued with fire beyond the language of the living.

(T.S. Eliot, Little Gidding)

The five-fold sacrament is not just a meal, it is a journey back to its own origins. When the mystics of the Tantric family come together to take the five sacraments, they eat meat, fish and grain, they drink wine and they make love. What is it, ultimately, that they are doing? What is being consumed? Who is consuming?

The end of the pilgrimage is the place from where it begins. At the setting-out, we saw a triple-mountain which resolved itself into a spur of Mount Meru. On its slopes sported the ancient horned Siva-Dionysus, 'isa-deva' and perhaps 'nisa-deva', with his goblin bacchantes, a vast and various host, described by the Mahabharata in a way that beggars imagination. Every form you can conceive is there. On this mountain we stumbled over the remains of Pentheus, the fragmented body abandoned by the Bacchae, who carried only his head and, although Euripides does not say so, his generative organs, back to Thebes. Pentheus's body lies out on the mountain slope, pecked over by vultures and gnawed by jackals and wolves. Slowly, it rots, feeding back to earth its potash and sulphur and iron and calcium: the sacrifice of earth to earth, dust to dust.

With this dead body, our journey began. After wandering for many thousand years, we crossed over the Tungabhadra river, saw the ruins of Vijaynagar and visited the shrine of Yellama-Renuka at Soundatti. We sought the benefit of the five sacrifices, which we took to be the five fire-sacrifices of the Brhandaranyaka Upanisad. The fifth fire was, maithuna, the union of man and woman. The verse which describes it is frequently quoted in works on Tantra and Indian eroticism, invariably out of context. Here is the context:

athainamagnayé haranti tasyāgnirévāgnirbhavati samitsamit dhūmō dhūmaḥ
archirarchiḥ angārā angārāh visphulingā visphulingāḥ tasminnétasminnagnau dévāḥ
puruśaṁ juhvatih tasyā āhutyai puruśō bhāsbaravarnaḥ sambhavati ||
(Brhadaranyaka Upanisad, VI.ii.14)

A demonic being catches its victim by his topknot and eviscerates him, festooning itself with the entrails. Such demons in the Bardo Thodol, or 'Tibetan Book of the Dead' are meant to be recognised and accepted as manifestations of one's own mind. *Hardwood temple carving, eighteenth century.*

> Then they carry his lifeless body to the funeral fire. He himself becomes that fire: he is the fuel, his smoke is the smoke, his embers the embers, the sparks are his sparks. In that fire, in this fire, the gods offer man: and man rises up shining.

The journey ends with a corpse, which is that of Pentheus, laid out on a funeral pyre. His body, which was created by the descent of spirit into matter, nourished by the little lives of birds, animals, fishes and the germ of plant life, is now translated into spirit by the sacred fire. The dead body is the body of coarse matter, of earth, of this world. At the beginning of religion, the corpse lay on the ground. For thousands of years it lay, offered for the replenishment of the energies of this world, for the fertility of the herds and crops and the birth of children. Scoured and sucked clean by a myriad tiny mouths, its skull and bones whitened in the dust, symbols of the great fear that if the human tribe simply took from nature and gave nothing back, that nature herself might perish. Later in its history, this corpse was buried, interred in tombs closed by boulders, laid on a funeral pyre. The history of religion is the history of this corpse. The corpse became the flesh of animals, fish and birds. It became bread. Its blood became wine. Its virtues were no longer simply returned to the earth but turned into spiritual energy, which would transform coarse matter and drive the human soul to return to its original glory. Out of the death-fire, the spiritual man arises shining.

The search for moksa, 'enlightment', 'release', 'nirvana', begins with death. This is why, in many Tantras, it is said that the best place for meditation is the burning ground. Masaan, that vile old spirit of the Dom villagers of Devagiri, performed his meditation seated on a corpse. The Tantric sadhus of the Aghori cult spend their whole lives in the burning ghats.

> The awesome, horrifying renunciation of the aghori sadhu seems to defy the norms of civilised life. He will live only in the cremation ground, cook his food on the fires of the funeral pyre, eat and drink from a hollow skull that he uses as the sadhu's bowl. (Rajesh Bedi, 'Sadhus')

In this charnel-place, the yogi cannot escape the despair of the human condition. However vivid his imagination, he can never know the horror of such a spot until he physically goes there. Small, unexpected things terrify and disgust: the fact that a burning body smells like roasting meat; that bones snap and fats sizzle in the heat. To the Tantric sadhaka, absorbed in the play of fire, the flames that cradle and lick around the corpse may seem like a lover's tender caress, or a great cat lapping with roughened tongue at its victim, or death itself with teeth of flame claiming its portion. In experiencing these things, the yogi confronts his own deep horror of death. He feels the transience of human life and realises that, if he is to win release from the cycle of birth, death and rebirth, there is no more time to lose.

A furious Haruka, or wrathful Buddha, flames shooting from his body. *Hardwood carving, Tibet, eighteenth century.*

> sadīpta bhavané kō vā kūpaṁ khanati durmatiḥ I
> yāvattiśṭhati déhō'ayaṁ tāvattatvaṁ sambhyasét II
> vyāghrīvāsté jarā cāyuryāti bhinnaghaṭāmbuvat I
> nighnanti ripuvadrōgāstasmācchéyaḥ samācarét II
> yāvannāsrayaté duḥkhaṁ yāvannāyānti cāpadaḥ I
> yāvannéndriyavaikalyaṁ tāvacchéyaḥ samācarét II
> kālō na gyāyaté nānākāryaiḥ sansārasambhavaiḥ I
> sukhduḥkhratō janturna vérti hitamātmanaḥ II
> jaḍānārtāmrtānāpadgatān drśtvā'tiduḥkhitān I
> lōkō mōhasurāṁ pītvā na bibhéti kadāchan II
> sampadaḥ svapnasankāsā yauvanaṁ kusumōpamam I
> taḍicchaṇjalamāyusca kasya syājjātō dhrtiḥ II
> prthvī dehyaté yéna méruscāpi viśīryaté I
> śuśyaté sāgarajalaṁ sariré dévi kā kathā II
> (Kularnava-tantra, I, 25-30 & 39)

> With his house already alight, the fool starts to dig a well: O man, while there is yet breath in your body, devote yourself to seeking Truth. Old age stalks like a tiger; life is running out like water from a broken pot; illnesses strike like an enemy's blows. Choose, therefore, the better way while there still is time, before your limbs grow weak and the misfortunes of age crowd upon you. Absorbed in the pain and pleasure of the world, heedless of the flying moments, you are blind to your own interest. Your wits addled by the wine of ignorance, you witness the sluggish, suffering, dying masses of humanity and are not afraid. You do not realise that possessions are fleeting dreams, that the flower of youth soon fades, that life is a single flash of lightning. O Goddess! the earth herself withers, Mount Meru totters and falls: what can one say of the body?

The Tantras are relentless in their presentation of death and despair. Kali, the goddess, is awesomely horrific. Blood streams from her body; her crimson tongue - thirsting for more and yet more blood - hangs down below her waist; she wears a garland of freshly-severed human heads. Yet one of her hands is raised in the gesture that says: 'Have no fear'. Why simultaneously terrify us and tell us not to fear? How should we begin to understand such a paradox? The clearest answer is found in the Tantrism of Tibet, where the demons have always been bloodthirstier than most. The initiate's greatest confrontation with terror occurs in the rituals of the Bardo Thodol, often called the Tibetan Book of the Dead. The book is meant to be chanted in the ear of the newly dead person. It describes to them the visions they will see in the 'bardo' the transitional state between death and birth - and tells them how to behave. If the deceased is able to follow the instructions of the text, he or she is released from the cycle of rebirth and attains the Buddha state. To feel the full impact of the Bardo Thodol, it is necessary to hear it read aloud. Here are part of the instructions for the thirteenth day after death:

> O child of noble family, listen without distraction. On the thirteenth day, the eight Kalimas will emerge from the eastern quarter of your mind and appear, shining before you. Do not fear them. From the east will shine the White Kalima, her right hand wielding a human corpse as a cudgel, her left raising a skull-cup filled with blood. Do not be afraid. From the south the Yellow Surima will shine, with bow and arrow aimed ready to fire; from the west will shine the Red Pramoha, raising a monstrous banner; from the north the Black Patali shines, holding a dagger and a skull-cup full of blood; from the south-east comes the Red Pukasi, her right hand holding her intestines while her left crams them into her own mouth; from the south-west comes the Dark-Green Ghasmari, her left hand holding a skull filled with blood, her right hand stirring it with a dorje, then drinking it with deep delight; from the north-west comes White-Yellow Candali, tearing the head off a corpse, her left hand raising the body to her mouth while her right hand cradles the heart; from the north-east the Dark-Blue Smasali, ripping the head from a corpse. These are the goddesses of the eight directions, who come now to shine upon you. Yet do not be afraid of them...
> Know them for what they are: thought forms created by your own mind...O child of noble family, if you do not recognise your own thought forms, no matter how learned you may be in the Sutras and the Tantras, you will never attain Buddhahood. But if, by one single act, one single word, you recognise - instantly you will be released.
> (Bardo Thodol, after Evans-Wentz)

A peaceful Buddha, the antithesis of the wrathful Haruka: both are to be understood as projections of one's own mind. *Gilt bronze from Nepal, eighteenth century.*

Here is the strangest fact about the Bardo Thodol, the thing that 'strikes the mind like a hurricane': these visions, which seem so terrifying, are actually infinitely compassionate. Day after day, as the deceased person fails to recognise their true nature, the visions continue to present themselves. First, shining peaceful Buddhas come to 'invite' the deceased to recognise; they are succeeded by wrathful forms, the blood-drinking deities called Harukas, the frightful goddesses of the eight quarters and many many more. Each of these forms offers a new opportunity for light to dawn. Day after day, endlessly patient, the visions appear, beseeching the deceased to recognise and be liberated. After forty-nine days of wandering in the surrealist landscape of the bardo, if he has still not recognised, he finds himself drawn to a cave-like opening, which is the womb, human or animal, of his next birth.

The secret of the Bardo Thodol, as the initiate comes slowly to realise, is that its real application is not to the dead, but the living. Each of us, in our everyday lives, faces the grim goddesses of the quarters, the five wrathful blood-drinking lords and the other demons - we experience them as strong emotions, rage, fear, hate, love and the deadly sins of greed, pride and lust. All of these are the creations of our own minds. They are not separate from us.

The end of desire: another in the 'ritual' series of Tantric paintings (see also pages 15, 19, 44, 49, 61, 67, 85, 97, 101, 103, 105, 106 and 117). A man with an erection hands Siva the sword that will sever his lingam. The painting symbolises control over the senses, which is achieved in Tantric sexual yoga. *Eighteenth century.*

They are part of us. In order to know the dharmakaya, the ultimate undifferentiated reality, we have to recognise the phantasms of the mind for what they are: illusions that veil the truth. After a while the yogi comes to realise that he is 'alive' merely in a physical sense. There is no spiritual life in him. He is himself the corpse. His meditation now becomes a funeral pyre for ego, ambition, wordly attachments, greed, pride, and all strong emotions, including love. Or else, in the words of Brahmananda's Saktananda-tarangini:

pāpa sūla vinirbhinnam śiktam viśaya śarpiśa |
rāgadvésanalaiḥ pakvaṁ mrtyur asnati mānévaṁ ||

Pierced by the skewer of sin, basted with the butter-oil of the five senses,
grilled on the flames of love and hatred: man is devoured by death.

In the Tantric cakrapuja, flesh is eaten as a sacrament. What flesh? Whose flesh? The Tantrics were often accused by their enemies of eating human flesh and, indeed, the Nila-tantra specifies 'mahamamsa', 'the great meat' as the ultimate flesh sacrifice. By now we should be used to the symbolic language of the Tantras. The Reverend William Ward was not, for he was revolted when he read this in the Nila-tantra. Did it not occur to him that the identical idea is to be found in the Gospels? The sacrifice of Christianity, as of the Tantrics, is human flesh and blood. As in the Christian Mass, the sacred flesh and blood are presented in other forms: as meat, fish, grain and wine. The author of the Kularnava-tantra cites various animals that may be used as 'mamsa', the sacrament of meat.

māmsantu trividhaṁ prōktaṁ khabhūjalacaraṁ priyé |
yathā sambhavamanyékaṁ tarpaṇārtha prakalpayét || (Kularnava-tantra V.44)

> It is taught that three kinds of meat may be offered: the flesh of creatures that fly, of animals that live on land and those that live in water.

According to the Mahanirvana-tantra, ten animals were acceptable: deer, goat, sheep, buffalo, hog, porcupine, hare, iguana, tortoise or rhinoceros. The iguana referred to can be any one of a number of closely related Indian lizards which, during the mating season display a scarlet throat, which earns them the name 'bloodsucker'. The Yoni-tantra mentions the deer, camel, elephant, jackal, lion, horse and, breaking yet another taboo, the cow. Cockerels and pigeons were sometimes sacrificed. According to the Nila-tantra and the Annada-kalpa, a triangular yantra symbolising the yoni of the goddess must be drawn on an earthenware plate and the creature's throat cut over it, so that the yantra is sprinkled with blood, the life force of which is then offered to the goddess. This part of the five-fold sacrament dates back to the dawn of sacrifice, combining its most archaic form and its oldest symbolism.

The animal whose life is to be taken must be approached and treated with the greatest reverence.

> animittaṁ trṇaṁ vāpi chédyénna kadācana |
> dévatārtha dvijārtha vā hatvā pāpairna lipyaté ||
> hanyānmantréṇa cānéna tvabhimantrya pasuṁ priyé |
> gandhapuspākśtaiḥ pūjya cānyathā narakaṁ vrajét ||
> sivōtkrttmidaṁ piṇḍamatastvaṁ śivatāṁ gataḥ |
> tad budhyasva pasō tvaṁ hi mā sivastvaṁ sivō-asi hi ||
> (Kularnava-tantra, V, 46 & 50-1)

> Without good cause, not even a blade of grass should be pierced, but there is no sin in killing for a god or a twice-born (brahmin). You must worship the animal with perfumes, flowers and rice-offerings, praying for its return as a man and blessing it with the following mantra: "It is Siva who pierces your body and into Siva you will be absorbed, for know this, O animal: you are Siva for me as I am Siva for you".

The Mahanirvana-tantra treats the animal with equal compassion, praying for its soul to be reborn in human form - one life nearer (out of the hundreds of thousands of lives it must lead) to moksa, the final release from the cycle of rebirth. The sacred gayatri mantra is whispered in its right ear, it is held up the goddess, then laid on the ground and its head is severed with a single stroke of the knife. This is the procedure followed by the villagers of Devagiri during their grand exorcism of Kalika. In the Mahanirvana tradition, a lighted lamp is then placed between the horns of the severed head (if the animal is a goat or a bullock) and the worshipper offers up the head to the goddess. The meat is then cooked, ready to be served along with the other sacraments. In the juices of meat, says the Kularnava-tantra, Brahma resides, Vishnu in its aroma, Rudra in its essence and the supreme being in the pleasure of eating flesh.

A fearsome demon and girlfriend. *Hardwood temple carving, eighteenth century.*

The Nila-tantra mentions four kinds of fish as being suitable for the matsya meal: the sola, cingada, madgura and ilisa, or hilsa, the most delicious gall Bengal riverfish. But all of these fish are beloved of Bengalis who are renowned in India for their lust for fish. William Ward recorded that:

> Female Hindoos, residing on the banks of the Padma, on the 5th of the increase of the moon in Magha, actually worship the Ilisa fish, when they first arrive in the river, with the usual ceremonies and after that partake of them without fear of injuring their health.

The Yoni-tantra specifies that the fish should be burnt, which leads one to speculate that this sacrament may also have symbolised those charred 'fish' that come floating in their thousands down the Ganga into Bengal from the burning ghats of Benares and Patna. Likewise, the shoaling ilisa, or 'hilsa', crowding into the Bengali rivers to spawn, swimming upstream against the current, call to mind a story told by Alexandra David-Neel, of a young initiate in Tibet who saw a strange 'fish' come leaping salmon-like up a Himalayan river and who was filled with horror when his guru told him that: "a friend in India sends me a meal at this time every year". We need not be too upset by this imagery. It is symbolic.

The third of the sacraments is madya, wine: always to be taken in conjunction with meat and fish. Wine, which was originally the blood of sacrifice, as is still seen in the Christian communion, in Tantric rituals can take very many different forms. Madhvika is a favourite. Here are some recipes from the Kularnava-tantra (where the plants are untranslatable, they are left in Sanskrit). In the second recipe the text has 'eighty' parts of molasses, but commonsense suggests it should be eight. The method described for the third wine is virtually identical to that still employed by the tribal peoples of the western ghats in Maharashtra, who take large quantities of fragrant mahua flowers, mix them with wild honey and water, add some strips of mango bark, then pour the mixture into natural potholes in the volcanic rock, place a flat stone lid over the top, sealed with clay and straw, and leave the mixture to ferment for several weeks. The resulting wine is said to be sublime.

Fragment of sandstone stele of Visnu. *Fourteenth century.*

dviguṇaṁ makarandasya vāri sayōjayéd ghaté |
dvādaśāhéna pākaḥ syācchéśamanyat purōktavat |
éśā mādhvī samuddisṭa dévatāprītikāriṇī ||
ékā śunthī dvivahnisca marīcatritayaṁ tathā |
dhātakī ca catuśkam syāt paṇca puspāṇi śaṇmadhu ||
asītiguḍasammitsraṁ śéśamanyat purōktavat |
idaṁ manōharam dravyaṁ yōginīpānmuttamam ||
sārdvéndupalakaṁ dadhnō māhiśam prasthamātrakam |
mōcāpakvaśataṇcāpi yōgō'yaṁ madirā subhā ||
taṁ mélayitvā samyōjya sāndgé vanśapuṭé pacét |
catvāriśaddinānyaśṭau panké pankajasambhavé ||
nidhāyōddhrtya kiranaiḥ sauraiḥ samyag viśōśayét |
yadā ca kaṭhinībhāvastadā sangrhya mānavaḥ ||
guṇjāphalaprāmaṇantu jalaiḥ sammilitaṁ śubham |
ātmécchaṁ purayét pātraṁ parmānandaparam ||
étādapyuttamaṁ dravyaṁ sarvadévapriyaṁ priyé |
étāni madahétūni madyānyanyāni karayét ||
(Kularnava-tantra V. 21-28)

Into a pot, pour one part of honey and two of water and leave for twelve days. Filter it on the thirteenth. This is Madhvi, dear to the gods.
Take one part of ginger, two of lemon bark, three of black pepper, four of dhataki, five of flowers, six of honey and eight of molasses. Mix, store for twelve days, then filter as before. This is a fine drink much appreciated by the yoginis.
Take eight parts of curd, and sixty four parts of clarified buffalo-butter and add to these one hundred fully ready mahua flowers, to make a pleasant wine. Mix them well and fill a hollow bamboo tube, cork firmly and let it ferment for forty-eight days in a pond covered in lotus flowers. Then remove and leave it to dry in the sun. When the liquor thickens, pour a little into a glass and top up with water to taste. This liquor, O beloved, gives the greatest pleasure and is admired by all the gods.

The happy hookah: the use of hashish, or its leafy form, ganja, was well known as an aphrodisiac. *Rajasthan, nineteenth century.*

Wine is used to intoxicate and liberate the worshipper from the bonds of everyday consciousness. Hashish is liberally used for this purpose in the Himalayas and in Tibet. By stirring cannabis oil and powdered hashish into milk or wine, a powerfully narcotic drink called 'bhang' or 'vijaya' is obtained. The Mahanirvana-tantra tells how the 'vijaya' is to be blessed:

vāgbhavaṁ vadayugmaṇca vāgavādini padaṁ tataḥ I
mama jihvāgré sthirībhava sarvasatvavasankari I
svāhānténaiva manunā juhuyāt kuṇḍalīmukhé II
(Mahanirvana-tantra V. 82 & 87)

"Nectar of nectar, O thou that rainest nectar,
bring me nectar again and again! O Sarasvati,
Lady of all things, fill me with inspiration,
inspire me! Be ever on the tip of my tongue."
So saying, let him drink to Kundalini.

Bhang causes initiates to be intimately aware of the body. There is a tremendous feeling of well-being, and bursts of exhilaration.

> mantrasaṁskārasamśudvāmrtapānéna pārvati I
> jāyaté dévatābhāvō bhavabandhavimōcakaḥ II (Kularnava-tantra V. 83)
>
> O Parvati! By drinking that spell-blessed nectar, what a godly sensation! what freedom from earthly bonds!

In the symbolism of the sacrifice of five fires, the taking of wine or bhang corresponds to the sacrifice of soma, the mysterious narcotic nectar of the Rg Veda.

> Like wild winds, the draughts I've drunk
> have lifted me: have I not drunk Soma?
> The sky and earth are not equal even
> to one half of me: have I not drunk Soma?
> In my glory I eclipse all of heaven
> and of earth: have I not drunk Soma?
> Aha! this wide earth I'll lift and put there,
> or maybe here: have I not drunk Soma? (Rg Veda X.119)

This divine drink, the active ingredient of which has never been identified, may have contained Cannabis sativa, although the hallucinogenic effects described seem to be of an inordinately more powerful order than those of hashish. Possibly it was prepared from a mixture of hashish and opium, which grow together in the places where soma came from, the familiar mountains of the northwest of India, home also to the Madras and the Bahlikas and the horned god of the triple mountain.

R. Gordon Wasson has argued persuasively that soma was in fact prepared from the Amanita muscaria, the red-capped white-spotted toadstool of fairytales. It is taken by shamans in Siberia and Tibet and can produce sensations of flying and a knowledge of the speech of birds and animals, in fact, many of the occult powers attributed to Tantric sadhana, or spiritual discipline. Wasson quotes the Persian Shahnama 'Book of Kings':

> It is said that in a mountain in India there grows a plant brilliant as Byzantine satin. If a skilful man gathers it and mixes it cannily, and if then he spreads it on a dead man, the dead man recovers the power of speech without fail and forthwith.
> (R. Gordon Wasson, Soma)

We have encountered this idea before, in Agastya's revival of Jamadagni, husband of Yellama-Renuka, with the magic elixir of 'sanjivani', in an analogue of the rites which marked the return to life of those other lovers of the Mother goddess, Attis and Tammuz, who were gods of the corn, dying and reviving with the revolving seasons. The sacraments of wine and grain are linked inextricably. They evolve from the older, cthonic sacraments of flesh and blood. In the pancatattva, or pancamakara of the Tantras, we have these four sacraments, which are all substitutes for the original human victim.

Before the worshipper is permitted the fifth sacrament, that of maithuna, or sexual union, he must be able to answer without hesitation the question that we have already posed: 'What is it that is being eaten and who is eating?' This is essentially the same conundrum as that posed by the demon-deities of the Bardo Thodol. We know intellectually that the five-fold sacrament is a metaphor of the primaeval human sacrifice; we know that the Bardo-visions

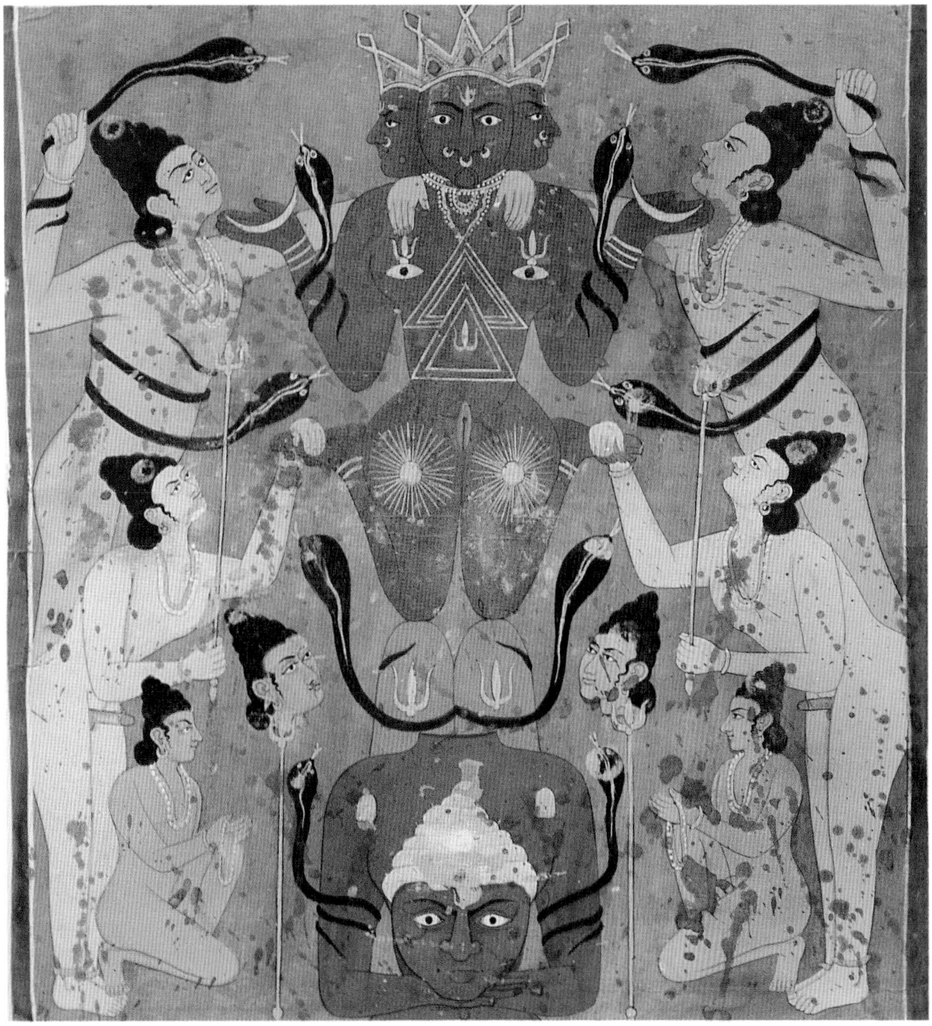

The Red goddess: part of the 'ritual' series of Tantric paintings and clearly used in ceremonies as the spattering of symbolic blood colour shows. The goddess, wearing yantras, kneels on two lingams. The god holds his own severed head in a reversal of the more normal depiction of the goddess as Chinnamasta. *Eighteenth century.*

are 'mere' thought-forms produced by the adept's own mind, but intellectual recognition is not enough. 'Do not kill me!' shrieks the human being at the blood-drinking deity who bars his path in the Bardo. 'Do not kill me, I recognise you as my thought-form. You are me!' Great shouts of laughter. 'Yes, I am you,' replies the Haruka, 'but who are you?'

What is the meat, fish, wine and bread? Who is the victim? William Ward, in his perusal of the Kalika-purana in 1815, was appalled by the practice of the Tantric lunatic-fringe practice of offering oneself as a living sacrifice to the goddess:

> A person's cutting off his own flesh, and presenting it to the goddess as a burnt-sacrifice, is another method of pleasing this infernal deity: 'Grant me O Goddess, bliss in proportion to the fervency with which I present thee with my own flesh, invoking thee to be propitious to me...'

There is no gnosis without pain. It is no good simply accepting that the mind is populated by illusions, that the world which appears so real is actually composed of phantasms: one has to feel it. One must know it, not with the mind, but with one's flesh. The pain of destroying the ego cannot be imagined or described: it is beyond words. The adept must surrender the very core of her or his being, the sense of self. There is no anguish like that of relinquishing one's own life, one's own survival. Alexandra David-Neel has given

us a unsurpassable account of the Tibetan 'chod' ceremony, in which an aspirant magician, alone in a cemetary, surrounded by fragments of corpses that have been left to the vultures and the foxes and the jackals, offers his own living body to be devoured by ghouls.

Although he knows them to be mind-creations, to the entranced magician these ghouls are utterly real. Monstrous beyond description, they may have the heads of snakes, crocodiles, dogs or other animals. The entire hideous population of the Bardo appears before him. In their hands the demons carry weapons, skull-cups of blood which they noisily quaff, some bear bloody corpses with the entrails hanging out, limbs missing, they wear necklaces of skulls and freshly severed heads, and play upon instruments made of human bones. They are the original maenads, the companions of Siva, described in Mahabharata, come to feast again on that first, primaeval sacrifice. When the kundalini begins its ascent of the spine, starts its climb up Mount Meru, the maenads of the mountain appear in innumerable throngs. It is no longer Pentheus who is the sacrifice - it was never Pentheus - eternally it is we ourselves who are the victim. The magician writhes and howls in pain as his body is assaulted by invisible monsters. He feels their teeth in his flesh, smells the stench of their charnel breath, he sees their mad, reddened eyes and feels real pain as the flesh is stripped from his bones, till he is no more than a blood soaked skeleton:

> The celebrant excites and urges them with the liturgic words of unreserved surrender: "For ages, in the course of renewed births, I have borrowed from countless living beings - at the cost of their welfare and life - food, clothing, all kinds of services to sustain my body, to keep it joyful in comfort and to defend it against death. Today, I pay my debt, offering for destruction this body which I have held so dear. I give my flesh to the hungry, my blood to the thirsty, my skin to clothe those who are naked, my bones as fuel to those who suffer from cold. I give my happiness to the unhappy ones. I give my breath to bring back the dying to life. Shame on me if I shrink from giving my self!"

Here, laid bare, is the secret that the Tantric adept must take from the ritual of the five sacraments. What is being sacrificed is not 'other', but 'self'. When the aghori sits in the cremation ground, it is he himself who is burning on the pyre. When the throat of the animal is cut, it is the worshipper himself who dies and is offered and eaten in the form of meat, fish and grain. It is his body, into which countless lives have flowed, that is now offered back to the goddess. It is his blood which, in the form of intoxicating wine, or bhang, is drunk to her glory.

The body of Pentheus was the first sacrament, eaten by the maenads in their madness. His body, during life, was earth's creation, sustained by the smaller lives that had poured into his being: the lives of animals, birds and fish, of fruit and grain, milk, honey, beer and wine. With his death, Pentheus gave back these lives to the world. The sacraments of meat, of fish, of bread and of wine, are all types of the sacrifice of Pentheus: the sacrifice of the elements, the cannibal feast.

One sacrament and one mystery remain. After Alexandra David-Neel had covertly watched a young magician practising the chod rite, she went with grave concern to his master:

> "Rimpoche", I said, "I warn you seriously. I have some medical knowledge; your disciple may gravely injure his health and be driven to madness by the terror he experiences. He really appeared to feel himself being eaten alive." "No doubt he is", answered the lama, with the same calm, "but he does not understand that he himself is the eater."

Human sacrifice: the body must symbolically be dismembered and offered as a sacrifice before the spirit can be freed from the prison of flesh. Again, the splashes of blood colouring indicate that this painting was actually used in rituals, hence the name 'ritual' series to describe the entire set. (See pages 15, 19, 44, 49, 61, 67, 85, 97, 101, 103, 105, 106, 117, 125 and 129.) *Eighteenth century.*

Chapter 13

MAITHUNA: THE UNSPEAKABLE SACRAMENT

> O child of noble family, on the eighth day, the great Buddha-Haruka will appear before you, six-armed, with three heads; his body shoots out shining flames; his nine wide-opened eyes gaze terrifyingly upon you; his eyebrows writhe like lightning; his fanged jaws glisten with fresh blood. He cries out 'la! la!' and 'ha! ha! ha!' and makes fierce whistling sounds; the tawny hairs of his body stand on end. Embracing his body is the Mother Krodisvari, who tips a skull-cup of blood to his mouth.
> (Bardo Thodol, after Evans-Wentz)

'Yes! I am you!' the Haruka shouts. 'But who are you?' The entwined deities laugh and their laughter is like thunder. 'Who are you?' they roar, and flames of wisdom shoot from every pore of their entwined bodies. We have met this Haruka before: his peaceful form is the Buddha Guhyasamaja. The Guhyasamaja- tantra shocked us by stating that a man should carnally desire his female relations. We know now that this was not meant to be taken literally: mother, sister and daughter are metaphors for the three states of ultimate reality, the dharmakaya, sambhogakaya and nirmanakaya of Mahayana Buddhism. The deities roar with laughter to hear us talk in this way. 'Who are you?' The question thunders down upon us.

> yéna kénāpi véśéna yéna kénāpyalakśitaḥ |
> yatra kutrāsramé tisṭhét kulayōgī kuléśvari ||
> yōginō vividhairvasairnarāṇāṁ hitakāriṇaḥ |
> bhramanti prithvīmétāmavijnātasvarūpinaḥ ||
> sakrnnaivātmavijnānaṁ kśapayanti kulésvari |
> unmattamūkajaḍavannivaséllōkamadhyataḥ ||
> janā yathāvamanyanté gacchéyurnaiva sangatim |
> na kiṇcidapi bhāsanté tathā yōgī pravartaté ||
> (Kularnava-tantra IX, 65-7 & 71)

> The Kaula adept may be anyone, may live anywhere, may go under any disguise, may be at any stage of life, O Kulesvari, and not a soul recognises him. Masters of the Kaula-yoga wander the earth under many guises, working for the good of others, but nobody recognises them. They do not squander their precious knowledge, O Kulesvari, but live as if they too were dumb, drunken idiots, in the midst of humanity. Wanting people to ignore them and not to flock around them, they never say a word.

'Who are you?' This question mocks the worshipper as she, or he, prepares for the ritual of the cakrapuja. Her feelings, as she steps into the magic circle, tremble between two realms. Outside is India, the twentieth century, rickshaws and buses, temples and burning ghats; inside is an empty space where these things have no reality. In the 'real' world, the

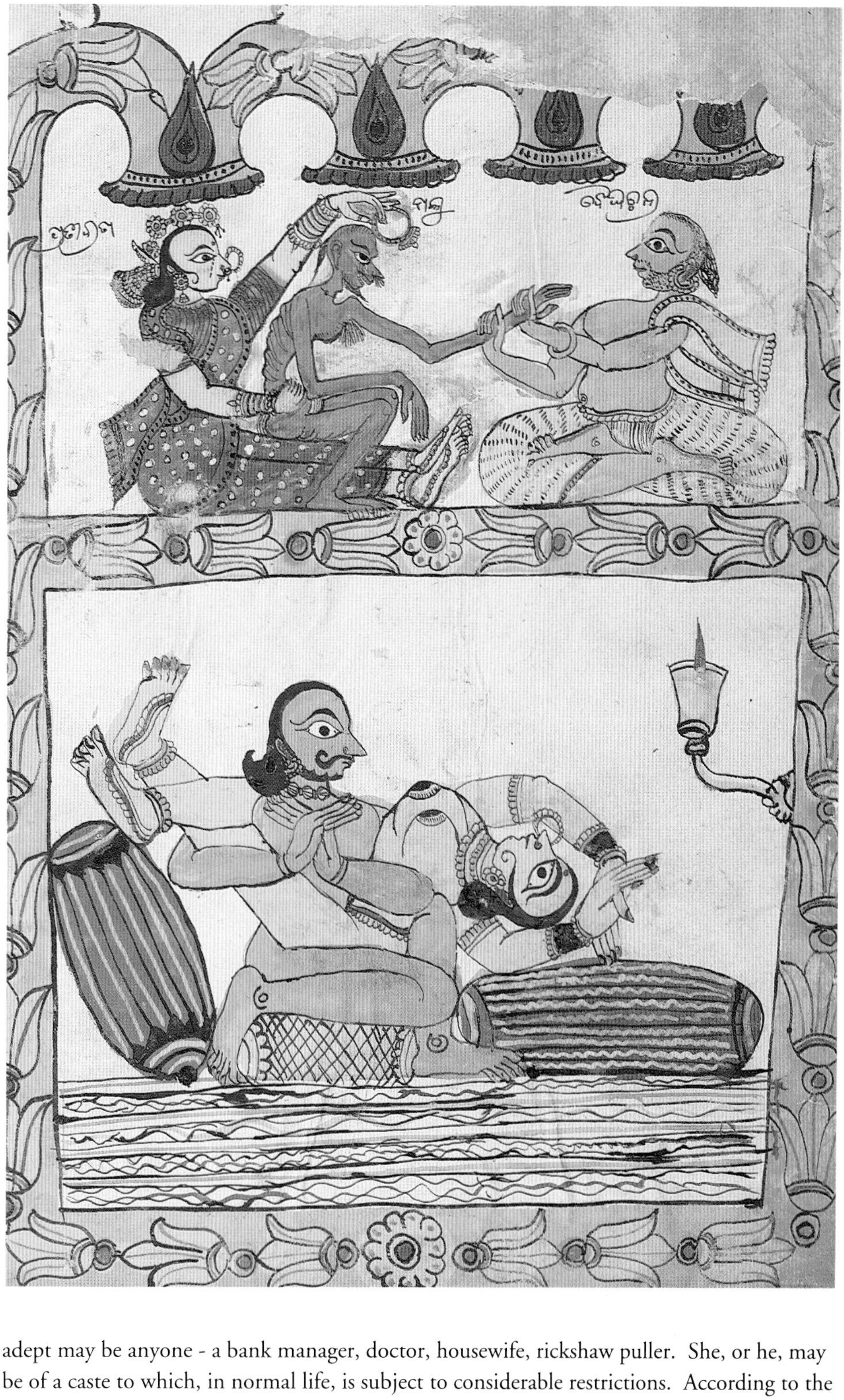

A well-fed priest wearing designer stubble and a female helper adorning an ugly old beggar and worshiping the godhead in him. Below a couple unite in a difficult Tantric sexual posture. *Orissa.*

adept may be anyone - a bank manager, doctor, housewife, rickshaw puller. She, or he, may be of a caste to which, in normal life, is subject to considerable restrictions. According to the rigid practices of caste Hinduism, a brahmin woman may not eat in the house of a candala, the candala may not let his shadow fall on her. At the edge of the circle these divisions vanish. Inside the cakra they are equal. When they eat, they will eat together, sharing the food, even taking morsels from one another's mouths, demonstrating that between them is no difference.

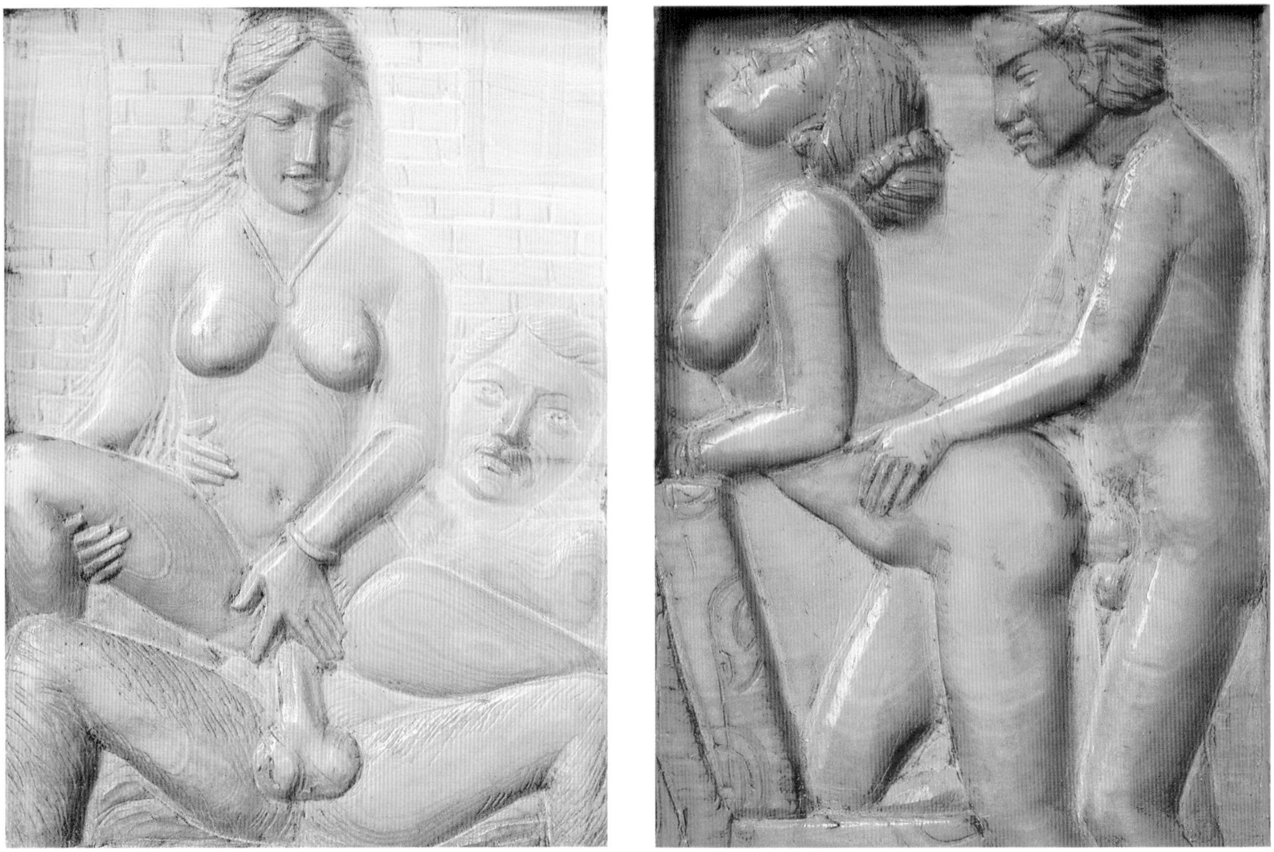

Ivory combs illustrating lovemaking. The work is very painstaking with the sculptor carefully etching every grouted joint in the stretcher-bond brickwork and the pattern on the cloth-covered chair. *Early twentieth century.*

The group of Tantrics who will celebrate the cakrapuja enter the circle in pairs, led by a guru, to whom at all times absolute respect and obedience must be shown. Before worship commences, bhuta-suddhi, the ritual which precedes all Tantric worship, must be performed. It is a ritual of the elements. The adepts visualise the earth element in the body dissolving into water which dissolves into fire which dissolves into air which dissolves into ether. The rituals that follow vary according to precisely what type of cakra has been convened. However the main thread is in all instances the same. The participants are seated, either in rows facing each other, or in a circle composed alternately of men and women.

> vāmé rāmā ramaṇakuśala dakśiné pānpātram I
> madhyé nyāstam marici sahitam śukarasyapi māmsaṁ II
> skandhé vīṇa lalitasubhāga sadguṇanām prapaṇcaḥ: I
> kaulō dharmāḥ paramagahanō yōgināmapyagamyah: II
> (Kaulavali-tantra)
>
> On the left a woman skilled in lovemaking, on the right a chalice of wine, spiced-pork in between; on the shoulder a lute which lasciviously unfolds a story of virtue: how deeply mysterious is this faith of ours, where the sacred and forbidden meet.

Women have two roles in the circles of the Tantrics. Some women, for example very young girls, or matriarchs, are worshipped as living forms of the goddess. In circles where maithuna, or ritual sex is to be performed, the women present are skilled in sexual arts. According to tradition, the former sit on a man's right and latter on his left, earning the name 'vamacari' or 'left-handed', for those who practised sexual rites.

The Kularnava-tantra, which addresses itself solely to the male worshipper, somewhat naively lists the qualities desirable in a woman who is to be brought into the circle as a sakti. She must be, it specifies, young, lovely, serious, pious, trusting, devoted, soft-spoken and mild-mannered. She must be dedicated to the service of the guru and the goddess, free of envy, greed and other flaws, of pleasing personality and a good character: in short, the girl every Hindu man dreams of marrying. Other texts are not so romantic. The Yoni-tantra, ever controversial, states bluntly that the best women for circle-worship are actresses, prostitutes, washerwomen, barber-women, the women of cowherds and garlandmakers. Are we to understand that respectable married ladies mingled in the cakra with these women of the streets? It seems so. Respectability is one of the things that must be left behind, like shoes at the temple door, at the perimeter of the Kaula circle.

piyā chāhé prém ras rākhā chāhé mān I
ék myān mé dō khaḍag dékhā sunā na kān II
(Kabir, 'Dohavali')

You cannot drink the nectar of
God's love and keep your pride.
Two swords in one scabbard,
never yet have been espied.

After a blessing of ritual implements and consecration of the wine, meat, fish and grain, the wine-cup passes from mouth to mouth around the circle. During the drinking of wine, in the Kularnava rite, the consciousness of the group rapidly changes. They are lifted up into a state of euphoria known as 'praudhanta-ullasa':

svābhīṣṭacéṣṭācaraṇaṁ prauḍhāntaḥ parikīttitaḥ I
prauḍhāntōllāsitāddévi mudité yōgimaṇḍalé I
yōginīmaṇḍale caiva kramādānandamuchyaté II
tadārūḍéśu vīréśu kāryākārya na viddhaté I
icchaiva śāstrasampattirityājnā paramésvari II
tatra yad yat krtaṁ karma śubhaṁ vā yadi vā'aśubham I
tatsarva dévatāprītyai jāyaté surasundari II
jalpō japaphalaṁ tandrā samādhirabhijāyaté I
vikriyā pūjanaṁ dévi uditaṁ bhairavīvaliḥ II
muktiḥ syācchaktisamyōgaḥ stōtraṁ tatkālabhāśitam I
nyāsō'avayavasansparsō bhōjanaṁ havanakriyā II
vīkśaṇaṁ dhyānamīśāni sayanaṁ vandanaṁ bhavét I
tadullāsé krtā nānā yā céṣṭā sā ca satkriyā I
kāryākāryavicārantu yaḥ karōti sa pātaki II
etaccakragatā vīrā vijnéyāḥ parayōginaḥ I
yénāsnuvanti manujāḥ sākśādbhairavarūpatām II
sammōdaḥ paramānandaḥ patanaṁ jnānavardvanam I
vénuvīnādivāddhaṇca kavitāracanādikam II
rōdanaṁ bhāśanaṁ pātaḥ samutthān vijrmbhanam I
gamanaṁ vikriyā dévi yōga ityabhidhīyaté II
cakré'asmin yōginō vīrā yōginyō madanamantharāḥ I
samācaranti dévaśi yathōllāsaṁ manōgatam II
śanaḥ prcchanti pārśvasthān vismrtyātmavivakśitam I
nidhāya vadané pātraṁ niviṇṇā nivasanti ca II

mattā svapuruśaṁ matvā kāntānyamavalambaté I
tathaiva puruśascāpi prauḍhāntōllāsasanyutaḥ II
puruśaḥ puruśaṁ mōhādālingatyanānganām I
prcchati svapati mugdhā kastvaṁ kāham imé ca ké II
kiṁ kārya vaymāyātaḥ kimarthamiha saṁsthitāḥ I
uddhānaṁ kimidaṁ hanta grhaṁ kim prānganaṇaṁ kimu II
mukhé āpūya madirāṁ pāyayanti striyaḥ priyān I
upadaṁśaṁ mukhé kśiptvā nikśipanti priyānané II
grhvantyanyōnyapātrāṇi vyaṇjanāni ca sāmmbhavi I
dhrtvā sirasi nrtyanti maddhabhāṇḍāni yōginaḥ II
ajnānakaratālāntamaspaśṭākṣaragītakam I
praskhalatpadavinyāsa nrtyanti kulasaktayaḥ II
yōginō madamattāsca patanti pramadōrasi I
madākulāsca yōginyaḥ patanti puruśōpari II
manōrathasukhaṁ pūrṇa kurvanti ca parasparam I
ityādivividhāṁ céśṭāṁ kurvanti kulanāyiké II
(Kularnava-tantra VIII.56-74)

When, O goddess, they reach 'praudhanta-ullasa', there is all kinds of merrymaking between the ecstatic yogis and yoginis in the circle. In this exalted state they have no thought of decorum but, O Paramesvari, as taught in the sacred texts, they act as the spirit moves them. Whilst in this ecstasy of mind, whatever they may do, whether fair- or foul-seeming, is taken, O Lovely Lady, to be for the pleasure of the Deity. In this divine delerium, O goddess, merely to speak is to chant sacred mantras; drowsiness becomes deep meditation; all acts become acts of worship; sexual union becomes the Great Release; to take the lower sacraments is to become Lord Bhairava himself; shouting out loud becomes the chanting of hymns; the touch of limbs becomes nyasa (invocation of deities into various parts of the body); to eat is to make an offering in the sacred fire; a casual glance becomes yogic concentration; even to sleep is to worship. In this euphoria, whatever is done is holy - it is a sin to think otherwise. Those who take part in the cakra are high yogis - Bhairava Himself. In their ecstatic high spirits - with their heightened awareness - they may play the flute and the vina, recite poetry, weep, give a speech, fall over, get up again, yawn and walk around - all these things, O goddess, are considered acts of yoga. In their exhilaration, O goddess, the initiated yogis and yoginis follow any whim of fancy. Growing distracted, they ask their neighbours to pass the wine jug and sit silently, holding it to their lips. Stirred by desire, ladies treat other men as their own lovers, clasping their necks for kisses. Sò too the men caught in the ecstasy of 'praudhanta-ullasa', some in their bewilderment even embracing other men. "Who are you?" amazed ladies ask their husbands. "Who am I?" "Who are these people?" "Why are we here?" "Why are we sitting here?" "Is this our home? Our garden?" O Sambhavi, the initiates eat food from one anothe's plates - they dance around with their drinking jugs on their heads. The men take mouthfuls of wine and make the ladies drink wine from their mouths. They take a bite of spicy food and then pass it from their own mouth to their lover's mouth. The Kaula women, out of their senses, clap, sing songs with slurred words, and dance in stumbling circles. The inebriated yogis fall joyfully on the ladies and the exhilerated ladies on the men. In this way, O Kulanayike, they satisfy their desires.

Enshrined in the very heart of this Tantric rite is the drunken revelry of the Madra women, described and condemned by Karna in the Mahabharata two millenia ago. At an

The goddess Sri, from the 'ritual' series of Tantric paintings. Sri is the essential cosmic form of the goddess, from which the world emerges in the evolution described by the Sri Yantra. *Eighteenth century.*

even deeper level stirs the old bacchic frenzy. The maenads and Madras both came from the same north-western mountains where cannabis, opium poppies and scarlet amanitas grow: the home of soma. (There is an argument to say that the whole history of religious dualism stems from an ancient quarrel over psychotropic plants, but that is another book.) Several features in the passage quoted above - for instance the dry mouth and reflexive yawning - suggest a drug experience rather than alcoholic stupor. We are back with Kubla Khan, floating in his opium trance: 'Weave a circle round him thrice, and close your eyes with holy dread; for he on honey-dew hath fed, and drunk the milk of Paradise.'

'Who are you?' The question which was thundered at us by the god and goddess, entwined in rapt union, is echoed by the mazed ladies in the cakrapuja circle. 'Who are you?' 'Who am I?' The name of their intoxication, 'praudhanta-ullasa', contains the clue to its purpose. 'Praudha' can simultaneously mean 'uplifted', 'standing out', and 'proud'. It is possible to interpret 'praudha-anta' as 'end-of-pride', or 'end-of-separation'. 'Who are you?' and 'Who am I?' strike to the heart of the Tantric ritual: they are not the questions of a befuddled drunk. The effect of this Tantric drinking is to blur the edges of self, to merge the worshipper into the divine, beyond division. Every man is Bhairava (Siva), every woman is Sakti. But Sakti is Siva and Siva is Sakti.

I am he as you are he
as you are me
and we are all together.
(The Beatles, "I am the Walrus")

The experience of the praudhanta-ullasa dissolves the boundaries of personality. For the same reason, food and wine are shared with an intimacy which uninformed commentators saw merely as further evidence of degeneracy. The passing of morsels of meat, fish and bread from one mouth to another is a genuine love-rite, removing the barriers between 'me' and 'other'. For this reason also, people of all castes are welcome in the cakra. There is no room for distinction. There is no 'you' and no 'I'. All are Siva and all are Sakti and in the union of Sakti and Siva there can neither be sin, nor any thought of sin. In order fully to realise this, the worshipper's identity and possessive sense of self must be annihilated. No name, no shame, no blame.

On entering the circle, the Tantric adept leaves behind everything that binds him or her to the personality he or she has left behind in the outer world. There can be no questions of 'me', 'mine'. Everybody is everyone's. This is why married women could participate without reproach in Tantric rites with men other than their husbands. It is why, in some circles, partners were chosen by lot; each woman, as she entered, removing her blouse and casting it into a drum; the men filing past, each picking out a blouse and pairing with the woman to whom it belonged. Pairing in the cakra, in order to be sacred, had to be indiscriminate and promiscuous.

Pornographic priestess
boy you been a naughty girl you let your
knickers down.
(The Beatles, 'I am the Walrus')

The texts themselves disagree about how far the idea of 'oneness' in the cakra could be allowed to sanction unions that would ordinarily be prohibited. In theory, no distinctions means no restrictions. Certain texts took this line, stating that if other skilled women were not available, a man could unite, calmly and without passion, with women of his own family. But this stretches the Kaula doctrine of non-duality to its extreme. Few Kaulas were radical or shameless enough, even in the circle, to break the deep- rooted taboo of incest. Most texts regarded it with horror and condemned it in the strongest terms.

Many Tantrics of the 'right-hand' path felt as strongly about 'left-hand' practices as ever Abbe Dubois or William Ward did, feeling that they debased the beauty and nobility of pure Tantric worship. But all Tantric practice is perilous. Even the Tantras themselves acknowledge that the Path is fraught with terrible dangers. It has been likened to walking the edge of a sword or riding a tiger. The practitioner of 'left-handed' Tantrism is takes an especially terrible risk, for he or she may be utterly destroyed by practices which can lead to illness, madness and even death. If the traveller in the Bardo does not recognise the real identity of the visions which haunt him - if he cannot answer the question 'Who are you? - they will tear him limb from limb. He will experience the pain and fear of the magician in the Chod rite, without understanding, and he will return, again and again, to the world of suffering.

Once again we must ask: were the instructions of the Tantric texts ever meant to be taken literally? Given what the Kularnava-tantra says of the praudhanta-ullasa, what can one make of the following?

mattā japanti dhyayanti stuvanti praṇamanti ca I
bōdhayanti ca prchanti nandanti jnāninaḥ priyé II
mattā bhramanti gurjanti hasanti vivadanti ca I
rudanti striyamicchanti nindantyajnāninaḥ priyé II
(Kularnava-tantra XI, 27-8)

In the cakra, O Beloved, the wise recite mantras and meditate; they worship with hymns of praise, and ask for guidance, or instruct others. Only the ignorant, O my Beloved, get drunk, roam about laughing and weeping and shouting, quarrel, yell obscenities and lust for women.

There are other strange contradictions in the Kularnava system. Verses VII.97-8 advise the worshipper to drink steadily and stop only when his vision, speech and movements start to be affected. To continue beyond this point is the behaviour of a pasu, or animal. However, verses VII.99-101 describe the method of drinking used by those who are fully initiated into the cult:

pītvā pītvā punaḥ pītvā yāvat patati bhūtalé I
utthāya ca punaḥ pītvā punarjanma na vidyaté II
ānandārtrpyaté dévi mūrccayā bhairavaḥ svayam I
vamanāt sarvadévāsca tasmātrividhamācarét II
(Kularnava-tantra VII.100-1)

The adept should drink, drink and drink again until he falls to the ground. If he gets up and drinks again, he will be freed from rebirth. His happiness enchants the goddess, Lord Bhairava delights in his swooning, his vomiting pleases all the gods.

To what sort of drinking might this refer? From the context of these verses, it is impossible that literal drunkenness, or real vomiting, is meant. For an answer, we should perhaps look to the enigmatic statement in the Kaula-jnana-nirnaya, a Bengali Buddhist Tantra attribute to the tenth-century teacher Matsyendranath, that to the pure in heart, everything is pure. Until now we have seen this idea as a sanction for illicit behaviour, but it may have been an instruction as to how the text should be interpreted. For the wise, the same Tantra continues, the joy of sexual union is itself moksa, but for the foolish moksa is sin. There is a pun here on the word 'moksa', which means both enlightement, and orgasm. Kaula-jnana-nirnaya is saying that gnosis, not sexual pleasure, is the aim of Tantric sex.

zāhid, sharāb pīné dé, mazjid mé baiṭ kar;
yā wō jagāh batā dé jahān par khudā na hō
(Hindi film song; 'Main nashe men hoon')

Priest, leave me be here in the temple to drink my wine.
Or else show me a place where God can't be found.

All Tantras are agreed that Tantric practice demands absolute purity of mind. Those who took part in the cakras were adepts, spiritually mature and expert in many branches of ritual. The disciplines which need mastering before the fifth sacrament of 'maithuna' can be taken include yantra, mantra, japa, nyasa, puja, pranayama, asana, bandha, knowledge of kundalini and the system of cakras. Yantra is meditation on symbolic designs, mantras are magical sound-seeds which detonate in the mind and dissolve it in gnosis. Japa is a programme of mantric chanting, nyasa the identification of various parts of the body with different aspects of divinity. Puja is ritual worship, pranayama is breath control. Bandhas are 'knots' associated with the body-seals, or mudras. Asana is posture. To become expert in any one of these takes considerable practice and presupposes a thorough grounding in mythology, symbolism, god-forms, perfumes, incenses, flowers to be used during worship. These techniques are not unique to Tantrism, and even within Tantrism, there are ways to attain moksa, nirvana, release, liberation, enlightenment - call it what one will - which do not involve sex at all. What Tantra, and only Tantra, offers is the experience of attaining transcendental union with a partner. All other systems are yogas-of-one. Tantra is the yoga-of-two.

> yōgī cénnaiva bhōgī syādbhōgī cénnaiva yōgavit |
> bhōgayōgātmakaṁ kaulaṁ tasmāt sarvādhikaṁ priyé ||
> (Yoni-tantra III.18)
>
> O my beloved, in other systems a yogi cannot be a bhogi nor a bhogi a yogi. But in the Kaula faith, both yoga and bhoga have a happy union.

The orgiastic circles were the outer forms of Tantric sexual worship, practised only by certain Tantric sects and condemned by others. The deeper sexual teachings are for one man and one woman. According to the Prapancasara-tantra, the sexual union of man and woman is to be viewed as a sacred sacrifice. It is the mystical union of ego and knowledge, ahamkara

Krishna and Radha, the perfect ideal of all human lovers: much erotic poetry and painting commemorates their illicit and tempestuous love affair.

A couple make love in the posture which Kama Sutra calls Indrani, named for the beautiful wife of the god Indra. *Nineteenth century.*

and buddhi. Each partner should treat the other with the utmost respect and reverence. The man must practise self control and do no injury to the vital breath, by which is meant, of course, that he should not spend his precious semen.

In tracing the evolution of sacrifice, we see that it began with the taking of human life and developed, via ritual castration, into various kinds of celibacy aimed at focussing and channelling the potent energies of ojas, the divine spark: sublimated in tiny amounts from semen and ovarian fluids, which must therefore be conserved. The most elementary of Tantric sexual practices is that of intercourse without emission - simple karezza - but the Tantrics surpassed themselves by inventing techniques that none but an Indian culture could have created, because no-one else had the necessary body-technology.

The techniques used in this sort of sexual union come partly from the tradition of the kamasastras and partly from hatha-yoga. Ultimately, all stem from the same source: Siva who is lord of sexual teachings, asceticism, yoga, music, dancing and all forms of intoxication. Given the need to maintain erection for long periods, skills such as the pompoir, which Vatsyayana in the Kama Sutra called the 'mare's trick', had to be perfected. The woman uses her vaginal muscles to trap and 'milk' her lover's penis. A number of different asanas (postures) and bandhas (knots) were practised. Commonly, the man would seat himself in padmasana, 'lotus posture', and the woman would sit astride, facing him, both backs straight. From this position, if both lie back until their heads are resting on the floor (this is a kind of yoga, remember) it becomes mula-bandha, the 'root-knot'. If the man lies on his back and the woman sits astride him, many varieties of viparita- rati, 'woman-on-top' are possible. According to Yoni-tantra, adept-women attain great success by this method. Alone among the kamasastras, Ratiratnapradipika has a posture called Kaularaki (= Kaula-rati), named for the Kaula Tantrics. Pranayama or breath control was used to prolong lovemaking without orgasm. To master these secrets was as difficult, it was said, as 'to tie an elephant with a spider's filament', or 'to immerse oneself in the ocean without becoming wet'. Few people in their lifetimes acquire such skills. In particular, tricks like vadavaka are hard to learn. Those women who knew these secrets were able to help their lovers remain erect and hard within them for the long periods needed for meditation. These skilled women were therefore much in demand.

The Niruttara-tantra says that the vesya who follows the Kaula path becomes the 'giver of moksa', or enlightenment. Moksa can of course also signify the orgasm, but this is the one thing it precisely does not mean here.

The techniques employed by the vesya include kissing, embracing and stroking her partner - using the techniques taught in the Kama Sutra and other sexual shastras. There is also a ritual described as 'rati-vigraha-darsana', which indicates a worship of the widely spread yoni, the most ancient and sacred of all religious symbols. The Yoni-tantra describes the yoni as though it were a sacred landscape, through which pilgrimage should be made. Ten spots within the yoni are sacred, says the Yoni-tantra, to different forms of the great Mother Goddess. Each yoni-tirtha has its own appropriate prayers and meditation. In the Mahanirvana-tantra too, we find mantras which are to be uttered by the man as he worships and kisses the yoni of his beloved. The Kubjika-tantra is another which enjoins the adept to worship his wife as a goddess. Having drunk together and become exhilerated, the wife should lie on their bed and the husband should repeat mantras 108 times, touching her heart with his heart, her vagina with his penis and her face with his face.

The most sophisticated of all the sexual-yoga techniques were the set of mudras, or gambits, (literally 'seals') designed not to prevent ejaculation, but to retrieve it. In the vajroli, or 'adamantine', mudra, the man uses his penis like a drinking straw to draw up the woman's vaginal fluids into his body. If this sounds extraordinary, the amaroli, or 'immortal', mudra is even more so: the man ejaculates into the woman's vagina, continues a slow intercourse which allows the fluids thoroughly to mix, and then draws the mixture back into his own body.

This, we may surmise, is the meaning of the repeated 'drinking' in the strange passage quoted above from the Kularnava-tantra. It is also the 'upward-flowing Jordan' of the gnostics which signifies a reversal of the normal downward flow, rather than mere retention of semen, which would at best be a kind of damming up. Whereas in the vajroli mudra the woman's vagina does not receive her partner's semen, the amaroli mudra allows both partners to benefit from the mingling of their vital body essences. Both will meditate on reabsorbing the prana or life energies into their bodies, charging the various cakras in preparation for the raising of kundalini. Here is the central secret of Tantric sexuality: when practising meditation alone, there is but one column of six cakras up which the kundalini lightning can flash.

Two bodies conjoined at the level of the svadisthana cakra - the genital centre - set currents of energy flowing between the two lovers. If they now kiss and allow their salivas to mingle, drinking the nectar from each other's mouths, the energy loops and swirls through their bodies at both points, purifying and rejuvenating.

The worshipper, in this rite of maithuna, aims to merge herself or himself directly with the deity. Thus the woman thinks of her partner as Siva and the man thinks of the woman as Sakti. Each must surrender completely to the other - surrender identity, pride, selfhood. Such a communion will take time to achieve and must be maintained for a long time. Therefore in Tantric sexual rites, the emphasis is not on quick arousal, but on long slow union, sustained at a high level of excitement.

If they can arouse each other and maintain their desire, feeling their bodies charge with pleasure, approaching orgasm yet never reaching it, using the breath and locks and seals and knots to stop just before the peak, then this bliss can go on and on without ceasing. If they can lose themselves in their lovemaking, no longer conscious of where their body end and their lover's body begins, like two blind ecstatic dancers, the dance itself the only reality; then they may, for just an instant, experience that they are one being.

A maharajah relaxes with palace women. It appears from the detail and character in the faces that the artist was painting a specific person and the painting probably was made for a private collection. *Early twentieth century.*

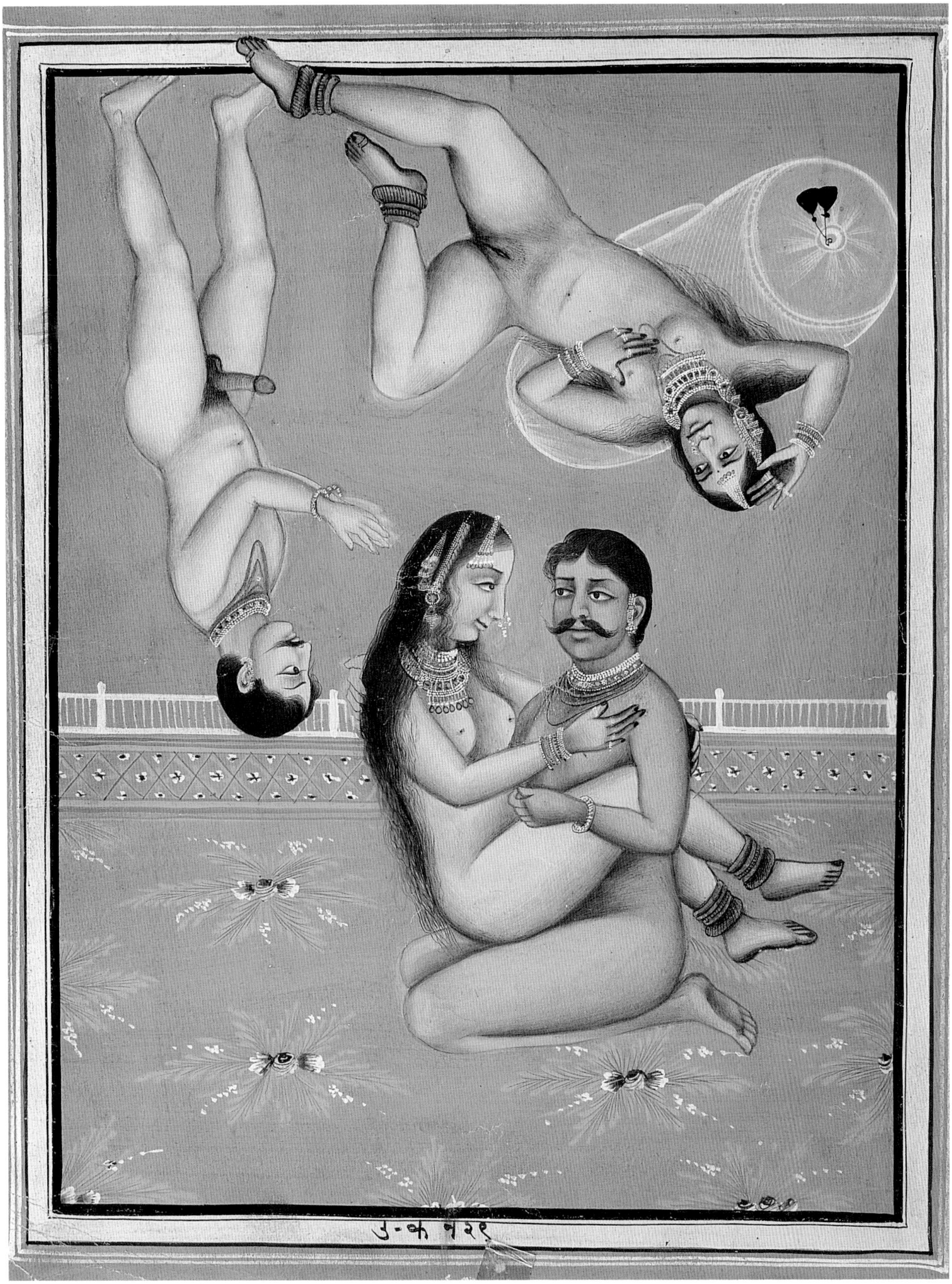

Siva and Parvati, the god and goddess, are immanent in every man and every woman: the message of Tantra. *Greystone carving, fourteenth century.*

> āmūlādhāramābrahmarandhraṁ gatvā punaḥ punaḥ I
> ciccandrakuṇḍalīśaktisāmarasya sukhōdayaḥ II
> vyōmapankajanisyandrasudhāpānaratō naraḥ I
> sudhāpānamidaṁ prōktamitaré madyapāyinaḥ II
> puṇyāpuṇyapaśuṁ hatvā jnānakhadagén yōgavit I
> paré layaṁ nayéccittaṁ palāśī sa nigadyaté II
> manasā céndriyagaṇaṁ saṁyamyātmani yōjayét I
> mattsyāśī sa bhavéhévi śéśāḥ syuḥ prāṇihiṁsakāḥ II
> apravudvā paśōḥ śaktiḥ pravadvā kaulikasya ca I
> śakti tāṁ sévayét yastu sa bhavét śaktisévakaḥ II
> parāśaktyātmamithunasamyōgānandanirbharaḥ I
> ya āste maithunaṁ tat syādaparé strīniśévakāḥ II
> (Kularnava-tantra V.107-113)

> From the cellar of the muladhara, the wine is taken up to the brahmarandhara, where kundalini pours blissfully into the moonglass of pure consciousness. To taste the wine flowing from this ethereal lotus - ah! - that is 'real wine-drinking'. Anything else is mere alcohol.
>
> To slaughter the beasts of praise and blame with the sword of knowledge and merge one's consciousness with the absolute: this is 'real meat-eating'.
>
> Who controls the senses with his mind, and yokes them to the imperishable, is a 'real fish-eater'. All others are merely killers of creatures.
>
> In men of animal-nature, Sakti sleeps, but in Kaulas is wide awake. He who honours Sakti is the 'real sexual worshipper'. Who knows the rapture of the soul's union with the Ultimate is a 'real adept of lovemaking'. All others are merely enjoyers of women.

In the end, these lovers will not need to make love in order to know this rapture. They will have no need even to touch one another. They will always be together, as they always have been, since the beginning. And now all that was hidden becomes clear. The holy well is once more holy. The women smile in the temple of Astarte. Agave shouts on the mountainside. Hearing the shameless laughter of the Madra women in the shadow of the triple-mountain, Alexander frowns. Prajapati howls, caught in the act by Rudra's arrow. Beware a dark man on the forest path. Thunder rolls over Lhasa and Luxor. Shaven headed priests of Isis and shaven headed Buddhist monks look up to the sky. Karna's anger flashes forth before the assembled armies. In the temple of Yellama a small girl looks for God and sees only a stone. This thought blasts the mind like a hurricane. O Goddess, the earth herself shakes, Mount Meru topples, falls. In a quiet room a world away, Wittgenstein writes: '7.00'.

If we look now at the dancing flames that surround Buddha Haruka and Mother Krodisvari, we see that they are laughing softly with compassion and delight. We are no longer afraid, for we know them - we have always known them - and every other thing since the beginning. 'Now I know who I am. I am you.'

ACKNOWLEDGEMENTS AND BIBLIOGRAPHY

In writing this book, I have drawn heavily on the published work of others. In particular, the chapter on Siva and Rudra owes much to Stella Kramrisch's excellent book The Presence of Siva. The chapter on Devagiri is based on the outstanding field-work of Tribhuvan Kapur, conducted among the remote villages of Kumaon, and published as Religion and Ritual in Rural India. For the information about the worship of Yellama and religious prostitution in Bombay, I relied on S.D. Punekar and Kamala Rao's A Study of Prostitutes in Bombay. Satish Kumar Sharma's Hijras: The Labelled Deviants, provided me with my information about the modern phenomenon of eunuchs in India. My understanding of Tantric symbolism owes a great deal to the work of Arthur Avalon - for the serious student of Tantra there is no finer writer.

I thank all these writers and their publishers and, in acknowledging my debt to them, hope that I have used the material I have gathered to make new connections, and to fill this book with new ideas. Unless otherwise indicated, all translations from the Sanskrit are mine.

Permission to quote from other published works has been sought wherever possible and I would like to thank A.J. Brill for permitting me to quote at length from the fine translation of 'The Thunder, Perfect Mind' by George W. MacRae, published in their The Nag Hammadi Library. Also Faber & Faber, for permission to quote from T.S. Eliot's Little Gidding and Robert Graves's The White Goddess; Sri Satguru Press for Thomas Coburn's Encountering the Goddess; Motilal Banarsidass, for Benoyttosh Bhattacarya's Buddhist Esotericism, Johann Jakob Meyer's Sexual Life in Ancient India and K.P.Bahadur's One Hundred Rural Songs of India; Pantheon Books for Erich Neumann's The Great Mother; The Gaia Atlas of First Peoples; Alan Ereira for permission to quote from The Elder Brother; Penguin Books for Phillip Vellacott's translation of Euripides' The Bacchae; Loeb Classical Library for Horace Leonard Jones' translation of Strabo The Geography, and J.Arthur Hanson's translation of Apuleis' Metamorphosis; Munshiram Manoharlal for permission to quote from Kisari Mohan Ganguli's translation of Mahabharata; The Illustrated Weekly of India; the publishers of The New English Bible; Jarrolds for B.Z. Goldberg's The Sacred Fire; Alan Lightman for Smile; Bantam Books for Gopi Krishna's Kundalini: The Evolutionary Energy in Man; Snow Lion Books for Glenn Mullin's translation of Mystical Verses of a Mad Dalai Lama; The Aquarian Press for Benjamin Walker's Gnosticism; Brijbasi for Rajesh Bedi's Sadhus; Oxford University Press for W.Y. Evans-Wentz's translation of the Bardo Thodol; Harcout Brace Jovanovich for R. Gordon Wasson's Soma: Divine Mushroom of Immortality; Abacus Books for Alexandra David-Neel's, Magic and Mysteries in Tibet; Northern Songs for John Lennon and Paul McCartney's I am the Walrus; and Rider for permission to quote the anecdote about the Zen master Ikkyu from Roshi Philip Kapleau's The Three Pillars of Zen.

To anyone reading this who is thinking of practising Tantra: please think again. Tantrism holds many dangers, psychological and spiritual, and should only be studied under the guidance of a respectable guru.

I have in my life only met three genuine siddhas, or adepts. One was a self-professed vamacari, or follower of the left hand way. In his company my wife and I felt ill at ease. We were glad to leave his museum-like house in an Indian city. The others were accomplished Buddhist meditators and are, though they would never claim this themselves, the nearest to enlightened beings that I have met. To be in their presence was to feel an immense sense of calm and well-being. They have been my friends for nearly twenty five years now and this book is dedicated to them - to John and Marie Ryder - with love, respect and gratitude.

Sanskrit and Vernacular Texts:

Ananga-ranga, Kalyana Malla, Ed. V.P. Bhandari, Chowkhamba, Varanasi, 1923
Ananga-ranga, Kalyana Malla, Ed. Ramchandra Jha, Chowkhamba, Varanasi, 1973
Arthasastra, Kautilya, III Vols, Motilal Banarsidass, New Delhi, 1965
Atharva-veda, Ed Devi Chand, Munshiram Manoharlal, New Delhi, 1980
Babhravya-karika, Babhravya-Muni, Chowkhamba, Varanasi, 1967
Brhadaranyaka-upanisad, Ed. with English translation, Sri Swami Sivananda, The Divine Life Society, Tehri-Garhwal, 1985
Brhad-viman-sastra, Maharsi Bharadvaja, Sarvadesik Arya Pratinidhi Sabha, New Delhi, 1977
Devi-bhagavata, with Nilakanthas commentary, Sri Venkateswar Press, Bombay, 1984
Guhyasamaja-tantra, India Office Library, London
Jnanasamkalini-tantra, Calcutta, 1891
Kadambarasvikaranasutram, Sri Rajarsi Pururavah, Chowkhamba, Varanasi, 1967
Kadambarasvikaranakarika, Sri Rajarsi Bharata, Chowkhamba, Varanasi, 1967
Kalika-purana, Venkateswar Press, Bombay, 1907
Kali-tantra, Ed R.D. Singh, Khemraj Srikrishnadas, Bombay, 1990
Kama-kala, Thakur Vijaybahadur Singh, Hindi Sahitya Kutira, Varanasi, 1954
Kama-kunjalata, Ed. Panditraj Dhundiraja Sastri, Chowkhamba, Varanasi, 1967
Kamasutram, Vatsyayana, Ms in Oriental Institute, Baroda
Kamasutram, Vatsyayana, Ed. Devadutta Sastri, Chowkhamba, Varanasi, 1964
Kamasutra-parisilan, Vacaspati Gairola, Chowkhamba, Varanasi, 1989
Kama-tantra-kavyam, Sri Devagnasuryavarya, Chowkhamba, Varanasi, 1967
Kaula-jnana-nirnaya, Ed. P.C. Bagchi, Calcutta, 1934
Kelikutuhalam, Pandit Mathuraprasada Dikshita, Gopal, Delhi, 1954
Kokasaravaidyaka, Ed. Narayana Prasad, Khemraj Srikrishnadas, Bombay, 1960
Kularnava-tantra, Ed. Ram Kumar Rai, Varanasi, 1983
Kumari-tantra, Ed. R.D. Singh, Khemraj Srikrishnadas, Bombay, 1990

Mahanirvana-tantra, Ed. Adi Brahmasamaj, Calcutta, 1876
Mahanirvana-tantra, Ed. with English translation, Arthur Avalon, Ganesh & Co, Madras, 1929.
Matrkabheda-tantra, Ed. C. Bhattacharya, Calcutta, 1933
Narmakelikautukasamvadah, Kaviraja Mukutadandi, Chowkhamba, Varanasi, 1967
Niruttara-tantra, Ed. R. Chattopadhyaya, Calcutta
Pancasayakam, Sri Jyotirisvaraviracitam, Chowkhamba, Varanasi, 1967
Paururavasamanasijasutram, Sri Jayakrishna Dikshita, Chowkhamba, Varanasi, 1967
Prapancasara-tantra, Ed Arthur Avalon, Motilal Banarsidass, Varanasi, 1935
Ratikallolini, Sri Dikshita Samaraja, Chowkhamba, Varanasi, 1967
Ratimanjari, Sri Jayadeva, Chowkhamba, Varanasi, 1967
Ratiratnapradipika, Sri Praudha Devaraja, Chowkhamba, Varanasi, 1967
Rudrayamala-tantra, Bombay, 1983
Saktapramodah, Raj Devananda Singh, Khemraj Srikrishnadas, Bombay, 1990
Saktisamgama-tantra, Ed. B. Bhattacharya, Baroda, 1947
Satcakra-nirupana, Ed. with English translation by Arthur Avalon, Ganesh & Co, Madras, 1918
Saundaryalahari, Sankaracarya, Ed V.K. Subramaniam, with English translation, Motilal Banarsidass, Delhi, 1977
Smaradipika, Sri Minanath, Chowkhamba, Varanasi, 1967
Srngararasaprabandhadipikamanjari, Kumara Harihara, Chowkhamba, Varanasi, 1967
Uttara-tantra, Maitreya, Ed. H.S. Prasad, Sri Satguru, New Delhi, 1991
Yogini-tantra, Ed. K. Misra, Bombay, 1983
Yoni-tantra, Ed. J.A. Schoterman, New Delhi, 1980

Greek and Latin Texts:

Apuleis, Metamorphoses, Vols I & II Ed. and translated J. Arthur Hanson, Loeb Classical Series, Harvard, 1989
Ovid, Ars Amatoria, translated by J.H. Mozley, Loeb Classical Series, Harvard, 1935
Martial, The Epigrams, translated by James Michie, Penguin, London, 1973
Strabo, The Geography, translated by Horace Leonard Jones, Loeb Classical Library, 1917

Works in English:

Anonymous, Ophiolatreia, privately printed, c.1890
Allegro, John, The Sacred Mushroom and The Cross, Hodder and Stoughton, London, 1970
Avalon, Arthur, The Great Liberation, Ganesh & Co, Madras, 1927
Avalon, Arthur, The Serpent Power, Ganesh & Co, Madras 1918
Avalon, Arthur, Principles of Tantra, II vols, Ganesh & Co, Madras, seventh edition, 1991
Avalon, Arthur, Sakti and Sakta, Ganesh & Co, Madras, 1927
Bahadur, K.P., One Hundred Rural Songs of India, Motilal Banarsidass, New Delhi, 1978
Banerjee, S.C., A Brief History of Tantra Literature, Naya Prokash, Calcutta, 1988.
Banerjee, S.C. and Banerjee, R., The Castaway of Indian Society, Punthi Pustak, Calcutta, 1989
Basham, A.L., Origin and Development of Classical Hinduism, OUP, New Delhi, 1990
Basham, A.L., The Wonder That Was India, Sidgwick and Jackson, London, 1954
Bedi, Rajesh, Sadhus, Brijbasi, Delhi, 1991
Besant, Annie and Leadbeater, Reverend C.W., Occult Chemistry, Theosophical Publishing House, London, 1919
Beyer, Stephan, The Cult of Tara, University of California Press, Berkeley, 1978
Bharati, Agehananda, The Tantric Tradition, Rider, London, 1965
Bhatt, M.S., Vedic Tantrism, Motilal Banarsidass, New Delhi, 1987
Bhattacharya, B., An Introduction to Buddhist Esotericism, Motilal Banarsidass, Delhi, 1980
Bhattacharya, B., Towards a Tantric Goal, Sterling, New Delhi, 1989
Bhattacharya, N.N., History of Sakta Religion, Munshiram Manoharlal, New Delhi, 1974
Burkert, Walter, Ancient Mystery Cults, Harvard, 1987
Burton, Sir Richard, The Kama Sutra of Vatsyayana, George Allen & Unwin, London, 1963
Camphausen, Rufus C., Encyclopedia of Erotic Wisdom, Inner Traditions, Vermont, 1991
Churton, Tobias, The Gnostics, Weidenfeld and Nicholson, London, 1987
Clifford, Terry, Tibetan Buddhist Medicine and Psychiatry, Samuel Weiser, Maine, 1984
Coburn, Thomas R., Encountering the Goddess, Sri Satguru, Delhi, 1992
Coleridge, Samuel Taylor, Select Poetry, Prose, Letters, Nonesuch, London, 1971
Danielou, Alain, The Ragas of Northern Indian Music, The Cresset Press, London, 1968
Dastur, J.F., Useful Plants of India & Pakistan, Taraporevala, Bombay, 1964
David-Neel, Alexandra, Initiations and Initiates in Tibet, Rider, London, 1931
David-Neel, Alexandra, Magic & Mystery in TIbet, Abacus, 1977
Dubois, Abbe J.A., Hindu Manners, Customs and Ceremonies, Oxford, 1905 edition. Original 1807.
Dyer, Louis, The Gods in Greece, Macmillan, New York, 1891
Edwardes, Allen, The Jewel in the Lotus, Julian Press, 1959
Eliot, T.S., Complete Poems, Faber & Faber, London, 1969
Evans-Wentz, W.Y., Ed. The Tibetan Book of the Dead, OUP, 1960
Evola, Julius, The Metaphysics of Sex, East-West Publications, London & The Hague, 1983
Feuerstein, Georg, Yoga: The Technology of Ecstasy, Crucible, Los Angeles, 1990
Fraser, Sir James George, The Golden Bough, Macmillan, London, 1922
Frazer, R.W., British India, Fisher Unwin, London, 1896

Ganguli, Kisari Mohan, Mahabharata, XII volumes, Munshiram Manoharlal, New Delhi, 1970
Goldberg, B.Z., The Sacred Fire, Jarrolds, London, 1931
Graves, Robert, The White Goddess, Faber & Faber, London, 1961
Griffith, Ralph, Hymns of the Rg Veda, Vols I & II, Munshiram Manoharlal, New Delhi, 1987
Gross, Robert Lewis, The Sadhus of India, Rawat, New Delhi, 1992
Jhingran, Saral, Aspects of Hindu Morality, Motilal Banarsidass, Delhi, 1989
Johns, Catherine, Sex or Symbol?, British Museum Publications, London 1992
Joseph, G.G., The Crest of the Peacock: Non-European Roots of Mathematics, Tauris, London, 1991
Jung, C.G., Memories, Dreams, Reflections, Collins, London, 1963
Kaplan, Aryeh, Meditation & Kabbalah, Samuel Weiser, Maine, 1982
Kapleau, Roshi Philip, The Three Pillars of Zen, Rider, London 1965
Kapur, Tribhuvan, Religion and Ritual in Rural India, Asia Publishing House, 1988
Kramrisch, Stella, The Presence of Siva, Princeton University Press, 1981
Krishna, Gopi, Kundalini for the New Age, Ed. Gene Kieffer, Bantam Books, New York, 1988
Lal, B.B. and Gupta, S.P. (Ed), Frontiers of the Indus Civilization, Books and Books, New Delhi, 1984
Levy, G.R., The Gate of Horn, Faber & Faber, London, 1948
Mackay, Ernest, Early Indus Civilization, Eastern Books, Patna, 1989
MacRae, George W., The Thunder, Perfect Mind, English translation, E.J. Brill, London, 1977
Majumdar, A.K., General Editor, The Vedic Age, Bharatiya Vidya Bhavan, Bombay, 1951
Mani, Vettam, Puranic Encyclopaedia, Motilal Banarsidass, Delhi, 1975
Mardia, K.V., The Scientific Foundations of Jainism, Motilal Banarsidasss, Delhi, 1990
Mark, Mary Ellen, Falkland Road: Prostitutes of Bombay, Thames and Hudson, London, 1981
Masters, John, Nightrunners of Bengal, Michael Joseph, London, 1951
Meyer, Johann Jakob, Sexual Life in Ancient India, Motilal Banarsidass, Delhi 1971
Miles, Rosalind, The Rites of Man, Paladin, London, 1992
Mookerjee, Ajit, Ritual Art of India, Thames and Hudson, London, 1985
Mookerjee, Ajit, Tantra Asana, Ravi Kumar, Basilius Press, Basel, 1971
Mookerjee, Ajit and Khanna, Madhu, The Tantric Way, Thames & Hudson, London, 1977
Mullin, Glenn H, Kalachakra, Snow Lion, New York, 1991
Murphy, Paul E., Triadic Mysticism, Motilal Banarsidass, Delhi, 1986
Narain, J, and Arya, Aditya, Khajuraho: Temples of Ecstasy, Lustre Press, New Delhi, 1986
Neuman, Erich, The Great Mother, Pantheon Books, New York, 1963
Nou, Jean-Louis, Hindu Temples, Editions Delroisse, Boulogne, 1982
Pandit, M.P., Gems from the Tantras, Ganesh & Co, Pondicherry, 1975
Possehl, Gregory L. (Ed), Ancient Cities of the Indus, Vikas, Delhi, 1979
Punekar, S.D, and Rao, Kamala, A Study of Prostitutes in Bombay, Lalvani, Bombay, 1967
Radha, Swami Sivananda, Kundalini Yoga for the West, Shambhala, Boston, 1978
Radice, Betty (Ed), Hindu Myths, Penguin, London, 1975
Rawson, Philip, The Art of Tantra, Thames and Hudson, London, 1973
Richlin, Amy, The Garden of Priapus, Yale, 1983
Riviere, J. Marques, Tantrik Yoga, Rider & Co, 1934
Rhie, Marylin, and Thurman, Robert, The Sacred Art of Tibet, Royal Academy of Arts, London, 1992
Roney-Dougal, Serena, Where Science & Magic Meet, Shaftesbury, 1991
Sastri, S. Krishna, South Indian Images of Gods and Goddesses, Asian Educational Services, New Delhi, 1986
Satya Prakash, Swami, Parables and Dialogues from the Upanisads, S. Chand & Co, New Delhi, 1975
Shankaranarayanan, S., Sri Chakra, Dipti Publications, Pondicherrry, 1970
Sharma, Satish Kumar, Hijras: The Labelled Deviants, Gian, New Delhi, 1989
Sinha, Indra, Kama Sutra, English translation, Spring Books, London, 1980
Sivapriyananda, Swami, Secret Power of Tantric Breathing, New Delhi, 1983
Tagore, Rabindranath, Collected Poems, Macmillan, London, 1936
Upadhyaya, S.C., Vatsyayanas Kama Sutra, Taraporevala, 1961
Vellacott, Phillip, Euripides: The Bacchae, English translation, Penguin, London 1973
Walker, Benjamin, Gnosticism, The Aquarian Press, Wellingborough, 1983
Ward, William, The Hindoos, 1815
Wasson, R Gordon, Soma: Divine Mushroom of Immortality, Harcourt Brace Jovanovich
Wightman G.B.H, and al-Udhari, A.Y., Birds through a Ceiling of Alabaster: Three Abbasid Poets, Penguin, London, 1975

Reference Works:

Apte, V.S., English-Sanskrit Dictionary, Motilal Banarsidass, Varanasi, 1969
Encyclopaedia Brittanica, Chicago, 1989
Partridge, Eric, Origins: An Etymological Dictionary of Modern English, Routledge, London, 1958
Williams, Sir Monier Monier, Sanskrit Dictionary, Oxford, 1899

INDEX

A

B

C

D

E

F

G

N

O

P

Q

R

S

T

U

V

W

Y

Z